Justin McCarthy

The Story of Gladstone's Life

Justin McCarthy

The Story of Gladstone's Life

ISBN/EAN: 9783743344334

Manufactured in Europe, USA, Canada, Australia, Japa

Cover: Foto ©ninafisch / pixelio.de

Manufactured and distributed by brebook publishing software (www.brebook.com)

Justin McCarthy

The Story of Gladstone's Life

WILLIAM EWART GLADSTONE

From a painting by the late Sir John Everett Millais, P.R.A., considered by members of the Gladstone family to be the most truthful and satisfactory likeness of any. The portrait hangs in the dining-room at Hawarden Castle.

Frontispiece

THE STORY OF

GLADSTONE'S LIFE

BY

JUSTIN McCARTHY

AUTHOR OF " A HISTORY OF OUR OWN TIMES," " THE FOUR
GEORGES," ETC.

New York
THE MACMILLAN COMPANY
LONDON: MACMILLAN & CO., Ltd.
1897

CONTENTS

vii

LIST OF ILLUSTRATIONS

FULL-PAGE ILLUSTRATIONS

ILLUSTRATIONS IN THE TEXT

THE STORY OF GLADSTONE'S LIFE

CHAPTER I

" THE GLEDSTANES "

I THINK I may take it for granted that Mr. Gladstone is the greatest English statesman who has
appeared during the reign of Queen Victoria.
This, indeed, seems to me a statement of fact and
not a question for argument. We may all have our
different opinions as to the policy involved at this
time or that in the statesmanship of Mr. Gladstone.
Some of us may admire him more in his earlier
days, some of us in his later, or even his latest.
He may be charged with inconsistency — a charge
which has naturally to be made against any great
statesman, for the essence of statesmanship consists in the recognition of imminent tendencies and
actual facts. Nobody can possibly be called a
statesman who starts in life with a pack of political
nostrums which he proposes to apply inveterately
to the cure of every constitutional malady in the

B   1

State.   A mind like that of Mr. Gladstone is inex-
orably compelled to go on studying the changing
conditions of things, and is absolutely prohibited
from applying remorselessly the remedies of the
day before yesterday to the troubles of to-day.
Many years ago John Bright said to me that Gladstone was "always struggling towards the light."
Such might indeed be the statement of Gladstone's
whole career.   He has been "ever a fighter," like
Robert Browning's hero — ever struggling towards
the light.   I propose to tell, as best I can, the story
of his rich and noble life.   Of course I can tell it
only from the outsider's point of view; but I may
perhaps say in excuse of my enterprise that I have
followed and studied with the deepest interest,
since I came to know anything of public affairs, the
career of Mr. Gladstone — that I sat in the House
of Commons with him for many years, and that I
was fortunate enough to have much interchange of
ideas with him — and I may perhaps say I was
admitted to his friendship.

William Ewart Gladstone is an Englishman only
by birth.   He was born on the 29th of December,
1809, in Rodney Street, Liverpool, one of the chief
residential streets of the city — a street which was,
and still is, much occupied by leading merchants,
barristers, and physicians.   But Mr. Gladstone's
family came from Scotland.   Many generations

ago the family bore the name of Gledstane. My friend Mr. George W. E. Russell, in his monograph on Gladstone, which belongs to the series called "The Prime Ministers of Queen Victoria," a very delightful little book, explains the meaning of the name. The family had had their abode from very early times in Lanarkshire. "The derivation of the name," says Mr. Russell, "is obvious enough to any one who has seen the spot. *Gled* is a hawk, and that fierce and beautiful bird would have found its natural home among the *stanes*, or rocks, of the craggy moorlands which surround the fortalice of Gledstanes." "As far back as 1296," Mr. Russell tells us, "Herbert De Gledestane figures in the Ragman Roll as one of the lairds who swore fealty to Edward I." By degrees the family estates became less and less, and at last became practically nothing at all. The latest surviving son of the family removed into a neighboring town and set up in business as a maltster. By the time this man's grandson had been born the family name had been changed into Gladstones. Yet a little later and it became that which we all know as one of the most illustrious names in English history — Gladstone. By something like an accident, John Gladstone, then the eldest son of the house, having been sent to Liverpool on business, attracted the attention of a leading corn merchant of the town,

and by his advice settled there for good. He became one of the great merchant princes of Liverpool, a member of Parliament, and a baronet. He
was a pure Lowland Scotchman, and he married
a Highland Scotch woman. The pair had six
children, and the third son was William Ewart Gladstone. John Gladstone was a man of great ability and energy — a man to make his way through any difficulties
and to win the honor and respect of any community.

MR. GLADSTONE'S BIRTHPLACE.
62 Rodney Street, Liverpool

In the public and political sense he stood in somewhat the same relationship towards his son William
Ewart Gladstone that the first Sir Robert Peel occupied with regard to his son, the great Sir Robert
Peel.

One of William Gladstone's elder brothers I remember well in Liverpool, where as a very young

man I spent several years. This brother, Mr. Robertson Gladstone, was a man of singular energy and force of character, of genuine ability both in politics and finance, a powerful and impressive speaker, a sort of rough-hewn model for his younger and much greater brother. He was a man of somewhat uncouth appearance and eccentric ways, about six feet seven inches in stature, and people turned their heads to look after him in the streets of London, although, of course, in his native Liverpool he was too well known to be stared at. He had, as I have said, eccentric ways, but he had no ways that were ignoble or unmanly. He was as straightforward a politician as ever lived. He had begun life as a Tory, but he gradually became a Liberal, and, indeed, an advanced Radical. If he were living in our time, he would be a powerful and uncompromising opponent of Jingoism. It was the common belief in Liverpool, and probably is the common belief there still, that Robertson Gladstone assisted his brother William in the preparation of his budgets when William was again and again Chancellor of the Exchequer. He was eloquent in a strong, unshapely sort of way, with a half-poetic gleam of feeling glancing every now and then through his speeches.

The eldest brother, Sir Thomas Gladstone, passed through life without advancing from his old-world

politics, and made no particular mark upon his
time. I have often thought that nature resolved
to make a decided advance in the family history

SIR JOHN GLADSTONE

by the creation of Robertson Gladstone, and that,
not yet quite satisfied, she tried again and gave
William Ewart Gladstone to the world.

Sir John Gladstone, the father, was one of those

men who, like his illustrious son, seem destined never to grow old. There is an interesting description given of his ways with his children which may perhaps help to account for the extraordinary aptitude for debate of William Ewart Gladstone. One of his friends has told us that nothing was ever taken for granted between Sir John Gladstone and his sons. He started and kept alive a constant succession of arguments on small topics and on large. His family circle appears to have been what the King of Navarre in Shakespeare's play says his court shall be — "a little Academe." Every lad was put on his mettle to defend his own case or to damage the case of another. It was all done in the most perfect good humor and with the full and unflagging enjoyment of those who took part in it. It must have been capital preparation for the Oxford Union and for the debates in the House of Commons. Sir John Gladstone was a great friend and admirer of George Canning. Young William Gladstone was sent to begin his education at the vicarage of Seaforth, a place in the neighborhood of Liverpool. Here he had as one of his fellow-pupils the late Dean Stanley, of Westminster. The friendship between these two lasted to the end of Dean Stanley's useful, refined, and gracious life. Gladstone did not remain long at Seaforth. At the age of eleven he was sent to Eton.

CHAPTER II

It would not, perhaps, be easy to convey to any untravelled American an idea of the glamour and the fascination which Eton exercises over the mind of a schoolboy who has any feeling for the picturesque, the venerable, and the poetic. Eton College stands within the very shadow of Windsor Castle. England has nothing to show more beautiful than the landscape which spreads around on every side. There is witchery in the river, in the woods, in the old historic Castle. One might almost say that the whole current of English history streams on with that noble river. I am not certain, so far as my travel goes, whether anything quite like those Windsor landscapes, including with them the historical memories and associations, can be found anywhere outside England. So far as one can judge, the whole effect impressed itself deeply on the mind of the schoolboy William Gladstone. All through his life he could become fired with enthusiasm at the mere mention of Eton and its studies and its memories. He seems to have worked hard

as a student, and, indeed, earned a certain amount
of unpopularity by his persistence in regarding
serious study as part of his business and his duty.
He was untiring at Greek and Latin, and occupied
his holiday time in studying mathematics. He
never, I believe, became a great classical scholar in
the narrow and pedantic sense. Probably no one
whose scholarship took that limited and practical
form ever really appreciated the beauty of the great
authors whom he studied. You cannot appreciate
Shakespeare if you are always occupied in trying to
parse him. Young Gladstone soon came to have
the most magnificent appreciation of the soul and
spirit and form and phrase of the great Greek and
Latin authors whom he loved. He persisted while
at Eton in being an unostentatiously pious and religious student. He would not join in or countenance any mockery or levity about things which he
had been taught to regard as sacred. Yet there
was nothing whatever of the "prig" about him, and
his force of character even then was such that he
compelled the most light-minded to respect him
and his ways. Nor would he stand any frolicsome
cruelty to dumb animals. "He stood forth," says
Mr. Russell, "as the champion of some wretched
pigs which it was the custom to torture at Eton
Fair on Ash Wednesday, and, when bantered by
his schoolfellows for his humanity, offered to write

his reply in good round hand upon their faces."
This is the sort of boy whom even schoolboys
must admire.

The merits of the system of education and of
discipline adopted at Eton have been the subject
of much criticism and complaint. The education
given there is said by some commentators to consist of nothing but Latin and Greek, and of these
superficially taught, and without any attempt to
instruct the learners in mathematics, physics, or
metaphysics. I shall not attempt to go into the
subject further than to accept it as highly probable
that Eton is, or was in Mr. Gladstone's school-
days, a place where a boy who loved learning
could acquire as much knowledge as he wanted,
but where a boy disinclined for severe studies was
left free enough to indulge his indolent inclinations. A man of eminent authority was once
asked whether a boy would be looked down upon
at Eton for being industrious in his studies. The
answer was significant: " Not if he could do something else well." Such a school would probably
suit the peculiar mind and tastes and aptitudes of
a boy like young William Gladstone. He would
soon find out for himself what studies suited him
best, and he was free to apply himself to these
with all his might. On the other hand, a school
with different modes of training might merely force

a pupil along some broad and common way without giving any opportunity to his natural peculiarities to assert themselves. Certainly Mr. Gladstone's predilection all through his life was rather for what may be termed literary studies than for mathematics or physics or metaphysics. One thing to be said in favor of Eton is that all its best and most distinguished students have looked back upon it with love and affection during the whole course of their lives in the outer world. "Floreat Etona" may be called the motto of the school. It is the pious wish of every student of Eton whom I have ever met. Such a fact in itself speaks for the school "with most miraculous organ," whatever its past or present defects of training or of discipline. It was probably just the place from which young Gladstone would draw all the best it could give.

Sir Roderick Murchison, the famous naturalist, has left it on record that Gladstone was "the prettiest little boy that ever went to Eton." Most of us can testify from our own knowledge that Mr. Gladstone lately is the handsomest old man who ever went to Eton or anywhere else. Visitors to Eton are shown, of course, the name of Gladstone carved into a wall or a woodwork here and there. But, naturally, no one ever goes to any place where a famous man once lived without being

shown his name carved, as it is confidently af-
firmed, by his own hand.

At Eton Gladstone's closest friend was that
Arthur Hallam to whose gifts and virtues the late
Lord Tennyson has inscribed his " In Memo-
riam." Among his other mates were some whose
names will still be remembered in America — Frederick Tennyson, for example, brother of the poet
and himself a poet; Alexander Kinglake, the author
of " Eothen," and the historian of the Crimean
War; James Bruce, afterwards the famous Earl
of Elgin; Charles Canning, afterwards Earl Canning and Viceroy of India, the " Clemency Canning" of the Indian Mutiny — a nickname then
given to him in scorn by the panic-stricken vota-
ries of a policy of slaughter, but now remembered
to his honor and to his glory.

William Gladstone was not much of an athlete,
as the term was then understood. He did not
care for games of any kind, but was very fond of
sculling, and kept a boat for his own use, and he
was then, as ever since, a tremendous walker. He
walked very fast, and he walked great distances.
His delight was to wander about through all the
lovely places surrounding Windsor, in company
with a few boys of his own age and of his own
tastes. Outside this inner circle of his intimates
Gladstone was not well known at Eton. He seems

to have been neither popular nor unpopular — a
somewhat curious beginning in life for one whose
strength and energy of character made it in his
after years impossible for any one to avoid forming a very distinct opinion for or against him.

ETON FROM THE THAMES
(From a photograph by the London Stereoscopic Co.)

He distinguished himself decidedly in the debates
of the " Eton Society " and in the editorship of the
" Eton Miscellany." Mr. Russell tells us that the
Eton Society in Gladstone's day was " a remarkable group of brilliant boys." " Its tone was
intensely Tory. Current politics were forbidden

subjects, but political opinion disclosed itself through the thin disguise of historical or academical questions. The execution of Strafford and Charles the First, the characters of Oliver Cromwell and Milton, the 'Contrat Social' of Rousseau, and the events of the French Revolution, laid bare the speakers' political tendencies as effectually as if the conduct of Queen Caroline, the foreign policy of Lord Castlereagh, or the Repeal of the Test and Corporation Act, had been the subject of debate." We all know the tremendous earnestness which schoolboys throw into the discussions of their debating societies. Probably Mr. Gladstone was never more thoroughly in earnest at the very zenith of his statesmanship, and when a speech from him might decide the fate of a ministry or a policy, than he was when he addressed the Eton Society on the subject of popular education. He was the means of introducing Mr. Kinglake to this Eton Society. He took a prominent part in the starting of the "Eton Miscellany." He became its editor and its most prolific contributor. He was actually the author of a humorous ode to the shade of Wat Tyler!

Shade of him whose valiant tongue
On high the song of freedom sung !
Shade of him whose mighty soul
Would pay no taxes on his poll !

—and much more, in the same elaborate strain of the mock-heroic. Only the other day, it may be said, this humorous versical freak of a school-boy was rescued from oblivion by a serious Tory critic, who brought it up as conclusive evidence that Mr. Gladstone had been from his earliest years the consistent advocate of anarchy and rapine. Such a critic may well remind us of that contemporary of Swift who took the trouble to point out that there could be no such places and people in the world as those which Lemuel Gulliver professed to have visited in his travels.

Gladstone remained at Eton until the end of 1827. He then studied for a few months with private tutors, and he became fond of gymnastics, of turning, and of wood-carving. He still delighted in his rambles through fields and woods, in his long, rapid walks, and in his chosen companionships. In October, 1828, he went up to Christchurch, Oxford. There were many young men then at Christchurch who afterwards made distinguished careers for themselves in the Church and in law and in political life. Among the undergraduates at other colleges in Oxford were Henry Edward Manning, the late Cardinal Archbishop of Westminster; Sidney Herbert, afterwards one of Gladstone's closest friends and colleagues in Parliamentary life; Robert Lowe, afterwards Lord

Sherbrooke; and Sir George Cornewall Lewis, a man of wonderful gifts and acquirements, curiously forgotten by the Englishmen of to-day — a man who, but for his unhappy defects of voice and articulation, might have been one of the greatest speakers in the House of Commons.

OXFORD, CHRISTCHURCH COLLEGE
(From a photograph by the London Stereoscopic Co.)

There was some doubt in Gladstone's family as to whether he ought to be sent to Oxford or to Cambridge. Now, it would seem to most of us that there was an absolute necessity, for the sake of historical fitness, that he should have been sent, as he was sent, to Oxford. The entire atmosphere of the place, steeped in its peculiar traditions and its mediævalism, seemed exactly suited to the whole temperament and genius of the youthful Gladstone. Members of the two universities are constantly arguing as to which of the rivals can show the more splendid beadroll of great students. Into this controversy I have no inclination to enter. Each can produce a magnificent record; but I should think an unbiassed observer might be inclined one way or the other, according as his taste and temperament led him to the scientific, or to what I may call the literary and historical, field of study.

Certainly Mr. Gladstone seems to me absolutely in his place as a student in Oxford. He was a hard student during his career as an undergraduate, and he led a very temperate life. He did not object to a supper or a wine party, but he was distinctly abstemious in the use of wine, and his example in this way produced a good effect, not only on those who worked with him, but also on some of those who came after him. Naturally, he took a leading part in the proceedings of the Union Debating Society, of which he first became Secretary and afterwards President. In the days of Arthur Pendennis self-conceited members of the Union Debating Society lived in the firm belief that the Prime Minister of the time watched with keen attention the doings of the youths in the Union, with the object of picking out fit persons to become Cabinet Ministers.

c

The Premier at the time when Gladstone delivered his maiden speech in the Oxford Union might, with great judgment, have turned his attention in that direction. Predictions after the event are, as we all know, of little account; but Bishop Charles Wordsworth, as he afterwards was, who heard the speech, said that "it made me, and I doubt not others also, feel no less sure than of my own existence that Gladstone, our then Christchurch undergraduate, would one day rise to be Prime Minister of England."

The University of Oxford is a world in itself, and might in Gladstone's early days be described as a world all to itself. Its general principles were those of devotion to the State Church and to Toryism — a Toryism which, as Mr. George Russell says, was of a romantic and old-fashioned type, as far as possible removed from the utilitarian Conservatism of a later day. "The claims of rank and birth," says Mr. Russell, "were admitted with a childlike cheerfulness. The high function of government was the birthright of the few. The people had nothing to do with the laws except to obey them." Mr. Gladstone himself, a great many years after, when speaking at the opening of a Liberal club in Oxford in the December of 1878, said: "I trace in the education of Oxford of my own time one great difference. Perhaps it was my own fault, but I must admit that I did not learn when at Oxford that which I have learned since, to set a due value on the imperishable and the inestimable principles of human liberty. The temper which I think too much prevailed was that liberty was regarded with jealousy, and fear could not be wholly dispensed with." Still, as will be easily understood, there were as many different phases of Toryism at Oxford, even then, as there were minds and temperaments. In a great centre of education there cannot possibly be that stolid monotony of opinion and of conviction which may be found sometimes among the church-goers and the Tories of some country village. Then, again, each of the colleges in Oxford, as in Cambridge, had its own peculiarities, its own traditions, its own class, and its own aspirations. Christchurch College in Oxford was, perhaps, the most aristocratic in its members and in its tastes. It seems to have become, for some unknown reason, a training-school for Prime Ministers. Its history would well have justified the ideas of Arthur Pendennis and his friends. Christchurch College gave during the century seven Prime Ministers, not including Mr. Gladstone himself, to English government. Among these were Lord Liverpool, George Canning, Sir Robert Peel, Lord Derby, Lord Salisbury, and Lord Rosebery, Gladstone's own successor in the office of Prime Minister.

In his second term Mr. Gladstone was elected a member of the Oxford Union Debating Society,  in which he made the speech so glowingly commended by Bishop Wordsworth in the words we have already quoted. He defended Catholic emancipation in the debates of the Union, but he opposed the removal of Jewish

GEORGE CANNING

disabilities, and he argued against the immediate abolition of slavery, although he urged that every preparation ought to be made for its gradual extinction by the teaching and training of the slaves so as to fit them for self-mastery and for citizenship. These views, as we shall see, he afterwards expressed in Parliament when he came to be a member of the House of Commons. In the debates of the Union he again and again opposed the very moderate movements towards political reform which at that time were held by many people to be well-nigh revolutionary. Yet even in young Gladstone's strongest speeches against the reform movement he seems to have taken good care not to commit himself to any unqualified objection to reform as a principle. His mind, indeed, would appear to have been a

sort of mirror of the general mind of Oxford —
a veneration for the past, a love of tradition,
a romantic sentiment of reverence for the ancient
institutions of the country, and yet a mind open
to see the inevitable tendencies of the future.

Gladstone worked very hard for the Oxford
Union, of which he became first the Secretary
and afterwards the President. He was studying
hard for classical honors and for divinity. He
studied Hebrew as well. He worked for four
hours in the early day and then went out for exercise, chiefly walking and boating, with also a
certain amount of what we now call athletic training — more, at least, than he had taken in his Eton
days. Then he attended classes and lectures and
resumed his solitary readings for many later hours.
He always read for two or three hours before bed-
time. Nothing whatever was allowed to interfere
with the course of his reading and his studies.

Not content with his studies and the work of
the Union Debating Society, he founded and
organized a debating society all of his own device
and construction, which he named the Oxford
Essay Club, but which became after a while col-
loquially named the "Weg," a title taken, as will
readily be seen, from Gladstone's own initials.
Frederick Denison Maurice, afterwards famous
in English Church history, mentioned in 1870

that "the circumstance of belonging to a small society at Cambridge brought me into a similar one at Oxford, founded by Mr. Gladstone, to which otherwise I never should have been admitted." "The members of the Weg," says Mr.

FREDERICK DENISON
MAURICE.
(From a photograph by
Elliott & Fry)

Alfred F. Robbins in his "Early Public Life of Mr. Gladstone," "assembled in each other's rooms in turn to hear an essay from its occupant, and it is owing to this circumstance that so excellent an idea has been preserved of what Mr. Gladstone was like when at the University."

Gladstone also studied hard in mathematics, but the study seems to have left less impression on his style of thought than any other of his readings and his trainings. Of the original members of the Weg, I believe Mr. Gladstone himself and his friend, Sir Thomas Acland, to be the only survivors. At one of the meetings of this society Gladstone read an essay which endeavored to explain and define the belief of Socrates in immorality.

I have heard quite lately that Mr. Gladstone himself was rather disposed to underrate the amount of interest which he took, while at Oxford, in out-of-door pursuits. One or two of his few surviving contemporaries may have been heard to declare that Gladstone held as good a place among the Oxford athletes of his time as he did among the hard-working students. It is possible enough that in later days the mind of the great statesman and the great student may have lost its memory of the physical exercises which were less a passion of his temperament and his nature than the working of the intellect and the development of the brain. One can only say that it is hard to believe in Mr. Gladstone turning his attention to anything, physical or intellectual, without becoming more or less successful in the attempt.

It is a curious fact that when his office of President of the Oxford Union came to an end he was succeeded by his friend, afterwards Cardinal Manning. It is a curious fact, too, not unworthy of record, that among the friendships which he made at Oxford was that of Mr. Martin Farquhar Tupper. The general public now has lost all memory of Mr. Tupper. Tupper was, however, a man well known in his day. He was the author of a book called "Proverbial Philosophy," a book which probably had at one time a larger circulation than any of the novels of Dickens and Thackeray, or the writings of Carlyle, or even the essays of Lord Macaulay. It was a book composed altogether of gentle platitudes, each platitude carrying with it a well-meaning moral purpose. The genial platitudes ceased to interest after a time, and Tupper faded out of the minds of even the dullest among us.   I remember a friend telling me, many years ago, that he had just come from a literary party where he had been sitting between the two extremes of poetry: between Alfred Tennyson on the one hand and Martin Tupper on the other.   Tupper first adored Gladstone and wrote poems to him, then for a while he turned against him, and afterwards went back to his first love.   Gladstone was always kind to Tupper, invited him to his house, always read and answered his letters (which must have been terribly boring work), and proved that he had never forgotten his old associates at the University.

In December, 1831, Gladstone took his double first class.

CHAPTER III

GLADSTONE was an earnest student of the Bible
and of patristic literature in those boyish days,
as he continued to be down to his latest years.
He left Oxford before the full influence of the
movement led by the late Cardinal Newman had
begun to assert itself in the place. His strong
inclination then was to enter the Church, and he
pressed his father hard to allow him to become a
clergyman. But Sir John Gladstone, shrewd and
keen-eyed man of the world as he was, saw, no
doubt, in the genius of his son something different
from that which could find its best course in the
career of an ecclesiastic. In Mr. Gladstone's time
strict obedience to the wish of a father was an
essential part of a son's duty. Gladstone gave
up his desire to enter the Church, but, as every
one knows, he has taken during all his life a deep
interest in Church history and in subjects of theological controversy. Early in 1832 he left Oxford
and went to Italy for the first time — to that Italy
which in after years he loved so much and served

so well. It seems in the fitness of things, too,
that young Gladstone should have passed directly
from Oxford to Italy. After a few months of
Italian wandering he was called back from Italy,
as Milton had been, by a sudden appeal to him
to enter on a political and a Parliamentary career.
His time had come, and it found him out. Those
who have watched with ever-increasing interest
the later years of his public life must know, of
course, through what changes of opinion he struggled on to be a great political reformer. But
there may be many to whom it would be a surprise to hear that the invitation which Mr. Gladstone first received was given because it was
understood that he was one of the rising influences that made against reform; that he was determined to keep back if he could the onward
movement of the popular cause, and that he was,
as Macaulay afterwards described him, the hope
of the stern and unbending Tories of that day.
The very manner of his invitation to enter Parliament would be an anachronism and an impossi-
bility in our time.

The invitation came from the then Duke of
Newcastle. The Duke represented the old-fashioned principle which set up the landlord's absolute
right over the votes of a constituency in which he
possessed the most of the land. The passing of

the Reform Bill had shaken the strength of the old
feudal principle.   According to that principle, the
great landlord of any region where there was a
Parliamentary constituency claimed the right to
return to Parliament anybody whom he thought fit
to select for the representative position.   This
Duke of Newcastle, about whom I am now speaking, had asserted his claim in the most frank and
simple fashion.   He will be remembered in English
history chiefly by the manner of this assertion.
"Have I not," he asked, "a right to do what I like
with my own?"—"my own" being in this case the
constituency of Newark, one of the boroughs which
fell within his territorial sway.   The Duke was a
good-natured, honest, somewhat thick-headed sort
of a man, and he could see nothing absurd whatever in a ducal landlord setting up such a claim.
The Duke was naturally greatly alarmed by the
movements of the epoch.   The Reform Bill of 1832
introduced for the first time the great middle
classes and the great middle-class cities and towns
of England to the right of representation in Parliament and the right of the suffrage.   It abolished
many of the old "rotten boroughs," as they were
called, and the "pocket boroughs," and therefore
struck sharply at the privileges of the territorial
magnates.   The Reform Bill, although the Duke
of Wellington described it as "a revolution by due

course of law," set up in fact but a very limited suffrage, and left the vast mass of the working population entirely outside the pale of constitutional representation. But it seemed at that time to all Tory minds like a measure of portentous revolution. On the other hand, ardent Liberals wrote and spoke as if the Reform Act were destined to bring about a millennium.

The Duke of Newcastle looked around every-

THE DUKE OF NEW-
CASTLE

where for some rising man capable of representing Tory interests in the borough of Newark. His son, Lord Lincoln, had been a school and college friend of young William Gladstone, and had heard him deliver his speech against reform, to which I have already referred. Lord Lincoln recommended Mr. Gladstone to the Duke. The Duke eagerly accepted his suggestion. Mr. Gladstone was summoned home from Italy, and thus the greatest English reformer of our time came into practical politics as the advocate of the party which set itself against any and every manner of reform. Even under these conditions Mr. Gladstone could not bring himself quite down to the level of the Duke of Newcastle. In his address to the electors of Newark he declared that he was bound by the

opinions of no man and no party, but said that he
felt it his duty to watch and resist that growing
desire for change which threatened to produce,
"along with partial good, a melancholy preponder-
ance of mischief." The Duke of Newcastle probably would not have admitted that there was any
good, even partial, to qualify the melancholy mischief. Mr. Gladstone declared in his address that
if Englishmen were to look for national salvation
they must make it their first principle that the
duties of governors are strictly and peculiarly religious, and that legislatures, like individuals, are
bound to carry throughout their acts the spirit of
the high truths they have acknowledged. Mr.
Gladstone said a good deal about the condition of
the poor and the remuneration of labor. From the
opening to the close of his career he was always
inspired by a sincere and active compassion for the
condition of the hardly worked and very poor. It
seems somewhat strange to us now to learn that
part of the address touched upon the question of
slavery. It has to be remembered that slavery still
existed, a tolerated principle and practice, in certain
of the English colonies. Its abolition was one of
the results of that Reform Act which the Duke of
Newcastle and Mr. Gladstone so much condemned.
The Gladstones had large properties in the West
Indies, including, of course, a considerable slave

population, and when England emancipated her
slaves by paying off the planters, the Gladstone
family naturally, and quite rightly, came in for a
considerable share of the national purchase-money.

Liverpool was a town which had a good deal
to do with the slave system in the colonies, and
in my early days I remember hearing from old
playgoers of a declaration flung by Cooke, the
great tragedian, in the face of an indignant
theatre in Liverpool which had ventured to hiss
him for some oddity in his behavior, that "there
was not a stone in the walls of the town which
was not cemented by the blood of African slaves."
Mr. Gladstone, however, did not present himself
in his address as an advocate of slavery. He
contended that the system was sanctioned by
the Scriptures, but he insisted that the slaves
were to be educated and prepared for gradual
emancipation. That was as far as any Englishman, not a member of an abolitionist organization,
would have gone at the time. The Newark contest was fought out with much stubbornness and
a good deal of passion, and the two Tory candi-
dates were elected, Mr. Gladstone's name being
at the head of the poll. This, it should be
remembered, took place at a general election —
the first general election since the passing of the
Reform Act, the general election which was to

create the first Reformed Parliament.   The Reformed Parliament met on January 20, 1833, and
Mr. Gladstone took his seat in the chamber over
which he was destined to maintain for so long
an almost absolute ascendency.

He was then twenty-two years of age; he had a
splendid physical constitution, a striking and handsome face, a mass of dark hair and splendid radi-
ant eyes.   His face was pallid, almost bloodless,
and a passing observer might have fancied that
the young man was wanting in health.   The
fancy, however, would have had no foundation,
for then, as through all his career, Mr. Gladstone's
intellectual faculties were sustained by an indomitable physical constitution.   I am myself strongly
of opinion that Mr. Gladstone distinctly improved
in appearance as his life went on deepening into
years.   I cannot, of course, remember him as he
was in 1833.   I think I saw him for the first
time some twenty years later.   But although he
was a decidedly handsome man at that time, I
do not think his appearance was nearly so striking or so commanding as it became in the closing
years of his career.   I do not believe I ever saw
a move magnificent human face than that of
Mr. Gladstone after he had grown old.   Of
course the eyes were always superb.   Many a
stranger, looking at Gladstone for the first time,

saw the eyes, and only the eyes, and could think for the moment of nothing else. Age never dimmed the fire of those eyes.

We have now Mr. Gladstone at the very outset of his Parliamentary career — a young man endowed with the rarest gifts, having the sure prospect of ample fortune, with friends among the highest families of the day, and with a brilliant reputation earned at school and college. He seemed destined, as indeed he was destined, for nothing but success. He came into the House of Commons at a peculiar crisis in its history. The old order was changing, giving place to the new; the whole situation could not but have made a profound impression on Gladstone's thoughtful and half-poetic mind. It must soon have been borne in upon him that the days of privilege were gone, and that the days of political and social equality were fast coming in. Few men could then have expected, even among the friends who admired him the most, that he was destined to play a supreme part in the expansion of the new era.

CHAPTER IV

GLADSTONE'S FIRST PARLIAMENT

THIS Reformed Parliament, in which Mr. Gladstone made his first appearance, had some very remarkable men in both its chambers. The House of Lords was, of course, entirely unaffected by the changes which had so profoundly altered the character of the Representative Chamber. Reform does not touch the House of Lords. The right of a man to be a peer consists either in the fact that he is the eldest son of his father, who was a peer, or that

DUKE OF WELLINGTON
(From an old engraving)

he is called up to the peerage by the gracious summons of the Sovereign. The most conspicuous figure in the House of Lords at the time was that of the Duke of Wellington, the victor of Waterloo. The Duke of Wellington was a consummate soldier, although he had none of the dazzling genius of the great Napoleon. Napoleon was a man born for conquest and for aggression. The Duke of Wellington was the very symbol of cautious and hard-headed resistance. Napoleon was really defeated by himself, and by himself only. "The meteor of conquest," as Byron says, "allured him too far," and he fell into cureless ruin. The Duke of Wellington held a place in the House of Lords and in the public mind of England which might be considered absolutely unique. He was not a great statesman; he was not, indeed, a statesman at all in the true sense of the word. Apart from his gifts and instincts as a commander, he was not a man of any intellect. But he was a thoroughly honest and disinterested man. It was well known that his life was absolutely devoted to the service of his Sovereign and of his country. His bitterest enemy never imputed to him a sordid or even a selfish motive. He had good sense enough to see who were the men upon whom, from his own point of view, he could best rely for guidance. Sir Robert Peel was then and forever after one of those men. The influence of the Duke of Wellington in the House of Lords was always, of course, a Tory influence; but it belonged to a form of Toryism which was willing in the end to recognize facts and to make the best of any situation. When once it was made clear to the Duke that he could not maintain some particular Parliamentary position, he had no more hesitation in withdrawing from it than he would have had in his days of battle about retreating from some line of defence which it must soon become impossible to hold.

The next most prominent figure in the House of Lords was that of Lord Brougham, the great advocate, the great popular agitator, the undoubtedly great orator — a man devoured by a perfect passion for hard work, a man of inexhaustible energy and vast resources, whose weakness consisted in an unconquerable desire to master every subject and to become first in every field. Lord Brougham is curiously forgotten by Englishmen and Americans of to-day. Yet his might truly be called a great career. He put himself at the head of every movement for political or social reform. He was an orator of a somewhat rough, unhewn, and even uncouth order, but his power over the feelings of his audience was a living fact admitting of no possible question.

LORD LYNDHURST

Another eminent man in the House of Lords, much greater as a mere lawyer than Lord Brougham, but with nothing like Brougham's political influence, was Lord Lyndhurst. Lyndhurst was on the Tory side of affairs, but he had mental enlightenment enough to inspire him sometimes to go a little in the way of genuine

reform.   Brougham and Lyndhurst, on different
sides in politics, had become members of the House
of Lords by the same sort of regulation process.
Each had served his party well both as lawyer
and as politician, and each, when his party came
into power, had been rewarded for his services by
the office of Lord Chancellor, which takes with
it, although not always at the very moment, a
seat in the House of Lords.

In the House of Commons which Mr. Gladstone
entered for the first time the two most remarkable
men were, beyond all question, Sir Robert Peel
and the great Irish tribune, Daniel O'Connell.
Mr. Gladstone was very soon drawn by instinct
and by sympathy into a sort of devotion to Sir
Robert Peel.   There was a certain affinity between
the characters and the gifts of the elder and the
younger man.   Sir Robert Peel had begun life
as a stern and unbending Tory, and naturally a
rigid advocate of the system of protection.   He
had already been won over, by the growing force
of his own conscientious convictions, to become
the Parliamentary instrument of Catholic emancipation.   Later on, as we shall see, he was destined
to break away from his Tory party and to establish
the system of free trade.   Peel was undoubtedly,
what Mr. Disraeli called him, a "great member of
Parliament."   He was a great Parliamentary orator

and debater. No man in modern times, except Mr. Gladstone alone, has ever swayed the House of Commons by argument and by eloquence as Sir Robert Peel did for many years. Like Mr. Gladstone, he had a magnificent voice, a voice strong, clear, flexible, and sweet, making itself heard without strain or effort in the farthest row of the farthest gallery, and at the same time capable of expressing the most delicate tones and semi-tones of feeling and of persuasion.

DANIEL O'CONNELL

Mr. O'Connell had but lately made his way into Parliament, partly by his own tremendous energy and popularity in Ireland, partly because Peel's conscience had converted him, as I have said, to the principle of Catholic emancipation, and Peel had brought over the Duke of Wellington; and partly because the Duke of Wellington himself had made up his mind that further resistance to Catholic emancipation would mean civil war, and he declared that he had seen war enough in his time, and would have nothing to do with civil war, anyhow.

O'Connell was a great figure in the House of Commons, as he had been a great figure at the bar and on the popular platform. He, too, possessed a voice of marvellous strength and music.

Disraeli, in rendering justice to Sir Robert Peel's
voice, says that nothing like it had been heard
in his time, "except, indeed, the thrilling tones
of O'Connell." Mr. Gladstone was early drawn
towards O'Connell by a kind of sympathy, greatly
as the two men differed on many political questions.   Gladstone was in favor of the principle
of Catholic emancipation even in his most anti-
reforming days of ardent youth, and he found
much that was attractive in O'Connell's genial
bearing.   I talked with Mr. Gladstone some years
ago about his early memories of O'Connell, and
he spoke with a certain modest gratefulness of
O'Connell's kindness to him when a young man
just entering on Parliamentary life.   He told me
several stories about O'Connell's earnestness and
energy in trying to redress this or that individual
grievance, and of the trouble which he had taken
for such purposes, and of the generous warmth
with which he accepted and put to proof Mr.
Gladstone's offer of co-operation.   I asked Mr.
Gladstone about Mr. O'Connell's eloquence in the
House of Commons, and he told me it was so
great and so commanding that he was unwilling
even to offer a criticism upon it, but that his
impression was that of the three great opportunities which O'Connell enjoyed, the bar, the platform, and the House of Commons, the House of

Commons was not his greatest success. I asked Mr. Gladstone what he believed to be O'Connell's principal characteristic. He made me an answer in a magnificent phrase which does honor to the memory of O'Connell. He said: "I think O'Connell's principal characteristic was a passion of philanthropy."

Lord John Russell was undoubtedly one of the leading men of the new Parliament. He had been the principal worker in the preparation and the carrying of the Reform Bill. He was a man of great ability and of remarkable power as a keen, incisive debater. He never, perhaps, rose to the full height of genuine oratory, but I at least have not heard a man in my recollection who could get the better of him in the keen sword-play of debate. Lord Palmerston, although he had held office more than once, and just at this moment was Secretary of State for Foreign Affairs, had not yet made any real mark on public life. Lord Palmerston's influence was of the slowest growth, and when it came at last it came suddenly and almost as in a flash. Mr. Stanley, afterwards Lord Stanley, and later still Lord Derby, was one of the commanding figures in the House of Commons. He was a man of great energy and eloquence, possessing a rhetorical fluency which had not, perhaps, been equalled in a modern English Parliament until Mr. Gladstone came to the front. He had a power of "phrasing," if I may use such an expression, which told with immense effect on the debates of the House of Commons, where a happy expression, an epigram that "catches on," an epithet that clings to the public memory, is often much more effective than the soundest argument. Mr. Stanley had on more than one occasion stood up in direct Parliamentary antagonism to Daniel O'Connell, and, according to the opinion of the majority, had not been worsted. He had taken a great part in the passing of the Reform Bill, although he was an aristocrat of the aristocrats. Later on he quarrelled with the Liberals over their policy as regarded the Irish State Church, and he afterwards settled down into the position of an avowed Tory. Mr. Disraeli had not yet found a place in the House of Commons. But Macaulay, and Grote, the historian of Greece, and Edward Bulwer, the novelist, were there.

The Prime Minister at this time was Earl Grey, who had been, one might say, the parent of the Reform Bill. He, of course, sat in the House of Lords, and therefore had little influence over the course of events in the House of Commons. The real leader of an English Government must always be in the Representative Chamber. He is like a commander-in-chief. His directions and his commands must be ready at a moment's notice. Many a crisis occurs in the House of Commons on which the fate of a measure or of a Ministry may depend, and when there is no time to send messengers across town to hunt up the nominal Prime Minister whose House of Lords has probably dispersed hours and hours before. Down to the present day English Governments continue to have nominal

Prime Ministers in the House of Lords, but such a Prime Minister, whatever his abilities and his force of character, can in the very nature of things be only a figurehead. The condition is like that of a commander-in-chief who is twenty miles away

EARL GREY
(From an old engraving)

from the field of fight. Probably before long the system will be changed altogether, and it will become a matter of course that the Prime Minister shall be a member of the House of Commons and not the House of Lords. The real Prime Ministers within my memory have been Lord John Russell, Lord Palmerston, Mr. Disraeli, and Mr. Gladstone. All these, of course, sat in the Representative Chamber. The leader of the House of Commons and of the Liberal party at the time when Mr. Gladstone first entered Parliament was the Chancellor of the Exchequer, Viscount Al-

thorp. It is perhaps hardly necessary to explain
to most readers that the title in Lord Althorp's
case, as in so many others, was what we call a
" title of courtesy," and merely indicates that the
bearer of it is a son of a peer, and, not being a
peer himself, is free to be elected to the House of
Commons. But even very intelligent and well-
informed strangers are often much puzzled by our
various titles and the difficulty of understanding
why this man can and this man cannot be a member of the House of Commons. I remember explaining at some length to a stranger many years
ago that Lord John Russell could sit in the
Representative Chamber because he was only the
son of a duke and was not a duke himself, and
that the Marquis of Hartington was entitled to sit
as an elected representative for precisely the same
reason. But, then, my friend asked me, what
about Lord Palmerston? He surely cannot have
a father living, and how does he come to sit here?
The explanation was easy enough. Lord Palmerston's title belonged to the Irish peerage, and an
Irish nobleman, if he is not chosen by his peers to
represent them in the House of Lords, is quite free
to be elected a member of the House of Commons.

Lord Althorp, then, at this time led the Government and the Liberal party in the Representative
Chamber. He was not a man of much statesman-

WILLIAM EWART GLADSTONE

(From a painting by George Hayter)

like ability, but he was a good party manager, and when, later on, the death of his father compelled him to enter the House of Lords, the party suffered by his absence from the real battlefield. Lord Althorp had at this time a considerable majority of the House of Commons behind him. But, on the other hand, the Tory minority under Sir Robert Peel was all compact and of one mind, and was willing to follow a leader whose sagacity, strength, and debating power were beyond any question or cavil. A writer who describes the events of this opening Parliament says that " to one danger, indeed, Ministers were exposed, a danger, however, which they themselves had created : their performances must either fall greatly short of what they had promised, and produce disappointment, or they must throw themselves, to support their popularity, into a career of dangerous and unconstitutional change on which they did not voluntarily care to enter. The public agitation which they had created and fostered in the great mass of the people for the purpose of carrying the Reform Bill had produced extravagant expectations that the meeting of a Reformed Parliament would necessarily be followed by the redress of everything deemed a grievance and the cure of everything called an evil." This is, indeed, a very correct description of the foremost peril to which the

Ministers found themselves exposed at the first meeting of that Reformed Parliament from which so much was expected and so much was dreaded.

Mr. Gladstone came quietly and modestly into the debates of the session. He first spoke on what might be called a local rather than a public question. Later on the Government had been strongly pressed by some of its own supporters to deal with the condition of slavery in the colonies. The new Colonial Secretary, Mr. Stanley, who had just resigned the office of what I may call Irish Secretary, brought forward a series of resolutions intended to lead up to the extinction of slavery in England's colonial possessions. It was in the course of the debate that followed that Mr. Gladstone delivered his first really important speech. Yet it was not a speech on the broad and general subject, but rather a reply to a sort of attack made by Lord Howick, afterwards Earl Grey, on the management of Sir John Gladstone's plantation in Demerara. Mr. Gladstone warmly vindicated his father from any charge of countenancing hard dealing with the slaves on his plantation. Every one felt the most genial sympathy with the young man called on to defend in his first important speech the conduct of his father as an owner of property in slave labor. Two or three weeks after this Mr. Gladstone spoke again in the

same debate, but dealt with the general subject.
He expressed just the same views as he had already
set out in his election address to the constituency
of Newark.   He was entirely in favor of the extinction of slavery, but he held that emancipation
must come gradually and after proper steps had
been taken for the education of the slave.   From
all that I have read or could hear I am not inclined
to believe that the speeches made anything more
than a passing and a personal impression on the
House of Commons.   Certainly I have no reason
to suppose that they gave to the House any idea
of the great powers which the young orator was
destined before very long to display.   I remember
talking years ago to some very old members of the
House of Commons who told me that for some time
Gladstone's speeches were listened to with only the
respect which the House always pays to youth, mod-
esty, and knowledge of the subject under discussion.
In Gladstone's early days, as in subsequent days,
the House detested "bumptiousness"—self-suffi-
ciency, "cheek," ostentation, and the unwarranted
assumption of any manner of superiority.   Many
experienced members of Parliament consider it
rather an inauspicious omen if a young man should
begin with a very successful maiden speech.   The
idea is that probably the young man has, to use a
colloquial phrase, put all his best goods in the shop

window, and that nothing is left inside. There are notable instances that way, and notable instances also the other way. The younger Pitt's maiden speech was a great success. The maiden speeches of Sheridan and Disraeli were ghastly failures. There is not much of a theory to be established either way. But I am inclined to think that Gladstone's earlier speeches did not put much of the goods in the shop window, and did not, indeed, give any idea of the wealth of deposit that was in the shop itself. It is a curious fact that Mr. Disraeli, Gladstone's lifelong rival, happening at that time to meet Gladstone in London society somewhere, and hearing people talk about him, wrote to his sister and gave her his opinion that " that young man has no future before him." It is well to remember that Cicero thought Julius Cæsar would never make a soldier.

The truth probably is that from the very first Gladstone had an instinctive, intuitive knowledge of the conduct which best suits the House of Commons. That conduct undoubtedly is the policy of waiting until your real opportunity comes. It is almost always a mistake to try to create an opportunity — to thrust yourself into any controversy in the hope that you can make an eloquent speech. The one fact which young Gladstone soon impressed upon the House of

Commons was the fact that he would not intervene in a debate unless he had something to say. Thus from the very outset he made himself sure of the ear of the House. Everybody knew that he would not get up to talk for the sake of talking, and that when he had said all that he wanted to say he would wind up with a few effective sentences and then sit down. We have to take Mr. Gladstone's speeches in this early part of his Parliamentary career very much on trust. The reports in Hansard, the semi-official records of the House of Commons debates, give only leading men in the first person, and Gladstone had not at that time advanced to the dignity of the first person. So we read only that the honorable member for Newark said that he would not at that late hour of the sitting detain the House too long with the observations he had to make—and so on. We can gather, however, even from these oblique and colorless reports, that Gladstone's style was even then somewhat diffuse and rhetorical, that it was usually very happy in its phrasing, that it was very fluent, and that the manner of the speaker was animated without being too dramatic. Mr. Gladstone, in fact, did not take the House of Commons by storm, and did not try to do anything of the kind. His great Parliamentary rival, Mr. Disraeli, did a few years later try to take the House by storm, and made a dismal failure of the attempt, and was thrown back consequently for many sessions in his Parliamentary career. One especial gift Mr. Gladstone very soon showed the House — his wonderful skill in the arrangement of figures. He came of a great commercial family, and he might be said to have been cradled in finance. To paraphrase Pope's famous line, he lisped in numbers, for the numbers came. He had some early opportunities of showing his capacity for such work, and thus he soon recommended himself to the attention and the favor of Sir Robert Peel. Peel might be said in a certain sense to be a Gladstone without imagination. In later years Gladstone used to be called a pony Peel, so much was he thought to have borne a resemblance to the great free-trade Minister. Now it is to the praise of Peel to liken him with his pupil Gladstone. So does perspective alter even in the practical life of Parliament.

CHAPTER V

THE principal events in Gladstone's first Parliamentary session were the division over the choice of a Speaker — a rare event in the House of Commons — the measure which put a limit to the system of slavery in the colonies and which provided compensation to buy out the owners of property in slaves, and the measures brought in to deal with the conditions of the Irish State Church and to repress agrarian disturbances in Ireland — Ministers having at that time no idea of any way of dealing with agrarian disturbances in Ireland other than the introduction of new coercion bills. I do not purpose to go into all these subjects. The task I have set myself is to tell, in the best way I can, the story of Mr. Gladstone's life. I am not engaged at present in writing a history of the doings in Parliament or out of it during Mr. Gladstone's lifetime. I shall, therefore, give an account of public events only as they serve to illuminate the story of that one great career. It is, however, of much significance to notice that during his very first session of Parliament the House had the ominous, portentous Irish question before it again and again. "The Irish spectre," as it was sometimes called, came thus across Mr. Gladstone's earliest Parliamentary path. A long time had to pass before it became clear to his mind that there must be found some other way of dealing with Irish political disaffection and Irish agrarian trouble than the simple, stolid, and useless mechanism of successive coercion measures. But Mr. Gladstone was probably making the beginning of his education in that way even in that very first Parliamentary session. The kind of friendship he formed with O'Connell may have had, all unconsciously at the hour, something to do with the expansive nature of his feelings at a later date towards the story of Irish grievances. Gladstone's mind was eager for the truth, but from the first it required to have the grip of very certain facts in order to lead it on towards the change. Gladstone learned truths most effectively by figures in arithmetic.

Early in 1833 Mr. Gladstone took a fancy for becoming a student of law. It was then his wish to go to the bar and practise there. One can easily imagine what a success he would have made if he had only followed the bent of that inclination. One can imagine how he would

have cross-examined some evasive and reluctant
witness, how he would have argued a point of
law with the judge, and how he would have
carried the jury along with him by the force of
his impassioned eloquence. He did not, however,
pursue his design, and although he was a student at Lincoln's Inn for more than six years,
he never took any step towards getting called
to the bar, and at length requested that his name
should be removed from the books of the society,
on the ground that he had no longer any intention of becoming an advocate. In the meantime,
of course, everything had changed with him, and
he had found his real career lying straight and
shining before him. His great love for arithmetic and his consummate skill with figures naturally attracted before long the attention and the
admiration of Sir Robert Peel. A change took
place in the government. The Whigs went out
of office for the time. They were, in fact, bluntly
dismissed by the King, William IV. — the last
time that a sovereign of England ever made use
of his supposed royal prerogative which gives a
right to the peremptory dismissal of a Ministry.
The Duke of Wellington was called upon to
form an administration, and he insisted that he
must have the co-operation of Sir Robert Peel. Sir
Robert Peel was then in Rome, but he was sent

for and brought back, travelling as fast as he could in those days of diligence and post-chaise. Sir Robert Peel accepted office, and made Mr. Gladstone a Junior Lord of the Treasury — a position which, for all its grandiose name, has practically nothing to do with the more serious work of administration. It was, however, the first round of the ladder, and Mr. Gladstone had set his foot upon it.

Before long he was raised from the place of a Junior Lord of the Treasury to be the Under-Secretary for the Colonies. Mr. Disraeli has said in one of his novels that an Under-Secretary in the House of Commons, whose chief is in the House of Lords, is master of the situation. So it was with Gladstone. His official chief was the Earl of Aberdeen, who, of course, sat in the House of Lords, and thus the whole representation of the Colonial Department in the House of Commons came into the hands of the young member for Newark. He had to answer every question put to the Colonial Office. He had to make every exposition of its policy. He had to defend every one of its measures which might chance to be assailed. That time happened to be a season of some anxiety and some trouble in the Colonies, and Mr. Gladstone had many an opportunity of showing his skill, his eloquence, and his mastery of each subject.

His career as Under-Secretary for the Colonies lasted but a short time. Lord John Russell carried a resolution in the House of Commons in favor of an inquiry into the property and the finances of the Irish State Church — we shall hear of that State Church again and again in the course of this narrative — and Sir Robert Peel immediately resigned his office. Gladstone, of course, went with him. It is well to observe that Mr. Gladstone's occupation of office under Lord Aberdeen led to a friendship between the two which had much influence on the lives of both men. In more than one great crisis at a later day Lord Aberdeen and Mr. Gladstone worked side by side.

Mr. Gladstone then had an interval of rest from the worry and trouble of office. He spent his time pleasantly, and according to his own ideas of how a young man's life ought to be spent. He took chambers in the Albany, Piccadilly, a great resort of bachelors of good position, and there, as Mr. George Russell tells us, " he pursued the same even course of steady work, reasonable recreation, and systematic devotion which he had marked out for himself at Oxford." " He went freely into society," Mr. Russell says, " dined out constantly, and took his part in musical parties, delighting his hearers with the cultivated beauty of his tenor voice."

Then Mr. Russell goes on to mention the fact
that Mr. Monckton Milnes, the late Lord Houghton, a poet and a host, who in his later years
was well known to Americans in London, had
established himself at that time in the metrop-
olis, and used to gather around him "a society
of young men who were interested in theology
and politics." "He used to entertain them at
parties on Sunday evenings," and "this arrangement," Monckton Milnes says, writing on March
13, 1838, "unfortunately excludes the more serious members, Acland, Gladstone, and others. I
really think, when people keep Friday as a fast,
they might make a feast of Sunday." Acquaint-
ances of Lord Houghton in his later years were
apt to say, half in jest and half in earnest, that
there was a distinct dash of the pagan about him.
However that may be, he was an admirable host;
he made it his business to know everybody who
was really worth knowing; he held out an encouraging hand to every young and promising
author or artist, and he was probably the very
last leading man in London society who kept up
the old practice of inviting friends to a break-
fast party. I may say that the "Acland" referred
to in Lord Houghton's letter still "lives, a prosperous gentleman." He is Sir Thomas Acland,
whose son, Mr. Arthur Acland, was lately Min-

ister of Education in Mr. Gladstone's Government.
Mr. Gladstone and Sir Thomas Acland continued
during all their lives to be as good friends as
they were in the old days of the receptions
in the Albany. Mr. Russell also mentions the
interesting fact
that Mr. Glad-
stone on one
occasion enter-
tained Words-
worth at break-
fast "in a
charmed circle
of young ador-
ers."

SIR THOMAS ACLAND
(From a photograph by Maull & Fox, London)

Nearly sixty
years after
those happy
leisure days in
Mr. Gladstone's
life, and dur-
ing those other
happy leisure days which came when he had
spontaneously closed his political career, a me-
morial drinking fountain to the memory of
Wordsworth was unveiled in the public park of
Cockermouth, in Cumberland, where the poet was
born. On that occasion Mr. Gladstone wrote a

letter in which he said: "I rejoice in any and every manifestation of honor to Wordsworth. I visited his house when a boy, and when a young man had the honor of entertaining him more than once in the Albany. I revered his genius, and delighted in his kindness and in the grave and stately but not austere dignity of his manner. Apart from all personal impression and from all the prerogative of genius, as such, we owe him a debt of gratitude for having done so much for our literature in the capital points of purity and elevation." It will be seen from this letter that Mr. Gladstone kept up to the end his exalted views as to the purpose and province of literature. He recognized to the full the power of even misused genius, but he recognized it as one must recognize the strength and the beauty of a volcanic eruption or a destroying avalanche. His whole soul went out in admiration of the genius which is used for what he calls "the capital points of purity and elevation." Disciples of the principle which calls itself "art for art's sake" many a time disparaged Mr. Gladstone's literary and artistic criticisms on the ground that he studied the purpose rather than the form. Yet it would be impossible for any of them to make out that Mr. Gladstone's favorites in literature, in painting, in sculpture, and in architecture were not illustrations of genius in its highest form. There could have been nothing very sympathetic for Mr. Gladstone in the writings of Swift; yet I have heard him maintain more than once with earnestness and warmth that Swift was the greatest writer of English prose.

All the time, however, Mr. Gladstone was a hard worker. He busied himself constantly with that part of the duties of a private member which is least known or thought of by the public out of doors. Nothing could be a greater mistake than to suppose that the work of a member of the House of Commons is confined to the hours during which the House is sitting. The House of Commons undertakes through its committees much, and far too much, of the purely local business of every city, town, and hamlet in the United Kingdom. Local gas bills, water bills, railway bills, and all manner of miscellaneous subjects of the kind are referred to what are called the Private Bill Committees in the House of Commons. Attendance on one of those committees is compulsory when a member has been appointed to it. The committees meet at eleven o'clock, usually, and go on until four o'clock, when the business of the House itself begins. Until very recent years it was quite common for the House to sit until three or four or five in the morning, and the Private

Bill Committees met at eleven o'clock all the
same. A member appointed to one of those committees must be present at each of its sittings,

THE HOUSE OF COMMONS AS IT APPEARED IN THE OLD PARLIAMENT
BUILDING, BURNED 1834

(This cut appeared in Sir Walter Besant's "London." Published by F. A. Stokes)

and all the time it sits. If he failed in his
attendance even for part of a day, the fact had to
be reported to the Speaker of the House of Commons, and the poor delinquent was summoned to

appear in the House and explain and apologize
for his absence, or receive the rebuke of Parliament. Into this seemingly dreary drudgery Mr.
Gladstone voluntarily plunged himself. The study
of that part of the life of the House of Commons
was interesting to him, as indeed every other study
was.

In the meantime he did not neglect his books
and his regular attendance at church. "Then, as
now," says Mr. Russell, "his constant companions
were Homer and Dante, and it is recorded that
at this time he read the whole of St. Augustine
in twenty-two octavo volumes." I have heard it
said that Mr. Gladstone was not much attracted
towards German literature, and I do not suppose
he ever felt drawn towards Goethe as he did
towards Homer and Lucretius and Dante. But
at the same time I must say that some of the
happiest quotations I ever heard Mr. Gladstone use
were taken from German literature — from Goethe
and from Schiller. I have heard it said, too, that
with all his passion for Greek literature, he never
cared much about Aristophanes. That may be so,
but I have to add that in my own hearing he once
delighted and amused the House of Commons
by an admirably appropriate citation from one of
the comedies of Aristophanes. Quotation is becoming less and less common in Parliament of

late years, and it is indeed regarded now as a
somewhat pedantic performance. I have heard it
said that Mr. Gladstone was the only man who
could compel the House to listen to a quotation
from Lucretius. Whether the House has gained
or has lost by its growing impatience of even the
most appropriate literary quotation I shall not
venture to decide, although I may have my own
opinion. The speeches in the House are not
any the less lengthy because they are no longer
brightened by some words here and there taken
from the wit and wisdom of the world's great
classic authors.

But now an event occurred of much importance
to England and the whole of the Empire. The
old King, William IV., died, and Queen Victoria
succeeded to the throne. William IV. was not
in any sense a great sovereign, but on the whole
he turned out better than might have been expected from the acts and the ways of his earlier
career. He had been brought up as a naval
officer, and a less manageable naval officer never
was in the English service. He had shown himself over and over again so incapable and impatient of discipline that at last it became necessary
to withdraw him from active service altogether.
His manners were rough and overbearing. He
sat in the House of Lords as Duke of Clarence,

and he made himself highly unpopular by his opposition to the abolition of the slave trade, and, indeed, to most of the measures which were demanded by the growing enlightenment of the country. There were many scandals in his life, and no doubt worse things were said of him than he deserved. But he positively obtruded himself on the condemnation of the public, for he openly wrangled with some of his brothers in the House of Lords, and words were interchanged among the royal princes which would not be tolerated by any Speaker of the House of Commons in our time. Undoubtedly, however, when he came to the throne he turned out much better than his antecedents led the country to expect. He was already an old man when he succeeded his brother George IV., and he had not many years to reign. Responsibility certainly improved him, and his people became more and more reconciled to him as his life grew nearer to its close. But he never could understand the true principle of constitutional government, although he went nearer to the acceptance of it than his brother and his father had done. We have just seen how almost at the close of his life he still held to his supposed right to dismiss his Ministers at his own good pleasure. With his death the existence of personal government came to an end. Queen

Victoria is really the first constitutional sovereign who ever sat upon the throne of England. Through all her long reign she has never done or tried to do any act which could possibly be called unconstitutional. She has been guided throughout by the advice of her Ministers, and she has accepted her Ministers on the recommendation of the representative House of Parliament. The difference in this respect between the reign of Queen Victoria and the reign of any of the Georges or even of William IV. is so great that one has to think the matter over in order to feel assured that within that short time we have traversed so great a distance.

The public paid a decent homage of regret over the tomb of William IV., and then before long had forgotten all about him. The accession of the young Queen had, to begin with, the great advantage that it severed the crown of Great Britain and Ireland from that of Hanover. Through the history of what is called the Hanoverian line down to the reign of Queen Victoria, the King of England had been King of Hanover as well, and the connection had been almost absolutely hateful to the people of England. The crown of Hanover descended in the male line only, and therefore the coming of a woman as sovereign of England broke off the connection.

England has often since the accession of Queen Victoria had good reason to be glad that Hanover was no longer a part of her responsibility.

With the accession of a new sovereign, a new Parliament had to be convoked, according to the custom of that day, which has since been altered. Gladstone was now distinctly recognized as a rising man. He was put up as a candidate for Manchester without his own consent. He was not elected. But he had been put up also, and with his consent, as a candidate for his former constituency, Newark, and was again returned. His friends in Parliament were in what is called the cold shade of opposition. Lord Melbourne was Prime Minister when the Queen came to the throne. But most people saw clearly enough that the Whig Ministry could not last long. Melbourne was an indolent man, not by any means wanting in intellect, and capable even of statesmanship, if he could only have summoned up faith enough to believe in anything and energy enough to act on his belief. The foremost statesman of the day was, beyond question, Sir Robert Peel, and it was not likely that such a man could long remain what Edmond About once expressly described as "an unemployed Cæsar." It was only a question of time, people said, and what people said in that instance turned out to be true.

But in the meantime Mr. Gladstone had taken
to a new sort of work. He came out as an
author — as the author of a book on the connection between the Church and the State.

CHAPTER VI

THE full title of the book was " The State in its Relations with the Church." It was the first book Mr. Gladstone ever published. It created a great sensation at the time, all the greater because Macaulay attacked it in one of his most famous essays. Except as an illustration of Mr. Gladstone's intellectual development and his way of thinking on religious questions, a way which has never since materially altered, the book has little interest for the world just now. It effected nothing in the progress of human thought; it neither advanced nor retarded anything; but it gives us in the clearest style an understanding of Mr. Gladstone's peculiar views. Mr. Gladstone's mind has been from first to last suffused with religious faith, and also with faith in the practical working of religion. At the time when he wrote the book the position of the English Church was strongly assailed both from the side of Roman Catholicism and from the side of rationalism. No better illustration of this double-

bladed kind of assault can be found than in the
history of the two Newmans. "Where is the
truth?" exclaims Arthur Pendennis in Thackeray's novel, discussing some question with George
Warrington. "Show it me! I see it on both
sides. I see it in this man who worships by Act
of Parliament and is rewarded with a silk apron
and five thousand a year; in that man who, driven
fatally by the remorseless logic of his creed, gives
up everything, friends, fame, dearest ties, closest
vanities, the respect of an army of churchmen,
the recognized position of a leader, and passes
over, truth-impelled, to the enemy in whose ranks
he is ready to serve henceforth as a nameless
private soldier; I see the truth in that man as
I do in his brother whose logic drives him to
quite a different conclusion, and who, after having passed a life in vain endeavors to reconcile
an irreconcilable book, flings it down at last in
despair, and declares with tearful eyes and hands
up to heaven his revolt and recantation."

At the time when "Pendennis" was written,
many readers, especially American readers, might
have fancied that Thackeray was dealing with
imaginary figures, types of the two different forms
of revolt against the English Church. Now, of
course, we all know that he was dealing with the
then real and living figures of John Henry New-

THOMAS BABINGTON, LORD MACAULAY

(From a photograph by Maull & Fox, London)

man and his brother Francis W. Newman. These
two figures served to illustrate admirably the kind
of revolt which from two different quarters set in
against the State Church of England about that
time. Mr. Gladstone was thoroughly loyal to
the Church of England, and was a believer still
in the possibility of her taking a governing part
in English human affairs. Perhaps it is not too
much to say for him that, according to his nature and temperament, he would have preferred
any Church to no Church at all, any religious
sway to a sway without religion. His book, therefore, was a bold effort to prove that every State
must have a conscience, and with the conscience
must profess a State religion. He contended
that the Church of England was still in a condition to expound the religion of the State and
to make itself the guiding power of the nation.

Macaulay, in his exuberant rhetorical and yet
practical sort of way, made mince-meat of the
whole theory. He took the view of the political
essayist and of the House of Commons. He pat-
ronized Mr. Gladstone's general ideas. He compli-
mented the young man on his rising abilities, spoke
hopefully of his career, and paid him some compliments on his style. But, all the same, he proclaimed the practical politician's view of the whole
theory, and he defied any one to explain how the

State was to undertake to have a conscience, a conscience of a purely transcendental kind, wholly
apart from the changing condition of things and
the new arrangements demanded by new difficulties.   Time has in its rough and ready way settled
the whole controversy long since.   Few men in any
civilized country are now of the opinion that the
State can endow itself with a conscience which can
decide in advance how it is to act at any wholly
unexpected crisis.   Still, there are not many of us
who have not a certain sentimental affection for
the exalted theory which Mr. Gladstone formed in
those early days concerning the duties and capaci-
ties of a State.

Of course the whole principle of the theory consisted in the idea of a paternal government.
Macaulay detested a paternal government, and was
never tired of saying harsh and contemptuous
things about it.   It is really the old immemorial
controversy between those who believe that knowledge comes by intuition and those who believe that
knowledge comes by experience.   Mr. Gladstone
insisted that the Church Establishment must be
maintained in England " because the government
stands with us in a paternal relation to the people,
and is bound in all things to consider, not merely
their existing tastes, but the capabilities and ways
of their improvement; because it has both an in-

trinsic competency and external means to amend
and assist their choice; because to be in accordance
with God's mind and will it must have a religion,
and because to be in accordance with its conscience
that religion must be the truth as held by it under
the most solemn and accumulated responsibilities;
because this is the only sanctifying and preserving
principle of society, as well as to the individual that
particular benefit without which all others are
worse than valueless; we must disregard the din of
political contention and the pressure of worldly and
momentary motives, and, in behalf of our regard to
man as well as of our allegiance to God, maintain
among ourselves, where happily it still exists, the
union between the Church and the State." Mr.
Gladstone pushed his opinions at that time so far
that he was not even intimidated by the difficulties
which surrounded the existence of a Protestant
State Church in Ireland. But he was perfectly can-
did in his admission of all the difficulties, and I
cannot forbear from quoting a passage which
showed how the mind of the dreamer was never
allowed wholly to confuse the mind of the practical
statesman. "The Protestant Legislature of the
British Empire," says Mr. Gladstone, "maintains in
the possession of the Church property of Ireland
the ministers of a creed professed, according to the
Parliamentary enumeration of 1835, by one-ninth

of its population, regarded with partial favor by
scarcely another ninth, and disowned by the remaining seven. And not only does this anomaly
meet us full in view, but we have also to consider
and digest the fact that the maintenance of this
Church for near three centuries in Ireland has been
contemporaneous with a system of partial and abu-
sive government, varying in degree of culpability,
but rarely, until of later years, when we have been
forced to look at the subject and to feel it, to be
exempted in common fairness from the reproach of
gross inattention (to say the very least) to the interests of a noble but neglected people. But however
formidable at first sight these admissions, which I
have no desire to narrow or to qualify, may appear,
they in no way shake the foregoing arguments.
They do not change the nature of truth, and her
capability and destiny to benefit mankind. They
do not relieve government of its responsibility, if
they show that that responsibility was once unfelt
and unsatisfied. They place the legislature of this
country in the condition, as it were, of one called to
do penance for past offences; but duty remains
unaltered and imperative, and abates nothing of her
demand on our services. It is undoubtedly com-
petent, in a constitutional view, to the government
of this country to continue the present disposition
of Church property in Ireland. It appears not too

much to assume that our Imperial legislature has been qualified to take, and has taken in point of fact, a sounder view of religious truth than the majority of the people of Ireland in their destitute and uninstructed state. We believe accordingly that that which we place before them is, whether they know it or not, calculated to be beneficial to them, and that if they know it not now they will know it when it is presented to them fairly. Shall we then purchase their applause at the expense of their substantial, nay, their spiritual interests?"

There is something positively touching in the ingenuousness, the sincere simplicity, of this way of putting the question. The State knows better than the people what the people ought to believe in religious matters, and therefore the State is warranted in spending the money of the people in teaching the people what the State thinks they ought to believe. The State in a constitutional country means the sovereign, the administration, and, above all, the majority for the time in the Representative Assembly. Now, in the case of the British Empire the sovereign at the time about which we are writing, or, at all events, just before it, was William the Fourth. The Prime Minister might have been the Duke of Wellington, let us say, or Lord Melbourne. The majority of the House of Commons were elected to support one political party or the other. This, then, was the State which, according to Mr. Gladstone's ideas at that time, was qualified to teach the people what they ought to believe in matters of religion. It seems now only necessary to set forth the theory in order to dispose of it. But the interest of the theory is to us in the fact that it was then maintained, sincerely and eloquently maintained, by Mr. Gladstone.

I have said that Mr. Gladstone's way of thinking on religious questions has never altered materially since the publication of the book on "The State in its Relations with the Church." I do not know that this statement of mine needs any explanation, but perhaps I had better say that, according to my thinking, Mr. Gladstone has never modified the conviction which told him that religion in some form must be the one solid basis of every State. We all know how Mr. Gladstone afterwards came to modify his views as regards the State Church in Ireland. When we come to deal with that subject, it will be easy to vindicate Mr. Gladstone's general consistency. In the meantime it will be enough to say that Mr. Gladstone condemned the Irish State Church, not because it was carrying out his views of its purpose and its duty, but because it had utterly failed to fulfil the only purpose which could

possibly warrant its existence as a Church establishment sustained by the money of the State.
No one supposes that Mr. Gladstone would at
any time have desired to set up a State Church
in Bengal because he considered that the English
State was more likely to know all about the
truths of religion than the natives of that Indian
province.

Another passage from Mr. Gladstone's book
concerning the Irish Church may also be quoted.
" It does indeed," Mr. Gladstone goes on to affirm,
"so happen that there are also powerful motives
on the other side concurring with that which has
here been represented as paramount. In the first
instance, we are not called upon to establish a
creed, but only to maintain an existing legal settlement where our constitutional right is undoubted.   In the second, political consideration
tends strongly to recommend that maintenance.
A common form of faith binds the Irish Protestants to ourselves, while they, on the other hand,
are fast linked to Ireland, and thus they supply
the most natural bond of connection between the
countries. But if England, by overthrowing their
Church, should weaken their moral position, they
would be no longer able, perhaps no longer willing, to counteract the desires of the majority tending under the direction of their leaders (however,

by a wise policy, revocable from that fatal course)
to what is termed national independence.   Pride
and fear on the one hand are therefore bearing
up against more immediate apprehension and
difficulty on the other.   And with some men these
may be the fundamental considerations, but it may
be doubted whether such men will not flinch in
some stage of the contest should its aspect at any
moment become unfavorable."

Exactly.   There is just where, to use a colloquial
phrase, the trouble comes in.   The lofty head of
speculation, to quote some famous words, has to
bow to grovelling experience.   Statesmen of the
wisest class will not, as a rule, batter their heads
against stone walls.   If a subject people will not
stand the imposition of a State Church which does
not belong to their faith or their traditions or their
history, it soon comes to be a question whether the
doctrine is to be thorough, whether it is to be enforced at all risks, or whether it is to be quietly
modified.   All experience tells us that, sooner or
later, the doctrine has to be modified or that civil
war and separation must result.   Macaulay once
again showed himself the practical statesman, the
thorough man of the world, when he laid down the
law that the essence of politics is compromise.   Mr.
Gladstone was still too young in feeling, and still
too completely overborne by that religious enthu-

siasm which has always been an exalted part of his
nature, to accept the idea of compromise where
what he believed great and fundamental truths were
concerned. Gradually he came to recognize the
fact that a statesman must work with his materials,
to perceive the truth of that profound saying of
Burke's which is apt to be misunderstood at a first
reading, yet has only to be read again and again in
order to impress its thorough wisdom on the mind,
that the human system which is founded on the
heroic virtues is doomed to failure and even to corruption. No race of men can always or long be in
the mood of heroic virtue, and human systems that
are to last must admit some compromise with
man's weaknesses and occasional wrongheadedness
and passion, and also with men's diversity of faith
where religious questions are concerned. All the
same, Mr. Gladstone's exalted views in his book on
the relations of the Church with the State seem to
me to shine out with a peculiar attractiveness at a
time and among a set of men with whom there was
so little profundity, or even seriousness, as regards
religious questions. Of course I do not agree with
his views — I suppose nobody now accepts them.
To a man like Lord Melbourne or a man like Lord
Palmerston they would, no doubt, have appeared
exquisitely ridiculous. But to me it counts a good
deal in their favor that they could not possibly have

appealed to the feelings of men like Lord Melbourne and Lord Palmerston. Even Sir Robert Peel, a man who had an earnestness of character and a strength of belief far beyond anything possessed by Melbourne or Palmerston, is said, on good authority, to have expressed his wonder that a man like Gladstone, with such a career before him, should have taken the trouble to write books. This, however, came of a general objection to a rising statesman throwing away his energy on the writing of books, and not from any philosophical or theological objection to the opinions of Mr. Gladstone.

The book and its whole history are interesting if only as an illustration of Mr. Gladstone's insatiable ardor for intellectual work of various kinds. He was always looking out for new and different fields of labor. Goethe was not content to be a poet and a novelist, but he must also be a naturalist and a pioneer of the theory of evolution. Gladstone was not content with being an orator and a statesman, he must also be a theologian, a reverent critic of Homer and Dante, and a translator of Horace.

CHAPTER VII

In 1839 an event occurred of far greater and more abiding personal interest to Mr. Gladstone than the success or failure of any literary work could possibly have been. Gladstone was then, as he has always been since, a hard and constant reader. He had at this time seriously injured his sight by persisting in studying too much by candlelight.

His physicians recommended him a complete rest somewhere in the south of Europe, and he decided upon spending the winter in Rome. In Rome he came into companionship with his old friend Henry Edward Manning, afterwards Cardinal Archbishop of Westminster, and in Manning's company he visited Monsignor Wiseman, afterwards Cardinal Wiseman, whose appointment to the Archbishopric of Westminster caused such a commotion in England. Among the visitors in Rome that winter were Lady Glynne, widow of Sir Stephen Richard Glynne, of Hawarden Castle, Flintshire, Wales, and Lady Glynne's daughters.

Mr. Gladstone had already some knowledge of these ladies, for he had known Lady Glynne's eldest son at Oxford, and had visited him at Hawarden a few years before the winter in Rome.

LORD LYTTELTON

(From a photograph by Maull & Fox, London)

The result of the visit to Rome was that Gladstone became attached and engaged to Lady Glynne's elder daughter, Miss Catherine Glynne. On the 25th of July, 1839, he was married at Hawarden to Miss Glynne, and at the same time and place the younger daughter, Miss Mary Glynne, was married to George William, the fourth Lord Lyttelton. Miss Catherine Glynne, now Mrs. Gladstone, was sister of Sir Stephen Glynne, and in the event of Sir Stephen's death without offspring the Hawarden Castle and its property were to pass to her on behalf of her issue. Sir Stephen Glynne was the last baronet of his name, and on his death, much later on, Hawarden passed into the hands of Mr. and Mrs. Gladstone. Much of Gladstone's later life is associated in public memory with Hawarden Castle. We think of him, of course, first of all, in the House of Commons; then, perhaps, in the official residence, Downing Street, London, or Carlton House Terrace; and more lately in Hawarden Castle.

Without in the least degree invading the sacred domain of a great man's private life, it may be said that no marriage could possibly have been more happy than that of Mr. and Mrs. Gladstone. The pair were young together, became mature together, and grew old together. I do not merely mean to say that they passed their lives in the same dwelling, but what I do mean to say is that they were always thoroughly together in purpose and in spirit, in heart and in soul. There never could have been a wife more absolutely devoted to her husband and to his cause than Mrs. Gladstone. There was something unspeakably touching, even to mere and casual observers like myself, in the tender care which she always lavished upon him, a care which advancing years seemed rather to increase than to diminish. One was reminded sometimes of the saying of Burke, that he never had an outside trouble in his life which did not vanish at the sight

of his wife when he crossed the threshold of his
home. Gladstone had several children. Two of
his sons were at one time members of the House
of Commons. William Henry, the eldest son, has
long since passed out of life. Herbert Gladstone

HENRY N. GLADSTONE AND HERBERT J. GLADSTONE AS BOYS
(Photographed from water color originals painted by Mary Severn)

is, I hope and fully believe, destined to carry on
the renown of the name. A young man, whatever
his ability, is naturally overshadowed by the fame
of such a father as William Ewart Gladstone.
Herbert Gladstone has kept as far as he could in
the background, but he has undoubted capacity, a

cool judgment, a clear head, and a ready power in debate, while he has a voice that for penetrating capacity and melodious tone brings back sometimes a delightful recollection of his father.

Mr. Gladstone himself made quite lately a touching allusion to his connection with Hawarden Castle. It came about in this way. In March, 1896, he was present at the opening of a new line of railway between Liverpool and North Wales, the first sod of which he had cut in the October of 1893. In the course of a short speech which he delivered he recalled the memories of his boyhood in Liverpool, and spoke of his more recent connection with North Wales. " I remember," he said, " when as a little boy I used to stroll upon the sands of the Mersey, now occupied for the most part by Liverpool docks. I remember how we used to look across the Mersey upon the Hundred of Wirral, and upon the Welsh hills beyond, just as an Englishman standing upon the cliffs of Dover now looks across into France. In point of fact, that is a feeble illustration, because France is now far more familiar to an Englishman standing on the cliffs of Dover than either Cheshire or North Wales was to the inhabitant of Lancashire at the period of which I speak. That has all been changed by a long, a hard, and a manful struggle, and a hard, stand-up fight between the great com-

G

panies on the one side and the promoters of this,
to all appearance, comparatively limited enterprise
on the other. The good sense and the right and
the true interests of the people have been with
you. You have struggled and you have won. I
rejoice in it. You were good enough to connect
my name and the name of my wife with this enterprise, but we have no other merit than that of
simply having borne such testimony as we could
to the true and the right. It is quite true that
this enterprise has for me a particular interest. In
Liverpool, which may be considered one of its ter-
mini, I first drew the breath of life and saw the
light of heaven. With Hawarden, if it please God,
my last acquaintance with the light and with the
air is likely to be connected. These two places
are of great interest to me. I take them now
simply as symbols of the connection which it was
desirable to establish."

In 1841 the Liberal administration was getting
into trouble. The revenue was falling and the
budget showed a very serious deficit, something
like two millions sterling. Sir Robert Peel, with
his usual astuteness, saw that the time had come
for turning the Liberals out of office. Lord John
Russell, as representing the Government in the
House of Commons, brought forward various proposals for an alteration in the adjustment of taxes

so as to restore the equilibrium of finance. Sir Robert Peel opposed these measures successfully, and at last brought forward a direct motion declaring want of confidence in the Government, and rested this declaration on the whole financial policy of the Liberals. The vote was carried by a majority, but only a majority of one. The one was enough. Nothing was left to the Government but to dissolve Parliament and to appeal to the country at a general election. The result of the election was disastrous to the Liberals. The Tories came back with a large majority. According to the custom of those days, the Liberals still retained office after the declaration of the polls, and presented themselves to the House of Commons as an administration. The usage then and until much later was that a Government, although outvoted and defeated at a general election, should retain office until formally expelled by a vote of the House of Commons. The formal expulsion soon came. The debate on the Address, prolonged over three nights and finishing at three o'clock on the morning of the 28th of August, 1841, left the Liberal Government in a minority of 91. Sir Robert Peel was immediately sent for by the Queen, and undertook to form a Ministry. Mr. Gladstone had been once more returned for Newark, and was, of course, invited by Sir Robert Peel to join the new administration.

It has often been stated, I do not know with what truth, that Mr. Gladstone was very anxious to become Chief Secretary to the Lord Lieutenant of Ireland — in other and less technical terms, Irish Secretary. Many great English statesmen, Sir Robert Peel himself among the rest, began their public career, or at least the more responsible part of it, in the office of Irish Secretary. Sir Robert Peel, however, appears to have thoroughly understood that the first tendency of Gladstone's genius was towards finance. He, therefore, appointed him Vice-President of the Board of Trade and Master of the Mint.

Mr. George Russell cites an interesting description given by the late Baron Bunsen of a dinner about this time, at which Mr. Gladstone was present, on the occasion of the then King of Prussia's birthday. "Never," says Baron Bunsen, "was heard a more exquisite speech; it flowed like a gentle and translucent stream. . . . We drove back to town in the clearest starlight, Gladstone continuing with unabated animation to pour forth his harmonious thoughts in melodious tones." At that time Mr. Gladstone was greatly interested in the scheme for the setting up of an Anglican Bishopric at Jerusalem. Baron Bunsen was one of the most re-

markable men of his time. Of poor parentage
and obscure birth, he made himself famous as a
linguist and a scientific scholar. The "Edinburgh Review" said of him that he "was endowed
by nature with the warmest and broadest sympathies. His knowledge was vast and varied.
To no field of intellectual research was he a
stranger." He was for some twenty years Secretary to the Prussian Embassy at Rome, and at
the time when we met him in the company of
Mr. Gladstone he had just been appointed Prussian Ambassador to England. He had a great
love of ecclesiastical as well as of classical history,
and between him and Mr. Gladstone there would,
of course, have been a natural sympathy. "He
acquired," says the "Edinburgh Review," "a position and an influence in English society which
had never before been possessed by a German
diplomatist." There is something charming in
that description of the return to London "in the
clearest starlight, Mr. Gladstone pouring forth his
harmonious thoughts in melodious tones."

His new office was exactly the position for
which Mr. Gladstone was by nature best suited.
There was a revised tariff in 1842 which abolished or else greatly lessened duties in the case
of twelve hundred articles liable to be taxed.
Mr. Gladstone took the leading part in the prepa-

ration of this new tariff, and, of course, not only
in its preparation but in its exposition and its
defence. Then perhaps for the first time he displayed his extraordinary powers as a financier
and as a Parliamentary debater. He had to go
through every minutest detail of his scheme in
the House of Commons. He had to answer every
objection, to clear up every misunderstanding, to
reply again and again on the same question until
he had fully impressed his meaning on the intelligence of the House of Commons. He showed
the most minute acquaintance with every part
of the country's commerce. He proved himself
practically acquainted with even the smallest details of its commercial business, and the whole
House at once recognized in him a master of
financial statesmanship. All contemporary writers
unite in bearing testimony to the extraordinary
impression he produced on the House of Commons. For it has to be observed that a man
might have had all the commercial knowledge,
and all the mastery of facts, and all the skill of
argument, and yet not have been a fascinating
Parliamentary orator. But this was what Mr.
Gladstone then and forever after proved himself
to be. Tariffs and taxation and commercial comparisons are generally considered somewhat dry
and tiresome subjects. Even those who want

to know all about them will listen sometimes to
their careful exposition only because they want
to get the knowledge and have to listen while
it is being expounded. But Mr. Gladstone could
make dry bones of finance live again. He could
brighten the dullest financial subject with what
might almost be called the musical touch of
genius. That was the quality which he then
for the first time displayed in full to the House
of Commons. In this way he was like Peel.
People, indeed, then began to speak of him as
a "pony Peel." In after years the public began
to recognize that the pupil had surpassed the
master. From the time of the debates on the
revised tariff it was quite evident that Gladstone
was the great coming financial minister. It was
evident, too, that he was the great coming Parliamentary orator. His admission to the Cabinet
was only a question of opportunity. All the
time, however, he still kept up his studies in
ecclesiastical history, his readings in the great
classic poets, and his interest in all questions
that concerned education and social improvement.

From some of his letters written at the very
time when he was thus impressing the House
of Commons as the rising financial statesman of
England one might almost be led to believe
that he was thinking nothing about finance, that

tariffs and duties were matters of no concern to
him, and that he was wholly absorbed in patristic literature or in the mediæval schools of philosophy or in the art of the Renaissance or in
the marvels of the ancient and modern potteries.
Nothing that was interesting came amiss to him.
He was as fond of receiving as of giving out information. He delighted in meeting any stranger
who could give him some new idea or some new
suggestion. Life must have been radiantly happy
for him at that time, when, with all the world
to interest him, he must have had the consciousness that with him a great political career was
just about to begin. We shall see before long
how ready he was, on a point of conscience, to
risk the chances of that career.

In 1843 Mr. Gladstone obtained for the first
time a place in the Cabinet. His reputation
had been growing so steadily that every one took
it for granted that his elevation to Cabinet rank
was only a question of opportunity, and that the
first time the vacancy occurred the position would
be offered to him. So, indeed, the event proved.
Lord Ripon resigned his place as President of
the Board of Trade, and became President of the
Board of Control — a Board established by Pitt
to control the affairs of India — and Mr. Gladstone succeeded him in the Board of Trade, and

became a member of the Cabinet. His course now seemed to be clearly marked out. He had attained the position which every one had long believed him destined to occupy, and there was nothing for him but to go on rising and rising step by step. He had never pushed himself, he had never spoken in the House when there was not a genuine occasion for him to speak. He had kept himself in the background, so far as it was possible for a man of such gifts to be kept in the background; his success had not been a sudden blaze, but rather a steady growth of light. Now, however, that he seemed to have found his place, he was suddenly compelled to abandon it. No outer force of compulsion was applied to him but the working of his own conscience dictated and enforced the step he was to take. In the earlier days of the session of 1845 Sir Robert Peel proposed to advance a certain way towards the propitiation of Irish public opinion. Sir Robert Peel had had this course strongly pressed upon him for some time by the Irish National Representatives and by the Roman Catholic priesthood of Ireland. He resolved, therefore, to establish certain non-sectarian colleges in Ireland, and also to increase the grant to the College of Maynooth, a college intended for the exclusive education of Roman Catholics and especially for the

education of Roman Catholic priests. The College had had a small grant for a considerable
time, which was given chiefly with the hope of
encouraging Irish students for the Catholic priesthood to remain at home and get their teaching
there instead of seeking it, as so many of them
had had to seek it, in France and Italy and Spain.
Mr. Gladstone was no enemy to the Maynooth
grant, or even to its increase, as he afterwards
proved.   But he thought that the proposals of
the Government put him into a position of much
conscientious difficulty. Was he to pledge himself to support the measure which he had not
yet fully considered, or was he simply to retain
his place in the Cabinet, as so many another man
would have done, and let the Prime Minister
have his way, or was he to retire from the Government altogether?   Now, there is a strong
objection felt in England to any member of a
Government who suddenly retires from it because
of what the ruder public opinion regards as over-
conscientious scruples.   A man who takes such
a course is very apt to find himself left in almost
complete isolation. "You can't count on him,"
practical statesmen say.   "You don't know at
what critical moment he may find that his conscience is troubling him, and that he is bound to
abandon his post and go apart into a corner and

think the whole thing over in the depths of his
moral consciousness." To be considered eccentric
or quixotic is almost fatal to a rising administrator in the House of Commons, where the principle of what is called common sense is encouraged
in a domination which highly wrought temperaments and intellects sometimes find it impossible
to endure. Many of Mr. Gladstone's closest friends
strongly urged him to conquer his scruples and
to remain in the Cabinet. One of those who
gave him this advice was Archdeacon Manning,
who had not then passed over to the Roman
Catholic Church. Archdeacon Manning pointed
out to him that his influence in the Cabinet would
be of immense service to the Church of England,
and that his withdrawal from office could not fail
to do damage to its interests. The same sort of
advice was given to him by other friends, each
from his own different point of view. "If you
leave the Government just now," said one, "on
this particular question, you are committed to
oppose them on this particular question when it
comes to be discussed as a Government measure;
and there you are — your time and your gifts as
a financial administrator all thrown away on a
mere matter of religious agitation." "Think,"
said others again, "how much we all expected of
you in the way of genuine social and educational

reform, and now, because of some curious scruple,
you are going to kick over the traces and get
out of the administration altogether."

Gladstone, however, remained quite firm. The
opinions that other men regarded as mere fastidious scruples were sacred principles to him. He
remained fixed in his intention, and he explained
his feelings very fully and candidly. He intended,
he said, to resign his place in the administration
— his first place in the Cabinet — but he firmly
declared that his resignation of office was not
necessarily to be followed by an opposition to the
scheme of the Government of which he was no
longer to be a member. "My whole purpose
was," he explained in a letter, "to place myself
in a position in which I should be free to consider my course without being liable to any just
suspicion on the ground of personal interest. It
is not profane if I now say, 'With a great price
obtained I this freedom.' The political association in which I stood was to me, at the time,
the alpha and omega of public life. The Government of Sir Robert Peel was believed to be
of immovable strength. My place, as President
of the Board of Trade, was at the very kernel of
its most interesting operations, for it was in progress from year to year, with continually wax-
ing courage, towards the emancipation of indus-

try, and therein towards the accomplishment of another great and blessed work of public justice. Giving up what I highly prized, . . . I felt myself open to the charge of being opinionated and wanting in deference to really great authorities, and I could not but know that I should inevitably be regarded as fastidious and fanciful, fitter for a dreamer, or possibly a schoolman, than for the active purposes of public life in a busy and moving age." These words reveal the whole nature of the man.

Mr. Gladstone then resigned his position as a Cabinet member of his great friend's administration. But although he resigned his place, he nevertheless supported the increased grant to the College of Maynooth by voice and vote. Had he been a man of less original power and genius, such a course of action might have rendered him hopeless for his whole life as a leading member of any possible administration. Being a statesman of supreme genius and command, he had, of course, to be put later on into a position befitting his political and financial capacity. But what I especially wish to direct attention to is the fact that Gladstone was not by any means regarded at that time as a statesman of such supreme political and financial genius. He was accepted as a very rising man, who was almost sure to become before

long a Chancellor of the Exchequer. But he was
not regarded as what Lord Palmerston once called
" the inevitable man"; and there was no reason
why, if he had made a political mistake and shown
an over-fastidious mind, he should not have passed,
as others had done, out of the running for high
administrative office. Men had not then in England imported from the political life of the United
States the epithet "a crank." But the reality of
the description was quite understood. They had
in Parliament then, as we have now, many cranks;
and to be a crank is to be a failure. It might
have been thought at that time, which had not the
experience of our time, that William Ewart Gladstone was going to turn out a mere crank, when
for his scruples about the Maynooth grant he resigned his place in the Cabinet and in the administration of Sir Robert Peel.

I am very anxious to direct the especial attention of my readers to this, as it now seems, quite
unimportant episode in the career of Mr. Gladstone. It is necessary to begin at the beginning,
and this is the beginning of one chapter of illustration of Mr. Gladstone's character as a statesman.
If we do not understand him by this revelation of
his nature and his temperament, we shall never
understand him at all. The whole question then
at issue has been long since settled, and is all but

forgotten. As I have said, Mr. Gladstone actually supported the Government in the measure brought in to increase the grant to the College of Maynooth. He spoke at some length in support of the increased grant. Then why did he resign his seat in the Cabinet because a measure was to be introduced which on its introduction he cordially supported? Here we get at a study of the character of the man. He had not made up his mind as to the purpose of the bill when it was submitted to the Cabinet. He could not pledge himself to support it and to speak for it. He thought it quite likely that it would commend itself to his maturer judgment — and, at all events, he told all his friends that he had not the least idea of pledging himself to vote against it — but he could not just then see his way, and he preferred not to take any responsibility for the measure, of which up to the time of its expected introduction he had not been able to make up his mind altogether to approve.

Just think what an absurdity this must have seemed to the hack ministerialist of the time! Fancy what the Tapers and Tadpoles, the Wishies and Washies of Mr. Disraeli's novels, would have thought of it! Only fancy — this young fellow, Gladstone, who has just got into the Cabinet, already feeling scruples of conscience about obeying the dictation of his chief, and actually giving up his place in the Government just because his own absurd conscience doesn't quite see its way in that particular direction! Well, at all events, there is one comfort — we have heard the last of this young Gladstone! Nobody will ever offer him a seat in a Cabinet again! Sensible men can't do with fellows of that kind. He seemed a coming man — and now he's gone!

CHAPTER VIII

THE FREE-TRADE STRUGGLE

On the twenty-third of July, 1845, Mr. Gladstone wrote to a very dear and intimate friend of his a letter, some passages of which have a distinct historical interest. "Ireland," says Mr. Gladstone, "is likely to find this country and Parliament so much employment for years to come that I feel rather oppressively an obligation to try and see with my own eyes instead of using those of other people, according to the limited measure of my means. Now, your company would be so very valuable, as well as agreeable, to me, that I am desirous to know whether you are at all inclined to entertain the idea of devoting the month of September, after the meeting in Edinburgh, to a working tour in Ireland with me — eschewing all grandeur and taking little account even of scenery, compared with the purpose of looking from close quarters at the institutions for the religion and education of the country and at the character of the people. It seems ridiculous to talk of supplying the defects of second-hand information by so short a trip; but

though a longer time would be much better, yet
even a very contracted one does much when it is
added to an habitual though indirect knowledge."

I am sorry to say that the suggested trip never
came off.   I wish it had come off.   I wish Mr.
Gladstone could then have gone to Ireland and
seen with his own eyes the condition of the peasantry and the condition of the landlords.   It was
on the very eve of the famine which forced Peel's
hand and compelled him to allow foreign corn to
come freely into Ireland.   Mr. Gladstone, if he had
then gone to Ireland, would have seen with his
own eyes, even in the course of a month's tour —
would have seen it though he had never asked a
question by the way — that the Irish cottier tenant
was being utterly crushed by the rack-rent system.
The Irish cottier tenant, John Stuart Mill said,
was about the only man in the world he knew of
who could neither benefit by his industry nor suffer
by his improvidence.   If he was industrious and
raised the value of his tenancy, his landlord came
down upon him for an increased rent; and if he
was improvident, the worst that could happen to
him was to go into the workhouse or else to starve,
either of which might well happen to him in any
case.   Mr. Gladstone's Irish land legislation nearly
thirty years later on would have been in all probability much more effective, and would have stood

much less in need of expansion and emendation, if
he had visited Ireland in 1845, and seen her condition with his own keen, observant eyes. But the
visit did not come off, and it was not until a great
many years after that Mr. Gladstone paid a short
visit to Ireland. Even then he did not go with
any intention of studying the agricultural conditions of the country. He had introduced and carried the first of his schemes of land legislation for
Ireland, and it was characterized by a certain nar-
rowness and even timidity which in all probability
would not have been found in such a measure if it
had been inspired by the personal observation of
1845.

In the winter of 1845 Mr. Gladstone met with
a slight accident which left its mark forever. He
was fond of shooting, as he was fond of nearly all
out-of-door exercises and sports. One day his gun
suddenly exploded at the moment when he was
loading it, and so injured the first finger of his
left hand that the finger had to be cut off. Since
then he has always worn a black ribbon round the
hand and covering the stump of the amputated
finger. Strangers visiting the House of Commons
for the first time, when Mr. Gladstone still occupied his leading position there, were sure to ask
what was the matter with his left hand and what
was the meaning of the black ribbon.

This was the only serious accident, so far as I know, which Mr. Gladstone ever encountered. He was, indeed, much later on, attacked by a cow in Hawarden grounds, but he kept his nerves all right, and he managed to escape without any serious harm. His passion for the hewing down of trees came at a later date, and it probably did more than any other exercise could have done to strengthen his frame and enable him to withstand the wearying effects of a life so much of which was strictly sedentary. For it has to be impressed upon the mind of the reader that during all his life Mr. Gladstone was a man of prodigious study. He was always studying some author or some series of authors. He wrote criticisms on Homer, criticisms by the enraptured admirer rather than by the dry-as-dust scholiast. He grappled with whole libraries of patristic authors. He seemed to want to read everything and understand everything, and all the time his Parliamentary work was going on in full swing. Now, the regular work of the House of Commons is occupation enough for most men. If they are inclined to stick to it, they find that they have plenty to do, and the more they do the more they have yet to do. But Mr. Gladstone stuck to all the details of his life in the House of Commons, while at the same time he was an indefatigable student of

VIEW OF HAWARDEN FROM THE SOUTH
(From a photograph by A. P. Monger, London)

literature, of history, and of theology.   No subject
that could be of interest to humanity failed to have
an absorbing interest for him.   All the time, too,
he was getting the very most he could in the way
of outdoor exercise.   No doubt this was the secret

of his splendid and prolonged physical health —
that he never allowed himself to become the mere
member of Parliament, or the mere student, but
that he always remembered that he had fibres
and limbs to keep in healthy, vigorous action, and
that whenever there was a chance of outdoor
exercise he was a man to get it and to enjoy it.

His political opponents made in later years a
good deal of capital out of his love for the felling
of trees. "That is Gladstone all over," they said—
"to cut down something which he can never cause
to grow again; there is his one chief idea of statesmanship." But this, of course, was later on. Even
still, Mr. Gladstone was generally regarded as a
rising young Tory statesman.

In this year, 1845, he wrote a letter to the late
Bishop Wilberforce, in which he explained that
his views with regard to the Irish Established
Church were becoming less fixed and clear than
they had been before. Mr. George Russell
attaches, and I think justly, a great deal of importance to that letter. I will quote some sentences
of it.

"I am sorry," says Mr. Gladstone, "to express
my apprehension that the Irish Church is not in
a large sense efficient; the working results of
the last ten years have disappointed me. It may
be answered, Have faith in the ordinance of

God; but then I must see the seal and signature,
and these how can I separate from ecclesiastical
descent? The title, in short, is questioned, and
vehemently, not only by the radicalism of the
day, but by the Roman bishops, who claim to
hold the succession of St. Patrick; and this claim
has been alive all along from the Reformation,
so that lapse of years does nothing against it."
I am not quoting this letter either for its political
or its theological interest. The Irish Church
question has been settled long ago, and settled
by Mr. Gladstone. No man in his senses would
now think of looking for the State endowment of
a Church in a country the vast majority of whose
inhabitants conscientiously refuse to enter that
Church's doors. But it is a common charge
made against Mr. Gladstone by his political opponents that his changes of opinion were sudden and
were in the political sense opportune. I have
the strongest conviction the other way, and I am
taking pains to make it clear that Mr. Gladstone's
changes of opinion were of slow and steady
growth, long thought out, and at first resisted.
Therefore I quote these sentences in the letter
to Bishop Wilberforce in 1845. They prove that
so far back as that distant time Mr. Gladstone's
doubts as to the value and the claims of the Irish
State Church were already becoming serious.

CHAPTER IX

I NEED not go over again here the old familiar story of the struggle against the Corn Laws and in favor of free trade. The Anti-Corn Law League had become a popular power in England. For a long time it was able to command but a very poor support in the House of Commons. The movement in the House of Commons was led by Mr. Charles Villiers, who, I am glad to say, is still living and, in Homeric phrase, looking on the earth. Mr. Villiers was an aristocrat by birth, a member of the great Clarendon family, so famous at many periods of English history. For years he led the Parliamentary movement in favor of the abolition of duties on the importation of foreign corn. Later on he obtained the splendid assistance, first of Mr. Cobden, and then of Mr. Bright, who both obtained seats in the House of Commons. Still the movement, more powerful in the country, made but little advance in Parliament, and, indeed, its prospects seemed darkest at the very moment when events were coming to insure its rapid success.

In England, and perhaps in other States as well, an object-lesson is needed in order to secure the passing of any great reform. The object-lesson in this case was given by the Irish Famine. " Famine itself," said Bright, "against which we had warred, joined us." In the autumn of 1845 the total failure of the Irish potato crop set in; and the vast majority of the Irish working population depended absolutely upon the potato for subsistence. Under the conditions, it was all but im-

THE RT. HON. CHARLES PELHAM VILLIERS, M.P.

(From a photograph by Elliott & Fry)

possible to maintain the duty on the importation of foreign corn. There can be no doubt whatever that the mind of Sir Robert Peel, and the mind of his great rival, Lord John Russell, had been tending more and more for some time in the direction of free trade. Peel's Cabinet all but broke up on the question, and he had to bring in capable men to supply the places of those who could not work with him in his new policy. Mr. Gladstone had by this time become a thorough convert to the principles of free trade, and he was invited by Peel to accept the office of

SIR ROBERT PEEL.
(From an old wood cut)

Colonial Secretary in the room of Lord Stanley, afterwards the Earl of Derby, who found that he could not go further with Peel on the way to a repeal of the Corn Laws. A curious fact in the story is that Mr. Gladstone's accepting office led to his exclusion from Parliament for the whole of the memorable session during which Peel's free-trade scheme was debated in the House of Commons. It came about in this way: Mr. Gladstone's acceptance of office compelled him to offer himself for re-election to his constituency if he desired to retain his seat in Parliament. But then Mr. Gladstone was the representative of Newark,

a borough which was practically controlled by the
Duke of Newcastle, from whose influence and
patronage, as I have already explained, Mr. Gladstone had secured his seat. The Duke of Newcastle was a sturdy protectionist, and could not
be expected to give his influence in favor of a
free-trade candidate. Mr. Gladstone felt a natural
and an honorable scruple about opposing his old
friend and supporter, the Duke of Newcastle,
and he therefore made up his mind to retire
from the representation of the borough and to
remain out of Parliament until such time as an
opportunity could arise for contesting some other
seat.

He issued his retiring address to the Newark
electors on the 5th of January, 1846. " By
accepting the office of Secretary of State for
the Colonies," he said, " I have ceased to be your
representative in Parliament. On several accounts
I should have been peculiarly desirous at the
present time of giving you an opportunity to pronounce your constitutional judgment on my public
conduct by soliciting at your hands a renewal of
the trust which I have already received from you
on five successive occasions, and held during a
period of thirteen years. But, as I have good
reason to believe that a candidate recommended
to your favor through local connections may ask

your suffrages, it becomes my very painful duty
to announce to you, on that ground alone, my
retirement from a position which has afforded
me so much honor and satisfaction." Mr. Gladstone declared that he had accepted office only
because he held that it was for those who believed
that the Government was acting according to the
demands of public duty to testify to that belief,
however limited their sphere might be, by their
co-operation. The course he had taken, he declared, was taken in obedience to the clear and
imperious call of public obligation. Mr. Gladstone, it was well known, had been the chief
inspiration of Sir Robert Peel on this question
of free trade. Even when he was not actually
in office, the policy of Peel's Government had
been mainly moulded by his energy, his knowledge, and his guidance. It seemed, therefore,
a curious stroke of fate that the whole session of
debate on the free-trade scheme should have been
carried on without Mr. Gladstone's presence and
co-operation. It seems to me something like a
positive loss to the history of the English Parliament that Mr. Gladstone's wonderful eloquence
and marvellous power of arraying facts and figures
should not have been allowed a chance of influencing that great debate. Sir Robert Peel, of
course, carried his scheme in despite of the re-

sistance of nearly all his former Tory followers. But he fell from power in a moment. He had undertaken to introduce a measure for the establishment of a new coercion scheme in Ireland. On the very day when the Free-Trade Bill passed through its third reading in the House of Lords, Peel's Coercion Bill for Ireland was thrown out by a large majority in the House of Commons. Some of the Liberals and nearly all the Radicals in England had always made it a principle to oppose mere bills for establishing coercion in Ireland, if unaccompanied by serious and solid schemes of legislative concession and reform. All these, therefore, voted against Peel on principle. The Irish members, who followed O'Connell's leadership, were, of course, determined to vote against it. All depended on the Tories, and the Tories were now thinking of nothing but revenge upon Sir Robert Peel for his abandonment of the cause of protection. Mr. Disraeli himself frankly owned that "vengeance had triumphed over all other sentiments" in the minds of the Tory party. The field was lost, but at any rate there should be retribution for those who had betrayed the cause. So the Peel party was turned out of office at the very moment of its greatest triumph.

Mr. Gladstone did not reappear in the House of

Commons until the autumn session of 1847.   There
had been a general election, and Mr. Gladstone
was invited to stand for the University of Oxford.
There could surely have been no seat that he was
better qualified to represent, or which he could
have had greater
pride in repre-
senting. Oxford
had been the
home of his
younger days.
Its scenery, its
surroundings, its
buildings, its his-
tory, its tradi-
tions, were dear
to his heart; the
sweetest memo-
ries of his youth
belonged to it;
his definite am-

ONE OF MR. GLADSTONE'S LONDON RESIDENCES
No. 6 Carlton Gardens.   (A. P. Monger, London)

bitions were formed and cultured and guided in
it. Gladstone was elected for the University. He
did not come first on the list. Sir Robert Harry
Inglis, a bigoted Tory of the old-fashioned order,
led the way, Mr. Gladstone came next, and a man
whose very name is now forgotten by most people
was the defeated candidate.   Still, Mr. Gladstone

came in as a representative of Oxford, and the
University did herself honor by the choice. Later
on, as we shall see, it was Oxford's perverse fate to
deprive herself of the honor. But for the time, at
all events, Mr. Gladstone was the representative of
the University of Oxford, and was in his rightful
place. It was later on but a new mark of his political progress when he had to seek another constituency.

Mr. Gladstone's address to the electors of Oxford
is even still a document of great public and still
greater personal interest. It explains for the first
time the change which had been coming over his
convictions with regard to the relationship between
the Church and the State. He acknowledged that
in the earlier part of his public life he had been an
advocate for the exclusive support of the national
religion by the State. But he came to learn that it
would be futile to try to maintain such a position.
" I found," he wrote, "that scarcely a year passed
without the adoption of some fresh measure involv-
ing the national recognition and the national support of various forms of religion, and in particular
that a recent and fresh provision had been made for
the propagation from a public chair of Arian or
Socinian doctrines. The question remaining for
me was whether, aware of the opposition of the
English people, I should set down as equal to noth-

ing, in a matter primarily connected, not with our
own, but with their priesthood, the wishes of the
people of Ireland, and whether I should avail myself of the popular feeling in regard to the Roman
Catholics for the purpose of enforcing against them
a system which we had ceased by common consent
to enforce against Arians, a system, above all, of
which I must say that it never can be conformable
to policy, to justice, or even to decency, when it has
become avowedly partial and one-sided in its application." This address, then, shows us Mr. Gladstone in his new stage of mental and spiritual
development. The old theory about the relationship between the State and Church has had to give
way to the teaching of experience, and to the in-
born conviction that it is in vain to strive against
actual facts. The true fanatic, of course, learns
nothing from experience. He clings to his political dogma although he finds it wholly impossible
to maintain it in action. To this mood of mind a
man of Mr. Gladstone's genius and capacity for
receiving new ideas never could descend. Mr.
George Russell, commenting on this event in Mr.
Gladstone's career, observes that that career "naturally divides itself into three main parts. The
first of them ends with his retirement from the representation of Newark. The central part ranges
from 1847 to 1868. Happily, the third is still in-

complete." Mr. Russell's book was published in 1891. We have since then seen the completion of Mr. Gladstone's political career. The whole story has been told.

For some three years after the dissolution of 1847, Mr. Gladstone's life was not marked by any distinct political events, so far as his particular career was concerned. They were three years of what Robert Burns calls "sturt and strife" all over the European continent, and in England and in Ireland, but Mr. Gladstone's political action was not of great public importance. He was as careful as ever in his attendance to his Parliamentary duties, and he spoke on all manner of important public questions. He opposed the measure making lawful a marriage with a deceased wife's sister, on grounds at once social and religious, contending that "such marriages are contrary to the law of God, declared for three thousand years and upwards." In absolute contradiction to the opinions expressed in some of his former speeches, he advocated the admission of the Jews to Parliament; and, indeed, I may say that one of the most interesting and important events of the general election which brought Mr. Gladstone in for Oxford was the election of Baron Rothschild, a Jew, for the City of London. Mr. Gladstone supported Lord John Russell in a resolution passed by the House of

I

Commons which declared the Jews eligible for election to all places and functions for which Roman Catholics might lawfully be chosen. He defended the establishment of diplomatic relations with the

MRS. GLADSTONE

(From the portrait by E. R. Saye)

Papal court. He called for reform in the navigation laws, a reform which would make the ocean, "that great highway of nations, as free to the ships that traverse its bosom as to the winds that sweep it." Any one could see by following the records of his quiet career during those years that they were a time of development with him. On many subjects his path was perfectly clear, and his way was to lead onwards. But there still clung around him some of the traditions of that Toryism under which he had been brought up, and which even yet had for him an almost romantic fascination.

In 1850 the first pang of sorrow was brought into the happy life of himself and Mrs. Gladstone. In the April of that year Catherine Jessie, a child not yet five years old, lost her life. She had suffered long from a painful illness, during which she was tenderly watched over, not only by her mother, but by her father as well. This was the first intrusion of death into the household, and we may be sure that it was always remembered. There are wounds which never heal for natures like those of Mr. Gladstone and his wife.

CHAPTER X

THE "Don Pacifico question" was the occasion of a great debate in the House of Commons. Lord Palmerston and Mr. Gladstone divided the honors of the debate between them. It was the greatest speech Lord Palmerston had ever made up to that time. It was probably the greatest speech Mr. Gladstone had made up to that time. What was it all about? Who was Don Pacifico? Such questions might fairly be asked even by a well-read young man of the present day. Don Pacifico figured in the politics of that day very much as Monsieur Jecker did at the time of the French intervention in Mexico. Don Pacifico was the comet of a season. His claims went very near to bringing on European war, and they certainly caused for a time a feeling of estrangement and even anger between England and France. Don Pacifico was a Jew of Portuguese extraction, but he was born in Gibraltar, and was therefore a subject of the Queen. He was living in Athens, and in 1847 his house was attacked and plundered by

an Athenian mob. The wrath of the mob was
inflamed because Don Pacifico was a Jew, and the
Greek Government had made an order that the
familiar celebration of Easter by the burning of an
effigy of Judas Iscariot should not be allowed to
take place any more. The mob got angry, and
wreaked their wrath on Don Pacifico's house.
Don Pacifico made a claim against the Greek
Government for compensation, estimating his losses
at more than thirty thousand pounds sterling. He
did not make any appeal to the Greek law-courts,
but when his demand was refused addressed himself directly to the Foreign Office in London.

The Foreign Office had at that time various
complaints, more or less important, against the
Greek Government. No doubt the Greek authorities had been somewhat careless and free, but it is
right to say that they showed themselves perfectly
willing to come to any reasonable understanding
with England. Still, they seem to have been quite
staggered by the demand of more than thirty thousand pounds for the destruction of household
property in Don Pacifico's modest little dwelling.
An English historian says that Don Pacifico
charged in his bill one hundred and fifty pounds
sterling for a bedstead, thirty pounds for the sheets
of the bed, twenty-five pounds for two coverlets,
and ten pounds for a pillow-case, and the writer

adds that "Cleopatra might have been contented with bed furniture so luxurious as Don Pacifico represented himself to have in his common use." The Greek Government had no faith in the costly bedstead and the expensive sheets and coverlets. They declined to pay, and the Don, as I have said, did not seek his remedy in any court of law.

Lord Palmerston happened to be in one of his bumptious moods, and he had got it into his head that the French Minister in Athens was privately urging the Greek Government to resist all the English claims. So Lord Palmerston lumped up the whole claims into one national demand, and insisted that Greece must pay up the money within a short, definite time. The Greek Government still hung back, and the British fleet was ordered to Piræus, where he seized all the Greek vessels belonging to the Government and to private merchants which were found in the harbor. This high-handed course gave great offence, not alone to Greece — which would have been a matter of little importance — great powers do not generally care much about the feelings of small States — but to France and to Russia. France and Russia were powers joined with England in the treaty drawn up for the protection of the independence of Greece. The Russian Government wrote an angry and, indeed, a furious remonstrance. The French Government withdrew for a time their Ambassador from London. All Europe was thrown into alarm, and indeed it was only the trumpery nature of the whole dispute, which rendered it impossible that rational nations could take up arms about it, that averted a calamitous war. After a while the whole dispute was quietly settled. Don Pacifico was lucky enough to get about one-thirtieth of his demand, and no doubt was well able to restock his house with very decent bed furniture.

In the meantime, however, the attention of Parliament and the public in England was directed to the serious nature of the course which Lord Palmerston had taken. Lord Stanley in the House of Lords moved what was practically a vote of censure on the Government, and he carried it by a majority of thirty-seven. For this, of course, Lord Palmerston did not care three straws. The Peers might amuse themselves every night of their lives, if they liked, by voting a censure on the existing Government of the country, and the Government would go on just as if nothing had happened. But it was quite a different thing with the House of Commons, and Lord Palmerston very well knew that his conduct with regard to Greece was strongly condemned by some of the most powerful men in the Representative Chamber. He acted with his usual skill and dexterity. He did not put up a pledged follower of himself or his Government to vindicate the policy pursued in Greece. He got an "independent Liberal," as the phrase goes, the late Mr. Roebuck, to propose a motion

JOHN A. ROEBUCK
(From a photograph by Maull & Fox, London)

vindicating the action of the Government.

Mr. Roebuck was a man of great ability, but eccentric, with, in fact, a good deal of the "crank" about him. He had never attached himself to any Government or Ministerial party, and he had often attacked and denounced the policy of Lord Palmerston; but there was a strong dash of what we should now call "the Jingo" in him, and he had rather a liking for a high-handed assertion of England's power. On the 24th of June, 1850, Mr. Roebuck proposed in the House of Commons a resolution declaring that the general foreign policy of the Government was calculated to maintain the honor and dignity of the country, and in times of unexampled difficulty to preserve peace between England and the various nations of the world. The resolution was ingeniously worded. It gives the mere Greek question the go-by, and talks only of the general policy of Lord Palmerston's Government. The principal interest of the debate for us now turns upon the speeches of Lord Palmerston and Mr. Gladstone. Sir Robert Peel made his last speech in that great debate, but the speech was memorable mainly because it was his last. But Palmerston lifted himself in his speech to a higher position than he had ever occupied before. It was not a speech of great eloquence in the oratorical sense, but it was a masterpiece of dexterity and plausibility. It appealed to every prejudice which could possibly affect the mind of the ordinary Briton.

He insisted that the foreign policy of the Government had been ruled by the principle which inspired the policy of ancient Rome, and by virtue of which a subject of that great empire could hold himself free from indignity by simply saying, "Civis Romanus sum." The quotation "fetched" the House, if we may use such a modern colloquialism. It probably secured to Palmerston his victory of forty-six, with which the debate con-

cluded. The whole speech occupied five hours
in delivery, and Lord Palmerston had not a single
note to assist him. Yet Mr. Gladstone's magnificent reply told upon the House, highly strung as
it was to impassioned self-admiration by Palmerston's rousing appeals. It was a great position
for Mr. Gladstone to hold when in such a debate
he had to maintain the principle of public and
private justice against so skilled, so plausible, and,
I must add, so unscrupulous an antagonist as Lord
Palmerston. Gladstone's was, both in argument
and in eloquence, by far the finer speech of the
two. It was a speech which glorified for States
as well as for individuals the principle of Christian dealing, of self-restraint, of moderation with
the weak, of calm consideration before a harsh
decision had been put in force. The speech, indeed, made the first full revelation of Mr. Gladstone's character as a statesman. It showed that,
above all things, he was the apostle of principle
in political as well as in private life. It was
nothing to him that a policy might be dazzling,
that it might be calculated to spread abroad the
influence of England, that it might make foreign
nations envious and English people elate with
self-glorification. What Mr. Gladstone asked was
that the policy should be just, that it should be
a policy of morality and of Christianity. John

Stuart Mill was said to have reconciled political economy with humanity. Gladstone endeavored always to reconcile politics with religion.

"Let us recognize," he said, closing his speech, "and recognize with frankness, the equality of the weak with the strong, the principles of brotherhood amongst nations, and of their sacred independence. When we are asking for the maintenance of the rights which belong to our fellow-subjects resident in Greece, let us do as we would be done by, and let us pay all that respect to a feeble State, and to the infancy of free institutions, which we should desire and should exact from others towards their maturity and their strength. Let us refrain from all gratuitous and arbitrary meddling in the internal concerns of other States, even as we should resent the same interference if it were attempted to be practised towards ourselves. If the noble lord has indeed acted on these principles, let the Government to which he belongs have your verdict in its favor; but if he has departed from them, as I contend, and as I humbly think and urge upon you that it has been too amply proved, then the House of Commons must not shrink from the performance of its duty, under whatever expectations of momentary obloquy or reproach, because we shall have done what is right; we shall enjoy the peace of

our own consciences, and receive, whether a little
sooner or a little later, the approval of the public
voice for having entered our solemn protest against
a system of policy which we believe, nay, which
we know, whatever may be its first aspect, must
of necessity, in its final results, be unfavorable
even to the security of British subjects resident
abroad, which it professes so much to study; unfavorable to the dignity of the country which the
motion of the honorable and learned member as-
serts it preserves, and equally unfavorable to that
other great and sacred subject, which also it sug-
gests to our recollection, the maintenance of peace
with the nations of the world."

I have thought it well to give this long quotation from the speech, partly because of its eloquence, its strength, and its beauty, but still more
because it marks a memorable step in the progress of the orator, and shows alike the reason
for his great triumphs and the reason, too, for
some of his passing defeats. Nothing could be
in broader contrast than the whole purpose of
Lord Palmerston's speech and the whole purpose
of the speech of Mr. Gladstone. Lord Palmerston appealed to certain national passions, which
have always in their inspiration a certain element
of selfishness and egotism, and even of vulgarity.
Gladstone addressed himself to the conscience

and to the hearts of men. He had not at that
time attained to anything like the supreme command over the Liberal party in the House of
Commons, and over his countrymen out-of-doors,
which it has since been his triumph to exercise
again and again with success. As we shall see in
the course of this narrative, Mr. Gladstone succeeded many times in prevailing upon England to
do some great act of justice sim-
ply because it was just. More
than a quarter of a century has
gone by since John Bright declared in tones of melancholy
conviction that the House of
Commons had done many things
which were just, but never anything merely because it was just.

SIR ALEXANDER COCK-
BURN
(From a photograph by
Basano, London)

Mr. Gladstone, later on, proved that a better order
of things might be attained. He induced the
House of Commons to do many things for no
other reason than because they were just. The
debate which I have been describing was illumined
by many powerful and brilliant speeches — the
speech of Mr. Cobden, of Lord John Russell, of
Mr. Disraeli, and of Mr. Cockburn, afterwards Sir
Alexander Cockburn, Lord Chief Justice of England. But the one speech of which it seems to
me history will take most account is the speech

of Mr. Gladstone. It was not merely a great
effort of reason and of eloquence. It marked an
era; it revealed a man; it foreshadowed a life's
policy.

That very day — for the debate lasted until
four o'clock in the morning — was marked by a
great national calamity. Sir Robert Peel, riding up Constitution Hill by the railings of the
Green Park, met with a fatal accident. His horse
threw Sir Robert, and then fell upon him. Sir
Robert was taken to his home, but could hardly
be said to have rallied for a moment. He died
on the second of July, in his sixty-third year. By
his death Gladstone lost the leader and patron
and friend on whom he had endeavored to mould
his own political character. Probably outside
Sir Robert Peel's own family no one felt the
loss more keenly than Gladstone did.

It is the custom in both Houses of Parliament
to publicly allude to the loss of some great member of either chamber. Mr. Gladstone delivered
a beautiful and touching speech in the House of
Commons on the evening of the third of July, in
which he told of the profound disappointment
which had filled the country because of the
premature close of such a life. "I call it," he
said, "the premature death of Sir Robert Peel,
for, although he has died full of years and full

of honors, yet it is a death that in human eyes
is premature, because we had fondly hoped that,
in whatever position Providence might assign
to him, by the weight of his ability, by the splendor of his talents, and by the purity of his virtues, he might still have been spared to render
us most essential services." Then he quoted
some especially appropriate lines from Sir Walter
Scott's poem, " Marmion ":

> Now is the stately column broke ;
> The beacon light is quenched in smoke ;
> The trumpet's silver voice is still ;
> The warder silent on the hill.

Not every one of Gladstone's audience understood at first the exquisite appropriateness of
these lines. They occur, indeed, in " Marmion,"
but they are lines on the death of William Pitt,
and are in the introduction to the poem.

The death of Sir Robert Peel had one important effect among ever so many others. It left
Mr. Gladstone free to follow whatever political
course his principles might dictate. The Peelite
party, so called, dissolved, never, as such, to co-
alesce again. It is impossible to suppose that
the influence of such a man as Robert Peel
would not have had some effect on Mr. Gladstone's individual action, and we do not know

whether Peel, with all his willingness to advance into new ideas, might have proved in his later years such a fearless advocate of reform as Mr. Gladstone showed himself to be. From this time forward we shall see that Mr. Gladstone shapes for himself the course of his political career. He was always a splendid second, a superb champion; but now for the first time men look to him for leadership, and the day is not far distant when he is to be recognized, whether in or out of office, as the foremost man in the House of Commons. Poor little Don Pacifico ought to be remembered kindly by English history for the mere fact that his preposterous claims gave Mr. Gladstone an opportunity of delivering his reply to Lord Palmerston, and claiming for England her sacred right to a policy of justice and of mercy. Thomas Moore, the Irish poet, spoke of Fox as one "on whose burning tongue truth, peace, and freedom hung." I have said in the House of Commons that the words would apply even more completely to Gladstone.

CHAPTER XI

THE NEAPOLITAN LETTERS

In the winter of 1850 Mr. Gladstone went with his family to Naples. One of his children was ill, and the doctors had advised that a southern climate should be tried, and so it was determined that a few months should be spent in Naples. Mr. Gladstone, no doubt, went with no other idea than to watch over the recovery of his child and to give himself a rest from political labor. Doubtless he was thinking much, too, about quiet and happy hours to be spent in the studies and with the books which he was growing to love more and more. But if he thought he was settling down for rest of any kind, he was doomed to be grievously disappointed. Yet I do not believe that in his heart he allowed himself to be disappointed, because his earnest nature sprang at every opportunity for doing any good to his fellow-man, and he never could resist the temptation of trying to right some wrong. " Rest elsewhere " was assumed as his motto by one of the great Netherland statesmen who joined in

resisting the domination of Philip II. and the
Duke of Alva.   Mr. Gladstone, too, might well
have taken the words "Rest elsewhere" as the
motto of his busy life.   He soon found that he
had other work cut out for him in Naples besides pensive loiterings among the ruins of Pom-
peii, or contemplating the outlines of Capri across
the blue bay, or climbing the sides of Vesuvius.

The kingdom of Naples was then one of the
worst-governed countries in Europe.   The dominion of the Spanish Bourbons was terribly
oppressive, and rebellion after rebellion was constantly going on.   I do not intend to enter into
all the questions involved in the relative merits
of Italian governments.   In all European countries then, including Great Britain, the common
idea was to stamp out rebellion as you might
stamp out the rinderpest.   Let us admit frankly
that the idea had not come up in Continental
States at that time — an idea which Mr. Gladstone afterwards powerfully impressed upon England — that the existence of rebellion was first
of all a reason for inquiring into the existence of
genuine grievance.   No doubt Mr. Gladstone
knew that political prisoners were treated harshly
in Austria, in Prussia, and in Russia, and that
they had been treated harshly in England and
in Ireland.   But, so far as I can judge, the gov-

ernment of King Ferdinand of Naples was more
harsh, on the whole, in its dealings with such
enemies than any other European State at the
time. In any case, Mr. Gladstone's was peculiarly a temperament to be impressed by the
propinquity of events. And here he found that
in the Naples where he settled for rest there was
going on a system of mediæval cruelty in the
treatment of prisoners of state. A large number
of Neapolitan public men who formed the opposition had been either banished or imprisoned.
Many thousands were lying in the jails on
charges of political disaffection, and were there
subjected to gross severity and insult. At once
there was an end of Mr. Gladstone's holiday.
He was determined to study the question for himself, and from the life. He obtained the means
of visiting the prisons. He saw the men in their
chains. He learned who they were and what
they had done. He found that some of them
were men of the highest personal character and
honor — patriots, statesmen, valuable citizens to
any State which showed itself worthy of their
co-operation. As the result of his inquiries and
his observation, Mr. Gladstone, on the second
of April, 1851, addressed, nominally to his friend
Lord Aberdeen, afterwards Prime Minister of
England, but really to the whole civilized and

Christian world, a letter in which he described and denounced the abominations which he had seen, and, indeed, the whole system of King Ferdinand's government. He followed this up with other letters, and the effect which they produced was an almost unparalleled sensation throughout England and throughout Europe.

He explained in his first letter that he had not gone to Naples with any idea of criticising the system of government there, or of looking out for grievances in its administration, or of propagating any political creeds or theories whatever. He said that the work which he had undertaken had been forced upon him by his conscience, and that even after he had returned to his own country he felt only stronger and more imperative the duty of proclaiming his views.

He very judiciously declined to go into any question as to the validity of the title possessed by the existing Government of the Two Sicilies. Whether the title was one of law or of force was not a matter for his consideration. He laid down three propositions: " First, that the present practices of the Government of Naples in reference to real or supposed political offenders are an outrage upon religion, upon civilization, upon humanity, and upon decency. Secondly, that these practices are certainly and even rapidly doing the

work of republicanism in that country — a political creed which has little natural root in the character of the people. Thirdly, that, as a member
of the Conservative party in one of the great
family of European nations, I am compelled to
remember that that party stands in virtual and
real, though perhaps unconscious, alliance with
all the established Governments of Europe as
such, and that according to the measure of its
influence they suffer more or less of moral detri-
ment from its reverses, and derive strength and
encouragement from its successes." He explained
that he had deliberately abstained from making
any British agencies or influences, diplomatic or
political, responsible for his utterances. The
charge he made against the Government of
Naples was not one of corruption among some
of its officials, of occasional harshness or even
cruelty to its prisoners, or the imprisonment of
men on charges not, in his opinion, sufficiently
proved. Charges such as these might in disturbed
and trying times be made, with occasional justice,
against any State in Europe. Mr. Gladstone's
indictment against the Government of the Two
Sicilies was that it deliberately violated its own
constitution and trampled on its own laws. This
point ought to be strongly impressed on the mind
of the reader. Mr. Gladstone did not merely ac-

cuse the Neapolitan Government of making the
full cruel use of laws which were in themselves
cruel. His charge against the Neapolitan Government was that it broke its own code of laws
for the purpose of inflicting on its enemies a
severity of punishment which the laws did not
allow, and that it obtained convictions by methods
which the laws themselves condemned. One striking passage from Mr. Gladstone's letter has, indeed, been quoted often and often before, but I
cannot refrain from quoting it once again:

"It is such violation of human and written law
as this, carried on for the purpose of violating
every other law, unwritten and eternal, human
and divine; it is the wholesale persecution of
virtue, when united with intelligence, operating
upon such a scale that entire classes may with
truth be said to be its object, so that the Government is in bitter and cruel, as well as utterly
illegal, hostility to whatever in the nation really
lives and moves, and forms the mainspring of
practical progress and improvement; it is the
awful profanation of public religion, by its noto-
rious alliance in the governing powers with the
violation of every moral rule under the stimulants
of fear and vengeance; it is the perfect prostitu-
tion of the judicial office which has made it, under
veils only too threadbare and transparent, the

degraded recipient of the vilest and clumsiest forg-
eries, got up wilfully and deliberately by the immediate advisers of the Crown for the purpose
of destroying the peace, the freedom, ay, and
even, if not by capital sentences, the life of men
amongst the most virtuous, upright, intelligent, distinguished, and refined of the whole community;
it is the savage and cowardly system of moral,
as well as, in a lower degree, of physical, torture,
through which the sentences obtained from the
debased courts of justice are carried into effect.
The effect of all this is a total inversion of all
the moral and social ideas. Law, instead of being
respected, is odious. Force, and not affection, is the
foundation of government. There is no association, but a violent antagonism, between the idea of
freedom and that of order. The governing power,
which teaches of itself that it is the image of God
upon earth, is clothed, in the view of the overwhelming majority of the thinking public, with all
the vices for its attributes. I have heard the strong
and too true expression used — 'This is the nega-
tion of God erected into a system of government.'"

This last phrase passed into history and into
literature. Mr. Gladstone gave it in the original
Italian in which he had heard it, and its fame
soon went abroad. Now, for the first time, Mr.
Gladstone had proved himself to be a leader of

truly Liberal ideas. Now there was clearly revealed in his nature that "passion of philanthropy"
which he himself had ascribed to O'Connell, and
which inspired him to the end. He was still far
from being a professed Liberal in politics. He
would still have put away from him the offer of
a place in a Liberal administration. But his ideas
were expanding beyond the narrow and hidebound
limits of the old-fashioned Toryism. Let it be remembered that there never was in Mr. Gladstone
any natural inclination towards republican sentiments. His whole feelings and reasonings went
with the monarchical form of government, and he
wrote, no doubt, with perfect sincerity when he said,
in his letter to Lord Aberdeen, that he complained
of the practices of the Neapolitan Government because, among other things, they were rapidly doing
the work of republicanism in Naples — "a political
creed which has little natural or habitual root in
the character of the people." He stood forth simply as a leader in the cause of humanity; that,
and that only, was the flag he unfurled.

The letter, as might be expected, created a profound sensation throughout Europe, and indeed
throughout the whole civilized world. A question
was put to Lord Palmerston in the House of
Commons on the subject, and Lord Palmerston
expressed his belief, derived from various other

W. E. GLADSTONE IN 1854

(From a photograph by Maull & Fox, London)

sources of information, that the statements contained in Mr. Gladstone's letters gave only too accurate a description of the condition of things existing in Naples. . Lord Palmerston added, however, that the British Government had not considered it a part of its duty to make any formal representations to the Neapolitan Government on a subject that belonged entirely to the internal affairs of the kingdom. But he announced that he had thought it right to send copies of Mr. Gladstone's letters, now embodied in a pamphlet, to all the English Ministers at the various courts of Europe, directing them to give to each Government a copy of the pamphlet, in the hope that, by affording them an opportunity of reading it, they might be led to use their influence in promoting Mr. Gladstone's object. There were, of course, numbers of replies, official and nonofficial, to Mr. Gladstone's charges. Some of the French papers made it a mere question of religion, and tried to convey the idea that it was only the case of a Protestant statesman denouncing a Catholic State. It is as well to point out that, in one of his letters to Lord Aberdeen, Mr. Gladstone distinctly exempts the clergy of the Roman Catholic Church in Naples, as a body, from any implication in the conduct of the Neapolitan Government. The whole mass of the re-

plies to Mr. Gladstone's letters had little or nothing
to do with the reality of the question at issue.

No doubt Mr. Gladstone was shown to have
made many mistakes as to dates and details and
persons. The most expert firm of lawyers could
not possibly have drawn up so long and compre-
hensive an indictment without making a mistake
here or a mistake there. All that Mr. Gladstone
had seen with his own eyes was beyond dispute,
and, in fact, never was disputed. But although
he had made the most searching efforts to get at
the literal truth of every statement submitted to
him, it was not possible that he could always be
proof against unconscious exaggeration, mistake,
or lapse of memory on the part of the narrator.
Yet the substance and the essence of his charges
remain absolutely immovable. Cruelties beyond
number were shown to have been inflicted by the
Neapolitan Government in absolute disregard and
defiance of the constitution and the laws of the
country. Mr. Gladstone frankly admitted the mistakes which he had made, but he showed with
clearness that the great bulk of his accusations
was established, and that he had in some cases
understated rather than overstated the gravity of
the charge. He published a letter in which he
once more vindicated his accusations. " The
arrow has shot deep into the mark," he said,

"and cannot be dislodged. But I have sought, in once more entering the field, not only to sum up the state of the facts in the manner nearest to exactitude, but likewise to close the case as I began it, presenting it from first to last in the light of a matter which is not primarily or mainly political, which is better kept apart from Parliamentary discussion, which has no connection whatever with any peculiar idea or separate object or interest of England, but which appertains to the sphere of humanity at large, and well deserves the consideration of every man who feels a concern for the well-being of his race in its bearings on that well-being; on the elementary demands of individual domestic happiness; on the permanent maintenance of public order; on the stability of thrones; on the solution of that great problem which, day and night, in its innumerable forms, must haunt the reflections of every statesman both here and elsewhere — how to harmonize the old with the new conditions of society, and to mitigate the increasing stress of time and change upon what remains of this ancient and venerable fabric of the traditional civilization of Europe."

Mr. Gladstone expressed a just pride in the knowledge that on the challenge of one private individual the Government of Naples had been compelled to plead before the tribunal of public opinion,

and to admit its jurisdiction. He even went so far
as to pay a compliment to the Neapolitan Government for having resolved on "the manly course of
an official reply," and declared himself not without
a hope that the result of the whole discussion might
be a complete reform of the departments of the
kingdom of Naples. Finally, Mr. Gladstone said:

"I express the hope that it may not become a
hard necessity to keep this controversy alive until
it reaches its one possible issue, which no power
of man can permanently intercept; I express the
hope that, while there is time, while there is
quiet, while dignity may yet be saved in showing
mercy, and in the blessed work of restoring Justice to her seat, the Government of Naples may
set its hand in earnest to the work of real and
searching, however quiet and unostentatious,
reform; that it may not become unavoidable to
reiterate these appeals from the hand of power
to the one common heart of mankind; to produce those painful documents, those harrowing
descriptions, which might be supplied in rank
abundance, of which I have scarcely given the
faintest idea or sketch, and which, if they were
laid from time to time before the world, would
bear down like a deluge every effort at apology
or palliation, and would cause all that has recently
been known to be forgotten and eclipsed in deeper

horrors yet; lest this strength of offended and indignant humanity should rise up as a giant refreshed with wine, and, while sweeping away these abominations from the eye of heaven, should sweep away along with them things pure and honest, ancient, venerable, salutary to mankind, crowned with the glories of the past, and still capable of bearing future fruit."

There can be no doubt that the publication of the letters and the vast-spreading controversy which sprang from it did much good, even to the political systems of the kingdom of Naples itself. No civilized Government can be thus compelled to plead its cause before the bar of universal public opinion without finding itself constrained to review its own actions and to revise some of its own practices. The prison system and the political trials of the kingdom of Naples began to improve a little from that day. But the kingdom of Naples was not allowed much time for improvement. Within less than ten years a revolution had swept it away; nor does there appear at the present moment the remotest prospect of a return of the Spanish Bourbons to rule in any part of Italy. Mr. Gladstone taught a lesson which it is necessary to teach to most Governments. I know, indeed, of no Government, except that of the United States alone, which is not under strong temptation

every now and then to deal harshly with its political
enemies, and even to strain the laws against them.
I have heard Mr. Gladstone's own words quoted
again and again in the House of Commons as a
lesson which ought to be an example to English
Governments in their dealings with political prisoners.   I can only say, so much the better.   The
moral of Mr. Gladstone's letters was never meant to
apply to the Government of Naples alone.   It applies to every State where, in times of disturbance,
the first thought is how to punish the enemy, and
all thought of finding out the grievance, if grievance there be, is waved away into the vague future.

I may remark that many even of Mr. Gladstone's
admirers, then and since, were of opinion that
there was something in the course he took which
was incompatible with the attitude assumed by
him in replying to Lord Palmerston on the Don
Pacifico question.   The course of reasoning is
somewhat curious.   Mr. Gladstone had denounced
in the House of Commons "the vain conception
that we, forsooth, have a mission to be the censors
of vice and folly, of abuse and imperfection, among
the other countries of the world."   It is pointed
out as something strange that a public man who
uttered such opinions should have almost straight-
way made himself the censor of vice and folly, of
abuse and imperfection, in the foreign kingdom

of Naples. Five minutes of reflection ought to be enough to show to any one that there is no inconsistency whatever between the one position and the other. Mr. Gladstone objected to the English Government, the English State, intervening in the affairs of Greece to set right certain defects of the Greek system, and with a strong hand seizing and confiscating Greek vessels to satisfy a preposterous claim for all but imaginary damages. What on earth has this contention to do with the right of a private individual to expose a terrible grievance seen with his own eyes in the prison system of a foreign country? We might as well say that Howard the philanthropist, because he visited foreign prisons and exposed the horrors of them, would have been inconsistent if he had objected to the English Government sending an invading army into each of these foreign countries in order to compel them to set their prison-houses in order. One might as well say, to come down to a smaller illustration, that the Member of Parliament who objected to our intervention in the domestic affairs of France or Italy is guilty of inconsistency if afterwards he writes a letter to the London newspapers to complain of the loss of his luggage on the French or Italian frontier. Mr. Gladstone acted with perfect consistency in these instances; and, indeed, the best possible way of rendering inter-

vention in the domestic affairs of foreign States
unnecessary is such an appeal to the public conscience of the civilized world as that which Mr.
Gladstone made when he brought the Neapolitan
Government, by his own voice and his own action, before the tribunal of European opinion.

He was then and since a strong friend and champion of Italian unity and therefore many accusations were made against him on that ground by
those who upheld the Austrian possession of Lombardy, and the rule of the King of Naples, and the
maintenance of the ducal systems of Tuscany and
Modena and other places. The whole controversy
is long since dead and buried, and I, for one, have
not the slightest wish to revive it. But one of the
charges made against Mr. Gladstone was that he
personally associated himself with Italian conspir-
acy, and that he was the intimate friend of Mazzini.
The only comment I have to make on this latter
charge is that I myself heard Mr. Gladstone, in
the House of Commons, many years ago, say,
with emphasis, " Mr. Speaker, I never saw Signor
Mazzini." I do not infer from these words that
Mr. Gladstone meant in any way to disparage
Mazzini or to associate himself with the charges
that were made from time to time against the
Italian leader. I merely note the fact that Mr.
Gladstone "never saw Signor Mazzini."

CHAPTER XII

Mr. Gladstone came out of one controversy into another. The excitement caused by the publication of his letters to Lord Aberdeen was thrown into the shade for the time by the passionate controversy in England on what was called the Papal Aggression. The then Pope, Pius IX., had made up his mind to give local titles to the Catholic Archbishops and Bishops in England. Ever since the days of the great Oxford Movement led by John Henry Newman, secessions had been going on among a certain class of devout and intellectual men from the Anglican Church to the Church of Rome. The Pope and his advisers might not unnaturally have been led into the belief that this movement indicated a tendency on the part of the whole people of England to become reunited with the ancient Church. As a matter of fact, the movement, as I have said, concerned only certain classes of pious, educated, and intellectual men. The whole vast bulk of the middle and lower classes of England had absolutely nothing to do

with it, and cared nothing about it. A very large,
far too large, proportion of the English lower-
middle and working class have little or no interest

JOHN HENRY, CARDINAL NEWMAN
(From a photograph by Mr. H. J. Whitlock of Birmingham)

in religion of any kind. But the Pope and his
advisers mistook the significance of the "Oxford
Movement," as it is called, and thought it meant
something like a national upheaval.

At any rate, the course taken by the Pope does not seem to us anything very formidable or stringent. Pius the Ninth issued a Papal Bull directing the establishment in England of a hierarchy of Bishops deriving their titles from their actual sees. The Bishops and Archbishops were there already, and were recognized and protected by the State; only they were called Bishops of Mesopotamia, or of Melipotamus, or of Emmaus, or what not, "in partibus infidelium" The Pope's Bull simply ordered them to call themselves Archbishops or Bishops of whatever division of England they happened to reside in. The first Archbishop appointed was Cardinal Wiseman, who now became Archbishop of Westminster. The Cardinal had been for ten years living quietly in England under the title of Bishop of Melipotamus. It is hard at this distance of time to get one's self back to any clear understanding of the mood of mind which made any Protestant care a straw whether Cardinal Wiseman was called Archbishop of Westminster or Bishop of Melipotamus. To make the whole agitation still more difficult to understand, the Catholic Archbishops and Bishops in Ireland always called themselves by their local titles, Archbishop of Dublin, Archbishop of Tuam, and so on, and nobody made the slightest objection.

But the truth probably is that the Pope's Bull

was issued at an unlucky time so far as regarded
the tempers of Englishmen, coming as it did just
in the wake of the Oxford Movement, which much
dismayed and offended the ordinary Englishman.
It was taken as an evidence that the Pope thought
that he had a right now to annex the whole of England to the Papal Church. Anyhow, a fury of anti-
Catholic passion flamed over the greater part of
England. Men usually calm and sensible lost their
heads over the affair. There were riots here, there,
and everywhere. Roman Catholic churches in
many towns were attacked and broken into; Protestant mobs were encountered by Roman Catholic
mobs, and a perfect saturnalia of disorder in speech
and in action prevailed throughout the Kingdom.

Lord Palmerston looked the matter very quietly
in the face. He did not attempt to conceal in private letters his contempt for the whole anti-Papal
agitation, but, like a cool man of business, he saw
that something would have to be done to satisfy the
public clamor. The Queen herself, in a letter to
her aunt, the Duchess of Gloucester, expressed
her deep regret at the "unchristian and intolerant
spirit exhibited by many people at the public meetings." "I cannot bear," she wrote, "to hear the
violent abuse of the Catholic religion, which is so
painful and so cruel towards the many good and
innocent Roman Catholics."

However, something had to be done, and I need
hardly say that useful legislation seldom is the
result of the vague conviction that something has
to be done. Lord John Russell was then Prime
Minister, and he brought in a bill prohibiting
under penalty the use of a title taken by a Catholic
Bishop from any see in England, or, indeed, from
any place whatever in Great Britain, and rendering
void all acts done by or bequests made to persons
under such titles. Probably never before in modern times has a measure been carried in the face of
so powerful and intellectual an opposition. Our
chief interest in it now attaches to Mr. Gladstone's
part in the long debates on the measure.

It may fairly be said that then, for the first time,
Mr. Gladstone assumed the position of a great Parliamentary leader. He led the opposition to the
bill simply as a question of public liberty. He
contended that if you tolerate the Roman Catholic
faith at all, you are compelled to allow it the use of
whatever forms and names and titles it thinks fit
to adopt. Men like Mr. Cobden, Mr. Bright, Sir
James Graham, Mr. Roebuck, followed with enthusiasm the leadership of Mr. Gladstone. Protestant
public men so intensely devoted to the interest of
their Church as Mr. Roundell Palmer, afterwards
Lord Selborne, and Mr. Beresford Hope, stood
resolutely by Mr. Gladstone's side. Mr. Disraeli

scoffed at the bill, although he declared that he would not take the trouble to oppose its introduction; but his language of contempt was as strong as that of Mr. Bright or Mr. Roebuck. On the other hand, some of the extreme Protestants like Sir Robert Inglis found fault with the bill on the ground that it did not go half far enough in its stringency. It would not be too much to say that, except for Lord John Russell alone, the whole intellect of Parliament was strongly against the bill. Yet the

ROUNDELL PALMER, FIRST EARL OF SELBORNE
(From a photograph by Maull & Fox, London)

measure was carried by an immense majority. Something had to be done to satisfy popular outcry. Lord Palmerston made the whole matter clear in one of his letters since published. "We must," he said, "bring in a measure. The country would not be satisfied without some legislative enactment. We shall make it as gentle as possible."

It proved in its application to be very gentle indeed. In fact, no attempt whatever was made to put it into practice. Cardinal Wiseman still called himself Archbishop of Westminster, and no one took any steps to prevent him from so doing. The strange popular outcry was satisfied, and it soon cried itself to sleep. Every thinking man saw, meanwhile, that out of those debates on the Ecclesiastical Titles Bill Mr. Gladstone had emerged a great Parliamentary leader. The most brilliant and impressive speeches he had ever made up to that time were delivered in opposition to Lord John Russell's measure. It has been said that Mr. Gladstone had decided leanings towards the Roman Catholic Church. No doubt a Church so venerable, with so picturesque and artistic a ritual, a Church "in whose bosom," as Thackeray put it, "so many generations of saints and sages have rested," could not but appeal to all that was poetic and all that was devotional in Mr. Gladstone's nature. But I do not believe that he had any sympathy with the especial doctrines of the Roman Catholic Church. It was at one time assumed by many that Mr. Gladstone was likely to be swept away by the Newman movement into Catholicism.

I have, however, spoken with men who were contemporaries of Mr. Gladstone at Oxford, who had themselves since become Roman Catholics, and who told me they never saw reason to believe that Mr. Gladstone was likely to join the Church of Rome. The whole controversy about the Ecclesiastical Titles Bill was with him only a question between genuine liberty and petty persecution. Nothing seems to me to be more honorable in the career of a public man than the part that Mr. Gladstone took in all those long and fierce debates.

Twenty years after, Mr. Gladstone had the satisfaction of quietly repealing the Ecclesiastical Titles Bill, which he had so earnestly and generously opposed.

We have no great concern now with the details of the struggles between governments and parties in the far-off days of the Ecclesiastical Titles Bill. The one direct interest, however, which we still have in those struggles is the fact that they pushed to the front two men who were destined to be almost lifelong antagonists. I speak, it need hardly be said, of Mr. Gladstone and Mr. Disraeli. Lord John Russell's Government was crumbling away, and, after a number of defeats, none of which was in itself of capital importance, Lord John Russell thought it necessary that he and his colleagues should resign. Lord Stanley was invited to form a

new administration, and so little certain was it even
then whether Mr. Gladstone had or had not severed
himself from his old Tory associations that Lord
Stanley, according to a rumor which every one believed, offered to Mr. Gladstone a place in the Conservative Government with the office of Foreign
Secretary.   Lord Stanley, however, vainly attempted to form an administration.   Lord Aberdeen was then invited to try his hand, and he, too,
could not see his way to success.   There was actually nothing to be done but for Lord John Russell
and his colleagues to return to office.   A Government thus set up again by sheer necessity, and because there was no other set of men who would take
the responsibility, never could be anything but a
failure in England.   Lord Palmerston did his best
to make the failure complete.   He was a most independent and, to use a modern slang word, "push-
ful" Foreign Secretary.   He did exactly what he
liked, without consulting anybody.   He had acted
repeatedly in defiance of Lord John Russell's warn-
ings and in defiance even of protests from the
Queen herself.   But he carried the joke a little too
far when he expressed to Count Walewski, the
French Ambassador in London, his entire approval
of Louis Napoleon's *coup d'état* of the second of
December, 1851.   Lord Palmerston was actually
dismissed from office — the last time, so far as my

memory serves me, that such an event occurred in
English history.   Nothing, however, could daunt
or dishearten Lord Palmerston.   He was up to the
front again after this tremendous blow, smiling, and
as if nothing particular had happened.   Within a
very short time
he managed,
with the Tories
to help him, to
defeat Lord John
Russell on a
measure that has
now no histori-
cal importance
other than in
that fact.   Lord
John Russell
went out of of-
fice, and was suc-
ceeded by Lord
Stanley, who had

EDWARD G. S. STANLEY, FOURTEENTH EARL OF
DERBY

(From an engraving by Mr. D. J. Pound)

now, on his father's death, become Earl of Derby,
with Mr. Disraeli as Chancellor of the Exchequer
and leader of the House of Commons.   This was
Mr. Disraeli's first appearance as a Minister of the
Crown.   People in general were greatly amused at
the notion of " Vivian Grey " becoming a Cabinet
Minister, " Sidonia " accepted as a British states-

man, " Coningsby " undertaking the responsibility
of Chancellor of the Exchequer. Disraeli's first
budget, however, was not a badly managed piece of
business, all things considered. The only object
was to carry the Government decently over the
session. Then there came a dissolution, and Mr.
Gladstone was again elected for Oxford with a
greatly increased majority. The results of the general election did not materially affect the balance of
parties, and the Government of Lord Derby returned to office. Mr. Disraeli now had to make an
attempt at a real working budget, and he certainly
did not succeed in the effort. Mr. Gladstone
stopped the way.

CHAPTER XIII

IN 1852 began the long Parliamentary duel between Gladstone and Disraeli, which ended only when, at the close of the session of 1876, Mr. Disraeli left the House of Commons and took his place, as he had always meant to do sooner or later, in the House of Lords. The debate was on Mr. Disraeli's budget, and it ended in the defeat of the Tory Government. Mr. Disraeli never, before or after, spoke with greater power and sarcasm and bitterness and passion than in his final speech in that debate. It was about two o'clock in the morning when Mr. Gladstone sprang up to reply to him. "Gladstone has got his work cut out for him," was the comment of one of the listeners when Mr. Gladstone rose to his feet. He had his work cut out for him, but he was equal to the work, and he soon made it quite clear that he was going to do it. Many members of the House and listeners in the strangers' galleries thought it hardly possible that, at that hour of the morning, and after such

a speech as Disraeli's, any further impression
could be made even by Mr. Gladstone. But before he had got far into his speech every one
felt that Gladstone was making a greater impression than even Disraeli had produced. It has
to be borne in mind also that Gladstone's speech
was necessarily unprepared, for he replied point
by point, and almost sentence by sentence, to
the speech of Mr. Disraeli. It seems to me that
from that moment Mr. Gladstone's position in
the House of Commons was completely established.

Then, as I have said, began the long rivalry
of these two great Parliamentary athletes. In
every important debate the one man answered
the other. Disraeli followed Gladstone, or Gladstone followed Disraeli. It was not unlike the
rivalry between Fox and Pitt, for it was a rivalry
of temperament and character as well as of public position and of political principle. Gladstone
and Disraeli seemed formed by nature to be antagonists. In character, in temper, in tastes, and
in style of speaking the men were utterly unlike
each other. One of Gladstone's defects was his
tendency to take everything too seriously. One
of Disraeli's defects was his tendency to take
nothing seriously. Disraeli was strongest in reply
when the reply had to consist only of sarcasm.

He had a marvellous gift of phrase-making. He could impale a whole policy with an epithet. He could dazzle the House of Commons with a paradox. He could throw ridicule on a political party by two or three happy and reckless adjectives. He described one of Cobden's free-trade meetings in some country place as an assembly made up of "a grotesque and Hudibrastic crew." It is not likely that one of Cobden's meetings was more grotesque or Hudibrastic than any other public meeting anywhere. But that did not concern the House of Commons; the description was

BENJAMIN DISRAELI

(From an old portrait representing him at the time of his entering Parliament)

humorous and effective; it made people laugh, and the adjectives stuck. Disraeli was never happy in statement. When he had to explain a policy, financial or other, he might really be regarded as a very dull speaker. Gladstone was especially brilliant in statement. He could give to an exposition of figures the fascination of a romance or a poem. Gladstone never could be, under any possible conditions, a dull speaker. He was no equal of Disraeli's in the gift of sarcasm and what Disraeli himself called "flouts and jeers." But in a reply he swept his antagonist before him with his marvellous eloquence, compounded of reason and passion.

I heard nearly all the great speeches made by both the men in that Parliamentary duel which lasted for so many years. My own observation and judgment gave the superiority to Mr. Gladstone all through, but I quite admit that Disraeli stood up well to his great opponent, and that it was not always easy to award the prize of victory. The two men's voices were curiously unlike. Disraeli had a deep, low, powerful voice, heard everywhere throughout the House, but having little variety or music in it. Gladstone's voice was tuned to a higher note, was penetrating, resonant, liquid, and full of an exquisite modulation and music which gave new shades of meaning to every emphasized word. The ways of the men were in almost every respect curiously unlike. Gladstone was always eager for conversation. He loved to talk to anybody about anything. Disraeli, even among his most intimate friends, was given to frequent fits of absolute and apparently gloomy silence. Gladstone, after his earlier Parliamentary

days, became almost entirely indifferent to dress.
Disraeli always turned out in the newest fashion,
and down to his latest years went in the get-up
of a young man about town. Not less different
were the characters and temperaments of the two
men.   Gladstone changed his political opinions
many times during his long Parliamentary career.
But he changed his opinions only in deference to
the force of a growing conviction, and to the
recognition of facts and conditions which he could
no longer conscientiously dispute. Nobody probably ever knew what Mr. Disraeli's real opinions
were upon any political question, or whether he
had any real opinions at all. Gladstone began as
a Tory, and gradually became changed into a
Radical. Disraeli began as an extreme Radical
under the patronage of Daniel O'Connell, and
changed into a Tory. But everybody knew that
Gladstone was at first a sincere Tory, and at
last a sincere Radical. Nobody knew, or, indeed,
cared, whether Disraeli ever was either a sincere
Radical or a sincere Tory. It is not, perhaps, an
unreasonable thing to assume that Disraeli soon
began to feel that there was no opening for him
on the Liberal benches of the House of Commons. He was determined to get on. He knew
that he had the capacity for success. He was
not in the least abashed by session after session

of absolute failure in Parliament, but he probably
began to see that he must choose his ground.
On the Liberal side were men like Palmerston,
Lord John Russell, Gladstone, Cobden, and Bright.
On the Tory side there were respectable country
gentlemen. Since the removal of Lord Stanley
to the Upper House there was not a single man
on the Tory benches who could for a moment be
compared, as regards eloquence and intellect, with
Disraeli. Given a perfectly open mind, it is not
difficult to see how an ambitious man would make
his choice. The choice was made accordingly, and
Mr. Disraeli soon became the only possible leader
of the Tory party in the House of Commons.

Now that it has all passed into history, and
has become merely a question of what might be
called artistic interest, I think we may be thankful that Disraeli made up his mind to cast in his
lot with the Tory party. We have, at all events,
the advantage from it that he was thus thrown
into permanent rivalry with Gladstone, and that
we have the long succession of Parliamentary
duels to read of and to remember. On more
than one occasion, too, Disraeli was able, according to his own phrase, to "educate his party" up
to some really liberal measure. In that way he
was able to serve the country, although most
likely his immediate idea was to keep his party

M

still in office. But I confess that, for myself, I
am not thinking so much of this fact when I express my thankfulness that Disraeli joined the
Tories. The liberal measures would have come
in due course of time whether Disraeli helped
them or tried to hinder them. But I cannot esti-
mate how much the Parliamentary history of recent
times would have lost in interest if Gladstone and
Disraeli had been on the same side in politics.
What would become of the chief interest and fascination of the Iliad if Achilles and Hector had
been allies and companions in arms?

Gladstone was needed to bring out all that
was keenest and brightest in the Parliamentary
eloquence of Disraeli. Gladstone, on the other
hand, would have been literally thrown away on
any Tory antagonist beneath the level of Disraeli.
Never since Disraeli left the House of Commons
has Gladstone found a Tory antagonist worth
his crossing swords with. Among other differences between the two men were differences in
education. Disraeli never had anything like the
classical training of Gladstone. The mind of
Gladstone was steeped in the glorious literature
of Greece and of Rome, about which Disraeli
knew little or nothing. Disraeli could not read
Latin or Greek; he could not speak French. In
a famous speech of his delivered in the House of

Commons at the height of his fame and in opposition to a measure of Gladstone's, Disraeli made
it plain that he thought the meaning of "university" was a place where everything was taught
—a place of universal instruction.   In another
famous speech he described John Henry Newman's "Apologia pro Vitâ Suâ" as an "apology"
for Newman's life.   When the Congress of Berlin
sat in 1878, and was presided over by Prince
Bismarck, the great Prussian statesman opened
and conducted the business in English.   Disraeli,
accompanied by Lord Salisbury, represented England at the Congress, and it was at first supposed
that Bismarck spoke English simply as a mark of
compliment to England.   But Bismarck kindly
spoke English because it had been made known
to him that Disraeli could not speak French.

It must be admitted, however, that all this tells
to a certain extent in Disraeli's favor.   Among
the contrasts between the lives and ways of the
two great rivals must be noticed the contrast
between the conditions under which they started
into public life.   Everything that care, culture,
and money could do had been done for Gladstone.   His father had started him in public life
with an ample fortune.   Disraeli was the son of
a very clever and distinguished literary man, who
was successful enough as a sort of *genre* artist

with the pen, but who could not give his son much of a launch in life. Disraeli got but a very scrambling education, and was for some time set to work in a lawyer's office. His early extravagances got him into much trouble at the outset of his career. He had luxurious Oriental tastes and fancies, and, besides, he was determined to get into the House of Commons at any cost, and the expenses of election in those days would seem almost incredible to our more modest times. It was no very uncommon thing for a man to spend 100,000 pounds in contesting a county. Disraeli at first contested only boroughs, but even a borough contest meant huge expenditure. He had therefore nothing like the secure and unharassed entrance into politics which was the good fortune of his great rival. Another difference between the two men was found in their attitudes towards general culture. Gladstone had a positive passion for studying everything, for knowing something about everything. He was unwilling to let any subject elude his grasp. He had tastes the most varied and all but universal. He loved pictures and statues and architecture and old china and medals and bric-à-brac of every kind, and he had made himself acquainted with the history of all these subjects. There was almost nothing about which he could not talk with fluency and with the keenest interest. He had a thirst for information, and it was a pleasure to him to get out of every man all that the man could tell him about his own particular subject. Although a great and indeed a tremendous talker, Gladstone was not one of the men who insist upon having all the talk to themselves. His thirst for information would in any case have prevented him from being a talker only. He knew that every man and woman he met had something to tell him, and he gave every one ample opportunity.

Disraeli possessed no such ubiquitous tastes and no such varied knowledge. He had travelled more than Gladstone ever travelled, but he brought back little from his wanderings. His life, indeed, ran in a narrow groove. Political ambition was his idol, and he lived in its worship. A writer of brilliant novels, he could hardly be called in the highest sense a literary man. His novels were undoubtedly brilliant, and brought him in every way a great success. He was probably the only English author who ever compelled his English public to read political novels. But he had no particular affection for literature or for literary men. Not very long after Thackeray's death Disraeli satirized the author of "Vanity Fair" most bitterly and recklessly in the person of one of the characters in "Endymion." Disraeli thor-

oughly enjoyed the life of the House of Commons
for its own sake. Gladstone probably enjoyed it
most for the opportunities which it gave him of
asserting his principles and pushing forward his
reforms. Of both men it is only fair to say that
during their long political struggle not one breath
of scandal touched their public or private life.
On one or two occasions when an accusation was
made against either man of having shown a spirit
of favoritism in some public appointment, the
charge was easily disproved, and indeed would
not have been seriously believed in by many
people in any case. Disraeli was once, while in
office, charged with having given a certain small
appointment to a political supporter. He was
able to prove at once, first that the recipient of
the place was the man best qualified for its work,
and, next, that the recipient of the place had
been a steady political opponent of Disraeli and
the Tory party. It is satisfactory to know that
in the higher walks of English political life the
atmosphere has for many years been pure and
untainted. The days of Bolingbroke and Walpole
and the Godolphins had long passed away, and
even the hard-drinking, reckless, gambling temper
of the times of Fox and Pitt was totally unknown
to the principal associates of Disraeli and Gladstone. In every way, therefore, these two great

rivals were worthy of the rivalry. I have often thought that of late years Mr. Gladstone in the House of Commons must have sadly missed his old antagonist.

Gladstone had a profound sympathy with Italy —a strong passion for Italy—very much like the passion which Byron had for Greece. He loved the language, the literature, the country, and the people. He spoke Italian with marvellous fluency and accuracy. An eminent Italian told me once that Gladstone, when speaking Italian, fell quite naturally into the very movement and gestures of an Italian. If Gladstone, he said, were to address the representative chamber in Rome, every one present would take him for an Italian — only it was possible that the Tuscan might think he was a Roman, and that the Roman would set him down as a Tuscan. Whenever he needed rest he almost always sought it under the skies of Italy. When, at a later period of his career, he visited the Ionian Islands as Lord High Commissioner on behalf of the Sovereign of England, he addressed all the public assemblies in the islands and on the mainland, in Athens and elsewhere, in Italian. The pronunciation of Greek which is taught at the English universities would have rendered it almost impossible for an English scholar, however well acquainted with the literary language of Greece, to make himself intelligible to a modern Greek audience. Gladstone spoke French with perfect fluency, but with a very marked accent. Indeed, his speeches in the House of Commons were always delivered with an accent which told unmistakably of the "North Countree." From his forbears he got the tones of Scotland; and then Lancashire has a distinct accent all to herself. I have a strong impression that some at least of the influence of Gladstone's finest speeches in the House of Commons would have been a little marred if they had been delivered in the commonplace accent of West End London society.

JOHN BRIGHT AS HE APPEARED IN 1853

(From a photograph by Maull & Fox, London)

CHAPTER XIV

THE Houses of Parliament have had in my memory three really great orators: the Lord Derby whom I have already mentioned, Mr. Gladstone, and Mr. Bright. All three came from the "North Countree." A high and mighty London weekly paper once said: "What a pity it is that Mr. Bright cannot catch the tone of the House of Commons!" The retort was obvious — What a pity it is that the House of Commons cannot catch the tone of Mr. Bright!

Gladstone and Bright soon became strong friends. The two men were curiously unlike in general ways and in bringing up. Bright was not, in the higher sense, a man of education — he certainly was not a man of culture. He had been quietly brought up, with what might be called a plain commercial education. He knew little of Latin, and next to nothing of Greek. He could read French, and could speak it fairly well. He was not widely read, but he had a marvellous appreciation of all the shades of mean-

169

ing which the English language was capable of
putting into expression. He was not a reader of
many books, but the books that he really cared
for he "loved with a love that was more than
love."   He adored the Bible and Milton, and he
learned to delight in Dante, although only through
the medium of a translation. One of his happiest
quotations was taken from Dante and made in a
speech on the condition of Ireland.

His style as an orator in the House of Commons was pure, simple, strong, and thrilling. He
had a voice which was perhaps, on the whole,
superior even to that of Gladstone himself. As
an orator, I should say that he now and then in
his greatest speeches soared to a height which
Gladstone never reached. But as a debater he
was not to be compared with Gladstone. As he
put it himself: "I can stand up to a fight well
enough every now and then, but Gladstone's foot
is always in the stirrup." One passion was common to both the men — the passion for following
in the path where justice and the improvement
of the condition of one's fellows seemed directly
to guide. For a long time Gladstone was a great
source of strength to Bright, and Bright was a
great source of strength to Gladstone. Bright did,
probably, his greatest work outside the House of
Commons, and Gladstone certainly his greatest

work inside it. Bright had a gift of rich Anglo-Saxon humor which Gladstone could not rival. It used to be noticed that Disraeli, great master of sarcastic phrases as he was, never would go in for a passage of arms with Bright. The hand of Bright had a terribly good-humored strength in its knock-down blow. It was like the buffet of Richard Cœur de Lion in Sir Walter Scott's "Ivanhoe." Bright was for many years of his life absolutely devoted to Gladstone's leadership in home affairs. He had little or no sympathy with Gladstone's enthusiasm about the cause of this or that foreign people. He never indulged in expressions of rapture about the national cause of Italy. This came in great measure from his not unreasonable conviction that the welfare of England herself and of her colonies ought to be the first consideration of English statesmanship. He was utterly opposed to most of England's interventions in foreign affairs. He justly condemned the policy of the Crimean War from the very beginning, and he was denounced and abused for his utterances, which now represent the opinion of all rational Englishmen. But he showed that his was not a merely insular mind when the Civil War in the United States broke out and when the sympathy of the vast majority of those who considered themselves "society" in

Great Britain was ostentatiously given to the Southern side. He stood up for the welfare of the people of India as opposed to the interests of those who went out there to push trade, to make money, or to earn distinction. He was for many years a friend of Ireland when friends of Ireland were rare figures in the Parliament House at Westminster. For years and years he stood up a brave, persistent, and splendid champion for justice to the Irish people. Nor even when, in his closing years, he fell away from Mr. Gladstone on this very question of Ireland's national claims, did the Irish people feel anything but a deep and poignant regret that the strong arm which had supported them so long should be for some strange reason suddenly withdrawn from them.

For the present, however, he stood by Gladstone's side, and was by far the most powerful supporter Gladstone had in the House of Commons or out of it.

CHAPTER XV

I MUST return to the duel between Mr. Gladstone and Mr. Disraeli and its immediate consequences upon English political life. Mr. Gladstone's speech completely crushed the whole of Mr. Disraeli's financial scheme. The budget was there one hour, and it was gone the next. When the division came to be taken in the early morning of December 17, 1852, the Government was found to be in a minority of nineteen.

Lord Derby at once wrote to the Queen announcing his resignation. It would be needless to say that the time was one of intense political passion. Mr. Greville, in his diary, gives us one curious and, let us hope, unique illustration of heated feeling among some of the Tories. On the twentieth of December, Mr. Greville tells us, "twenty ruffians of the Carlton Club"—thus he describes them, and no doubt justly—gave a dinner to a Tory political colleague who had been charged with bribery at an election and had got off without any serious condemnation. "After dinner,"

Mr. Greville says, " when they got drunk, they
went upstairs, and, finding Gladstone alone in the
drawing-room, some of them proposed to throw
him out of the window. This they did not quite
dare do, but contented themselves with giving
some insulting message or order to the waiter and
then went away." I cannot attempt to vouch for
the truth of this story, but I remember quite well
that the story was told at the time, and was generally believed to have some truth in it. As I
heard the tale at the time, the proposal was to
" fling Gladstone out of the window in the direction of the Reform Club," which is, in fact, the
very nearest public building. This version of the
story would make it seem more like a coarse joke
than like any proposal with a serious purpose.
But nothing can be more certain than the fact
that about that time Gladstone was bitterly detested by all the ignorant and infatuated followers
of the Tory party.

When Lord Derby and Mr. Disraeli and their
colleagues resigned, the men who came into power
had to form a coalition government. The Whigs
could not make a government of their own. The
Peelites were not strong enough to think of forming an administration; and the time for a Radical
Cabinet was still very far off. The new Government, therefore, was a combination of Whigs and

Peelites, with one or two "philosophical Radicals,"
as they were then called, sincere and earnest Radical speakers, that is to say, but not fighting men
like Cobden and Bright.   Lord Aberdeen became

WINDSOR CASTLE
(From a photograph by Mr. Wilson, London)

Prime Minister, and Mr. Gladstone, as Chancellor
of the Exchequer, had for the first time a full
opportunity of displaying his genius in the management of finance.   He had to fight a stiff battle
at Oxford.   And although he was elected, he was
elected by a majority seriously reduced.   His first
budget was introduced on April 18, 1853.   The

speech which he made in introducing his financial
scheme will be remembered forever in the House
of Commons.   Certainly since the days of Pitt no
financial exposition equal in point of eloquence had
ever been heard in Parliament.   Sir Robert Peel
at his highest level was distinctly surpassed by his
pupil.   It seems hard to understand how a man
could contrive to throw so much eloquence, fancy,
illustration, and humor into a statement of facts
and figures, but it is quite certain that Gladstone
then, and in all his succeeding budget speeches,
kept the House absolutely fascinated by the charm
of his style, entirely apart from the substantial
merits of the proposals he had to make.   The
clearness with which he explained all the details
of his subject was the gift of genius in itself.   The
faculties of the listener were never kept upon the
strain — and it may be said that there can be no
really great speech which keeps the faculties of the
listener on a perpetual strain.   The gift of lucid
explanation is like the gift of a fine voice.   If we
find it difficult to hear what an orator is saying, we
soon, whether we like it or not, begin to be weary
of his speech.   In the same way, if we are dis-
tressed by the difficulty of understanding the
arrangements and comparisons of facts and figures
which a Chancellor of the Exchequer is laying before us, we must only wait in patience for next

morning's papers in order to find out what the
plans of the financier really were. There was no
difficulty in Mr. Gladstone's case. One might not
agree with him, but no one could possibly pretend
that he did not understand. The budget speech
of 1853 lasted for five hours. I did not hear the
speech myself, but I have spoken with numbers of
men who told me that only a glance at the clock
in the House of Commons could have convinced
them that the orator had spoken for anything like
such a length of time. Mr. George Russell gives,
in a few lines, a very clear exposition of the principles of Mr. Gladstone's first financial scheme.

"It tended to make life easier and cheaper for
large and numerous classes. It promised wholesale remissions of taxation. It lessened the charges
on common processes of business, on locomotion,
on postal communication, and on several articles of
general consumption. The deficiency thus created
was to be met by the application of the legacy
duty to real property, by an increase of the duty
on spirits, and by the extension of the income tax
at fivepence in the pound to all incomes between
one hundred and one hundred and fifty pounds."
"The speech," says Mr. Russell, "held the House
spellbound. Here was an orator who could apply
all the resources of a burnished rhetoric to the
illustration of figures, who could make pippins

N

and cheese interesting, and tea serious; who could
sweep the widest horizon of the financial future,
and yet stop to bestow the minutest attention on
the microcosm of penny stamps and post-horses."

That was, indeed, the peculiar charm of Mr.
Gladstone's financial expositions. One never could
tell what curious illustration or quotation he
might not bring in next; by what odd fancy he
might light up some subject in itself unattractive;
by what happy phrase he might fasten attention
on some matter of merely commonplace interest.
One could not miss a word; one could not endure
to wait for the next morning's papers. The voice,
the intonation, the gestures, were in perfect keeping with the words. Every word was set off and
made emphatic by the manner and the tone.
The position of Mr. Gladstone was proclaimed
certain by the first budget speech. It put him
at the head of all the financiers of his day, and
it set him up as a financial orator superior to
Peel and at least equal to the younger Pitt. I
believe that most of Gladstone's great financial
expositions have been made without the help of
anything more than the barest memoranda in
figures. The orator was always ready to reply
to any interruption, to give answer to any question, to travel away for a moment from the main
track of his speech in order to remove difficulties

and to solve doubts which it might be convenient to deal with at once, and then to turn back to the main line of his argument and go on as if no break in its tenor had ever been caused. In truth, Mr. Gladstone could do whatever he liked with language, as certain great musicians have been able to do whatever they like with notes.

I am not now asking my readers to consider the actual effects of the financial scheme introduced by this brilliant and memorable speech. Monsieur Fould, the once famous minister of Napoleon the Third, said to his master on a certain important occasion: "Give me good foreign policy, and I will give you good finance." Mr. Gladstone might have said the same thing to his colleagues in the spring of 1853. He had given them good finance, and they marred it by a bad foreign policy.

CHAPTER XVI

THE first time I ever heard a speech from Mr. Gladstone was on the twelfth of October, 1853. It was on the occasion of the unveiling of a statue to Sir Robert Peel, erected in front of the Royal Infirmary in Manchester. On that occasion the freedom of the city was presented to Mr. Gladstone, and he delivered a speech in the Town Hall. That was a time when the Crimean War was impending but did not seem yet quite a certain fatality, and I well remember how intense was the interest with which everybody waited for any hint as to the possibility of peace that might be given by the Chancellor of the Exchequer. The speeches made by Mr. Gladstone on that memorable day were worthy of the man whom it commemorated, and of the man who was his most illustrious follower. I shall never forget the impression made on me by Mr. Gladstone's eloquence, and made still more, I think, by the sincerity and the earnestness of the orator himself. Commemoration speeches are apt to be

triumphs of phrase-making and of rhetoric, and
of nothing more. But in this instance the whole
soul of the orator seemed to inspire the language
of his speech. Mr. Gladstone appeared to be
simply pouring out his heart and thought to a
sympathetic audience. He spoke of Peel as he
alone was qualified to speak of him; but I think
every one who listened to Mr. Gladstone that
day felt convinced in his mind that a greater
statesman and a greater orator than Peel had
risen up to take the foremost place in the political life of England. As regards the Crimean
War, it was plain enough that Mr. Gladstone was
only hoping against hope. He still persisted in
a lingering longing to look for the maintenance
of peace, but nobody who heard him could have
doubted for a moment that Mr. Gladstone's belief
in the possibility of the maintenance of peace
was a faith which seemed very like despair.
Soon after, the country "drifted," to use a famous
expression, into the war with Russia, and on
March 27, 1854, the public announcement of the
war was made.

I am not now going back to the old story of
the Crimean War. The country had been lashed
into a passion for war, and there is no argument,
for any European population at all events, when
that passion for war lights up. The war had

been opposed in the most earnest and vigorous
manner by men like Cobden and Bright. Some
of Bright's speeches against the war policy are
models of reason, of feeling, and of eloquence.
But they only served to make Mr. Bright unpopular for the moment with the majority of his
countrymen, and he was burnt in effigy in several
places as the friend of Russia. Everybody knew
that Mr. Gladstone was, above all things, a votary
of peace, of economy, and of everything which
could add to the national prosperity. For him
there was no glory about war. At a much later
period of his career he declared that he did not
understand what was meant by national *prestige*.
He had to prepare a war budget, but even in
the speech which introduced it he took care to
express the profound dislike he felt to any war
that was not actually inevitable. Much, no
doubt, of the misery which the war entailed was
due to the fact that many of those who, like Mr.
Gladstone, were dragged into accepting it had
no heart in the war policy and no sympathy
with it. The Prime Minister of England himself,
Lord Aberdeen, was anxious to the very last to
keep out of the war. The trouble in all such
cases is that patriotic Englishmen naturally shrink
from abandoning the public service of their
country at a time when the country is on the

eve of a great campaign. Lord Aberdeen and
Mr. Gladstone remained, therefore, at their posts
after the war broke out.

There is not now, I believe, a single responsible public man in England who does not utterly
condemn the
policy of that
most unfort-
unate war. To
England it
brought nothing
but loss and mis-
ery. There was
no glory to be
gained out of it,
even if England
had wanted
glory of that
kind. Never be-
fore in all her

GEORGE H. GORDON, FOURTH EARL OF ABERDEEN
(From an engraving by Mr. D. J. Pound)

warlike history had England been so poorly served
by her commanders in the field. No Henry the
Fifth was there, no Duke of Marlborough, no Duke
of Wellington. The suffering inflicted on Englishmen was not the work of the enemy; it was the
work of their own military administration. The
mismanagement, the perverse blundering, the utter
incapacity of those who looked after the army

on the field, were absolutely without precedent.
The whole commissariat and hospital organization
utterly broke down. England, as Mr. George
Russell very truly says, "lost some twenty-four
thousand men, of whom five-sixths died from pre-
ventable disease and the want of proper food,
clothing, and shelter." With the help of the
French and the Sardinians, the English army
defeated the Russians time after time. Yet, when
the whole war was over and done, only one great
name came out of it, and that was the name of
the Russian general, Todleben, who defended
Sebastopol. If I were to mention in succession
the names of the English commanders, very few
of my readers now would know about whom I
was talking. The war propped up for a short
time the fabric of the French Second Empire.
It made the fortune of the House of Piedmont.
Count Cavour, not caring three straws about
either Turkey or Russia, had seen his opportunity with the eye of genius and volunteered the
alliance of Sardinia, and so obtained a right of
representation at the Congress of Paris, where
terms of peace were made, and thus laid the
foundation of a United Italy under the House
of Savoy. But for England the war did nothing
whatever except to bring vast loss of treasure
and vast sacrifice of gallant lives. No question

in which we were concerned was settled by that war.

What is called the Eastern Question remains unsettled still, or rather, indeed, I should say that it is in a far worse condition now than it was before the Crimean War broke out. The Ottoman Government, for whose sake we spent so much money and so much blood, has lately proved itself the most savage and tyrannical government known in civilization, and commits its Armenian massacres under our very eyes, metaphori-

CAMILLO BENSO, COUNT DI CAVOUR
(Signor Brogi, of Florence)

cally at least, and without the slightest regard to our expostulations. England fostered the Turkish Government to be an outrage upon civilization and a defiance to England herself. "We were fighting," said Mr. Bright, "for a hopeless cause and a worthless ally."

Meantime the condition of the English troops
in the Crimea began to be a public scandal and
horror. Mr. Roebuck announced in the House
of Commons his intention to move for the appointment of a Select Committee to inquire into the
state of our army before Sebastopol, and "into the
conduct of those departments of the Government
whose duty it has been to minister to the wants
of that army." There was no serious possibility
of resisting such a motion. Such was the conviction of Lord John Russell, who instantly resigned his place in the Cabinet. Mr. Gladstone
did not see his way to resign in the face of the
debate and division which were about to take
place. He even defended to the best of his power
the policy and conduct of the administration. The
result of the division was a majority of 157 against
the Government. The Ministry of Lord Aberdeen — the Coalition Ministry, as it was called —
broke down as a natural result of this declaration
of the majority of the House of Commons.

The Queen sent for Lord Derby, who tried to
form an administration, but could not succeed. He
offered a place to Mr. Gladstone, but Mr. Gladstone declined it. Two other eminent "Peelites,"
as they were called, Sir James Graham and Mr.
Sidney Herbert, also refused to accept office under
Lord Derby. All three gave as a reason that,

they had opposed the motion for a sort of amateur inquiry into the military organization in the
Crimea, and that they could not countenance it
by becoming members of the Government. There
was nothing for it but to make Lord Palmerston
Prime Minister. The Peelites were willing to
join him, but on the understood condition that
the amateur inquiry was not to take place. Mr.
Gladstone was offered the position of Chancellor
of the Exchequer, and accepted the office. Lord
Palmerston had once described himself very cor-
rectly as, under the conditions, the "inevitable"
Prime Minister. Mr. Gladstone was certainly the
inevitable Chancellor of the Exchequer. "He is
indispensable," said a keen observer at the time,
"if only because any other Chancellor of the
Exchequer would be torn into pieces by him."
It has to be observed that this was the first time
that Gladstone consented to take office under a
Whig leader. This was, therefore, a distinct advance on the way to Liberalism first, and to Radicalism afterwards. Lord Palmerston, of course,
was not much of a Liberal, and was nothing of
a Radical. Still, he stood up as an opponent to
Toryism, and professed to be a man of progress;
and therefore, when Gladstone joined his Cabinet,
there was clear evidence that Gladstone had done
forever with the "stern and unbending Tories,"

of whom, according to Macaulay, he was once
the rising hope. He did not, however, serve for
long under the new Government. As I have said,
Lord Palmerston's administration was formed on
the understanding that Mr. Roebuck's demand for
a sort of amateur inquiry into the carrying on
of the Crimean War was not to be granted. Lord
Palmerston, however, soon saw that the country
would not be satisfied without some form of inquiry. The mind and heart of England were
sick and sore because of the stories of military
maladministration and easily avoidable disaster.
Palmerston consented to the inquiry, and thereupon Mr. Gladstone, Sir James Graham, and Mr.

GEORGE CORNEWALL
LEWIS

Sidney Herbert resigned office.
They had been members of Lord
Palmerston's Cabinet about three
weeks. Sir George Cornewall
Lewis became Chancellor of the
Exchequer in place of Mr. Gladstone. Gladstone took his seat
on one of the back benches, behind the bench on which the members of the
Government have their places. I have many
times seen him rise from that seat and heard
him criticise the financial schemes of his successor. His criticisms had, it is needless to say, life
and vigor in them. He was master of every sub-

ject which could be included in a budget. He
knew all the details of every question. He could
at any moment pour out a flood of criticism which
dissolved the proposals of an opponent as a stream
of corrosive acid might have done.

I must say for myself that I always had a very
high idea of the ability of Sir George Cornewall
Lewis. He is a man who is almost wholly forgotten in our time; but I am convinced that he
was one of the most thoroughly intellectual men
of his day. I know that it may fairly be asked
of me, " How could a man come to be forgotten
if he had said or done anything worth remembering?" All I can say is that I quite admit the
fact that Sir George Lewis is personally forgotten,
but I insist upon it that he seemed to me to have
one of the greatest intellects of his time, and I
know that some of his sayings, witty and sarcastic, humorous and profound, have passed into our
common literature and our common talk, and are
quoted every day by people who have some faint
notion that they are citations from Dean Swift
or Sydney Smith. Lewis had a miserably poor
voice, and had no ideas about elocution, and the
House of Commons hardly ever takes to a man
whom it is difficult to understand or follow. In
no case whatever could he have been an equal
of Mr. Gladstone in financial argument, and he

must have had a hard time of it very often while
under the criticism of Mr. Gladstone. There
was, I am sure, a great deal of the genuine philosopher about him, and I have little doubt that
he said to himself now and again, "I am no
match for Gladstone, and I know it. I have
not the voice or the fluency or the eloquence.
But there is one thing I can do; I can thoroughly
admire Gladstone, and admit his superiority."

Gladstone, however, did not confine himself
to criticisms merely of financial policy. He
showed himself an independent critic on all subjects which aroused in him any question of principle. He made a great speech in the important
debate on the manner in which the English
authorities had behaved towards the Chinese in
the once famous question of the *lorcha* Arrow.
The Government was defeated on that question,
and Parliament was dissolved. But Lord Palmerston was quite safe. He had appealed to
what may be called the Jingo feeling of the country. He had denounced the Chinese Governor
of Canton as "an insolent barbarian," and he
came back into power with a strong majority.

Mr. Gladstone was returned without opposition
for the University of Oxford. He seemed to
many observers somewhat depressed and dis-
gusted by the condition of affairs, and by the

triumph of Lord Palmerston over what appeared
to Mr. Gladstone to be moral principle and national honor. On June the third, 1857, we find it
noted in Mr. Greville's journal that "Gladstone
hardly ever goes near the House of Commons,
and never opens his lips." He was destined,
however, before long to open his lips to some
purpose. The Divorce Bill was introduced by
the Government, and there was no subject in
human affairs on which Gladstone felt stronger
convictions than the introduction of a measure
to make divorce cheap and easy.

It is quite certain that Gladstone never liked
being under the leadership of Lord Palmerston.
It is quite certain that he was glad just at this
time to be released from such a leadership. The
natures of the two men were totally unlike. One
was earnest about everything; the other was earnest about nothing. But we may fairly assume
that Gladstone, having so suddenly withdrawn
from Lord Palmerston's administration, was not
anxious, was indeed very unwilling, to start up
in opposition to his late leader. The Divorce
Bill was, however, too much for him, and he felt
that he was bound to stand up and bear testimony against it.

It was not likely, in any case, that such a man
as Gladstone could remain long away from the

House of Commons, or, being there, could hold
his peace forever. At several periods in Mr.
Gladstone's career there came a short season
during which he seemed to have practically withdrawn from Parliamentary life; during which he
seldom came near the House of Commons, and
never opened his lips there. Such a season never
could have occurred in the career of a man like
Lord Palmerston or Mr. Disraeli. Palmerston
and Disraeli lived for the House of Commons
and in the House of Commons. To attend its
debates was a necessity to either man's existence.
It was not so with Mr. Gladstone. He went to
the House of Commons because it gave him an
opportunity of advocating some great measure of
national importance, or of opposing some scheme
which he believed to be wrong. Each short secession came to an end the moment when Mr.
Gladstone saw that there was work which he
ought to do. In 1857 Mr. Gladstone found himself drawn back to the House by his determination to oppose the Divorce Bill which was brought
in by Lord Palmerston's Government. He fought
this bill through its every stage with characteristic and indomitable energy. He spoke incessantly
in the debates on the measure, and he fought it
with a spirit and with a mastery of detail which
aroused the wonder even of those who knew him

W. E. GLADSTONE IN 1857

(From the painting by Mr. George Frederick Watts, R.A.)

THE CRIMEAN WAR

best. He opposed the measure first of all upon the high ground of principle. He contended that marriage was not only or mainly an arrangement of the nature of a civil contract, like the hiring of a house or the setting up of a mercantile partnership. He refused to admit for a moment the idea that marriage could be anything but a mystery of the Christian religion. He appealed to the law of God as to the inviolable sanctity of the marriage tie. That bond, he said, could not be severed in such a manner as to allow either of the parties to marry again. This was his first line of defence, and he sustained his position with splendid eloquence and perseverance.

Now, the House of Commons is not an assembly which is easily to be influenced or impressed by considerations of so exalted a nature. It is usually and for the most part a prosaic, man-of-the-world, half-cynical sort of assembly which is inclined to take human beings pretty much as they are commonly found in clubs and drawing-rooms and on race-courses, and is rather impatient of any appeal to what may be called the higher law. Yet it cannot be doubted that the magnificence of Mr. Gladstone's eloquence enthralled the House for the time, although it could not in the end carry the division. The most light-minded members of the House listened in

o

breathless admiration to those noble appeals to
the higher law for which nobody so well as he
could have obtained a hearing. Every one must
admit that, whether he was practically right or
wrong, he took in his argument the loftiest position that statesmanship or morality could occupy.

He fought his battle not only in the House of
Commons, but also in the public press. Mr.
Gladstone has always at every great crisis of his
career championed his cause in the journals and
the reviews as well as on the public platform and
in the House of Commons. He put his principles very clearly and emphatically in an article
which appeared in the "Quarterly Review," in
which he says: "Our Lord has emphatically told
us that, at and from the beginning, marriage was
perpetual, and was on both sides single." From
these opinions Mr. Gladstone has never since
receded in the least. He has changed his views
on many subjects, but on this question his opinions have undergone no change. When he had
fought the bill on its main principle, and then
endeavored to have it postponed for fuller public
examination and discussion, and had been beaten
on both those issues, he next applied himself to
amend the bill in its passage through committee.
As every one knows, the actual principle of a
bill is determined on its second reading in the

House of Commons. That principle is then taken
to be established, and thereupon the bill goes into
committee to be amended or modified or made
worse in its details. Mr. Gladstone applied himself to an unceasing effort for the elimination
from the bill of what seemed to him its worst and
most offensive purposes. He pointed out, for
instance, that there was a fundamental injustice
in that part of the bill which would entitle the
husband to obtain a divorce from an unfaithful
wife because of a single act of infidelity, but
which did not give the same right to the wife
against the husband, and did not entitle her to
obtain a divorce unless the husband had been
physically cruel as well as morally unfaithful.

The debates in committee were conducted on
the part of the Government by the Attorney-Gen-
eral, Sir Richard Bethell, afterwards Lord Westbury, one of the keenest and ablest lawyers ever
known in the House of Commons. Sir Richard
Bethell was master of every statute and every
clause which could have any bearing on the subject, and he had an unfailing resource of acrid and
even vitriolic sarcasm. It might well have been
thought by many people that even Mr. Gladstone,
with all his eloquence, would be no match for such
an antagonist on that antagonist's own ground.
But Mr. Gladstone never in his whole life showed a

more marvellous fighting power than he put forward
in this long controversy. To every reply he had
his rejoinder; to every citation of authority he had
another citation at the tip of his tongue. His
wonderful gift of memory came into surprising
play. He could repeat whole passages from a
statute without a scrap of a note to assist him.
One might have thought, to hear him, that he had
given up his entire life to the study of the marriage laws of various ages and nations, and had
never allowed

RICHARD BETHELL, BARON WESTBURY
(From a photograph by Maull & Fox)

his attention to be distracted from the subject by
finance or politics or the reading of Homer. He
did succeed in obtaining some slight improvements
in the measure, but the bill in its main provisions
was passed in spite of all his resistance. Old mem-

bers of the House of Commons will tell you to
this day of the effect produced by those splendid
passages of arms. Bethell, they all say, was great,
but Gladstone was greater, and it was Bethell's own
ground and not Gladstone's. The bill was passed
into law, and Mr. Gladstone has never ceased to
condemn it. Something, of course, has to be said
for the bill if we consent to come down from that
lofty religious principle which Mr. Gladstone maintained, and which some of the great churches of the
world have always maintained. It has to be said
that divorce existed in England long before the
passing of the Act Mr. Gladstone opposed, but it
was divorce obtained after a very different fashion.
A divorce could be obtained, first of all, by proving
the offence in a court of law, and then by passing a
bill through both Houses of Parliament to give
effect to the judgment of the court of law by the
dissolution of the marriage. This was an immensely costly process, and it made divorce the
luxury of the very rich. Mr. Gladstone did not
find his conscience or his mind attracted by the
prospect of facility or cheapness.

CHAPTER XVII

THE IONIAN ISLANDS

I venture to think that Mr. Gladstone never undertook a more congenial task than that which was offered to him by the Tory Government, which had turned out Lord Palmerston, when the Homeric scholar was invited to go out to the Ionian Islands for the purpose of conducting an inquiry on the spot as to the complaints and grievances of the islanders. The proposal was made under the inspiration of Sir Edward Bulwer Lytton, the novelist and dramatist, who had become Secretary for the Colonies in the Tory Government. Bulwer Lytton's career in Parliament had up to this time been little better than an absolute failure. He had been in the House of Commons from 1831 to 1841, and his attempts at Parliamentary debate had ended in almost absolute breakdown. But he was a man of indomitable perseverance, and he seems to have said to himself that he would not die until he had made a name as a Parliamentary orator. A debater he never could have been, because he was so deaf that he had to read a speech in the newspapers before he could attempt to reply to it. His articulation was, from actual physical causes, so defective that almost any other man would have considered himself utterly debarred from any attempt at eloquence. But Sir Edward Bulwer Lytton had a boundless confidence in himself — I should have called it a boundless self-conceit, if he had not made good his pretensions so far as popularity was concerned. One may smile at the extravagance of the style displayed in several of his novels, but it is impossible to deny that the novels had an immense popularity. He wrote a play, and was told by the critics that he had no dramatic gift. He accepted the fact that the play was a failure, but he said that he could do better, and he wrote the "Lady of Lyons," which, with all its preposterous faults, had for more than a generation a vast success, and even still holds the stage. Inspired by these successes, he seems to have made up his mind that he would conquer the House of Commons also. He did in the end conquer the House of Commons, after a fashion, very much as he had conquered the literary and the dramatic public. Even in the full popularity of Dickens and Thackeray he held his own with the literary public; even in the days of Gladstone and Bright and Disraeli he accomplished a marvellous success in the House of Commons. He was a master of the art of gorgeous phrase-making, elaborate no doubt, but very splendid. Whenever it was known that he was about to speak in a debate, the House was crowded.

I am really unable to explain the secret of his success, but the success itself was at the time a fact which it would be impossible to doubt. His speeches are well-nigh forgotten now in the House of Commons, and nobody any longer believes that he was a great orator. Some of us did not believe it even then; and even while we were under the influence of the spell we felt pretty clear that it was but a glamour and a magic destined to lose its effect. Still, we could not deny that Bulwer Lytton had conquered the House of Commons and held it for the time enthralled. Then he turned on to prove himself a practical statesman. He founded, for example, the Colony of British Columbia. But the mission of Mr. Gladstone to the Ionian Islands was something more in keeping with Bulwer Lytton's general tastes and tendencies. The seven Ionian Islands were united as a kind of commonwealth by the Settlements of 1815, and they were placed under the protection of England, which had the right of maintaining garrisons in them. England was represented by a Lord High Commissioner, who was usually a soldier, and who was Commander-in-Chief as well as civil Governor. The Republic of the Seven Islands had a Senate

and a Legislative Assembly. For many years
there had been growing complaints in the islands
against English administration. The complaints
admitted, in fact, of no real compromise. What the
islanders wanted above all things was to be Greeks
and to be united with the Kingdom of Greece. It
was futile to point out to them that their material
affairs were much better administered under the
English Government than they were likely to be
under the Government of King Otho, the dull, incapable ruler of the Greek Kingdom. It was of no
use to tell the islanders that they had much better
roads and harbors and lines of steamers than were
possessed by the inhabitants of the Greek Kingdom. Their whole ideas of life were not limited
to roads and piers and bridges and harbors. They
had an impassioned, romantic, indomitable desire
to be united with their brothers of the Kingdom.
Futile, unreasonable critics in this country tried to
convince them that the islanders, after all, were not
of kin with the Greeks of the mainland. It was
argued that the inhabitants of the mainland had
got so intermixed with other races that they could
hardly be considered genuine Greeks at all. The
islanders could not be reasoned out of their national
sentiments by any inquiries into the pedigree or
the family tree of the Grecian Kingdom. So there
was always some trouble in the Ionian Islands, and

the Lord High Commissioner every now and then
dismissed some more or less mutinous Parliament
and convened another by a general election, and
the new Parliament was in spirit just the same
as the old, and
things went on
exactly as they
had been going
before.

EDWARD GEORGE EARLE LYTTON BULWER,
BARON LYTTON

Bulwer Lytton
was, it would
seem, the first
statesman in of-
fice to whom it
occurred to ask
himself whether,
after all, there
might not be
something worth
considering in
the claims made by the people of the seven islands.
" Sir Edward Bulwer Lytton," says a modern writer,
" had not been long enough in office to become
soaked in the ideas of routine. He did not regard
the unanimous opinions of the insular legislature,
municipalities, and press as evidence merely of
the unutterable stupidity or the incurable ingrati-
tude and wickedness of the Ionian populations."

Therefore it occurred to him that it might be as well to send out some impartial statesman who could examine the controversy on the spot; and he could think of no one so well fitted for such a task as Mr. Gladstone. Every one knew that Mr. Gladstone was in strong sympathy with the general movement of Greece to accomplish a high destiny in Europe, and the mere fact that such a man was sent out would be enough in itself to prove to the islanders that no predetermined spirit of hostility was dictating the mission. The news of the offer was at first received in English society with incredulity, and then with a good deal of ridicule. Is it possible, wise and solemn people asked, that Mr. Gladstone could be induced to accept so crazy a mission? Mr. Gladstone, however, did not think the mission altogether crazy, and he at once accepted it.

Sir Edward Bulwer Lytton had made in his despatch an eloquent allusion to Mr. Gladstone's Homeric studies, and dry officials insisted that this was nothing short of an unwarrantable outrage on all the precedents of conventional diplomacy. "What are we coming to?" they asked. "We have a Prime Minister, Lord Derby, who goes in for Greek studies; we have a novelist as leader of the Government in the House of Commons; we have a novelist as Colonial Secretary;

and these three propose to send out a man on a
mission to the disturbed Ionian Islands for no
other reason than because he is fond of reading
Homer!"

Mr. Gladstone, however, was in hope that he
could do some good by accepting the mission, and
he went out to the Ionian Islands, arriving at Corfu
in November, 1858.   Up to that time I believe
he never had been in Greece.   It must have been
to him like the actual realization of youth's best
dream when he stood on the soil of Greece, when
he went from island to island of that enchanting
Greece for which nature and poetry and history
and tradition have done so much, when he saw
the home of Ulysses and the fabled rock of
Sappho, and, above all, when he climbed the
Acropolis of Athens and gazed upon the Parthe-
non, and, turning his eyes one way, looked on
Mount Hymettus, and turning another way saw
Salamis, and then, on a clear day, the outlines of
the steep of Acro-Corinth.

Even the most commonplace among us who
have in our early days been at all in love with
Greek poetry and Greek history, were it through
the blurring medium of translations and "cribs,"
have felt as we reached that enchanted soil rather
as if we were coming home to some familiar
scenes of our boyhood than as if we were enter-

ing for the first time into a foreign country. If that is so with the commonplace among us, how must it have been with a man like Mr. Gladstone, steeped to the lips in all the poetry, the history, and the traditions of Greece, and with an opportunity given to him now of visiting Greece, not merely as a tourist, however loving and devoted, but as a man intrusted with a mission to listen to the complaints of the Greek islanders and to endeavor to find some remedy for any genuine grievances of which they complained.

Mr. Gladstone, it is needless to say, went to the task he had undertaken for the British Government with the most genuine and exact loyalty. On December the third, 1858, he called together the Senate of the Septinsular Commonwealth at Corfu, and he explained to them the task which he had set out to accomplish if he could. At Corfu, and during all his public addresses in the Greek islands and the mainland, he spoke in Italian, which is the commanding foreign language once you leave Trieste on the way to the Levant. Mr. Gladstone did not attempt to speak in modern Greek. He could read modern Greek with perfect fluency, and has been heard to complain that he found some difficulty only when Greeks would write to him in a very bad hand and in "cursive Greek." But the hopeless incompatibil-

ity between the pronunciation of Greek taught
at Oxford and the Greek spoken in Corfu or in
Athens would have rendered it impossible for
him to make himself effectively understood if he
attempted to address in Greek a modern Greek
audience. Every one who has been in Greece,
and who knows anything at all of classic Greek,
must have found that, while it is easy enough
to make out the meaning of a leading article in
an Athenian newspaper, it is hardly possible to
make one's self understood by or to understand
the courteous Greek to whom one puts a question in the streets.

The effect of Mr. Gladstone's speeches in Italian
was something superb and electrifying. He told
the Senate of the Ionian Islands at Corfu that
the liberties guaranteed to the islanders by the
treaties of Paris and by the Ionian law were
absolutely sacred in the eyes of the Queen of
England. But, he said, on the other hand, "the
purpose for which the Queen has sent me here
is not to inquire into the British Protectorate,
but to examine into what way Great Britain may
most honorably and amply discharge the obliga-
tions which, for purposes European and Ionian
rather than British, she has contracted." Then
he made an official visit to all the islands, receiving deputations and delivering replies. He under-

W. E. GLADSTONE

(From a photograph by Samuel A. Walker)

took that a full inquiry should be made into every complaint or grievance, and that a thorough system of constitutional government should be established in the islands. As I have said, however, the Ionians had one uncompromising grievance — the grievance that they were kept from a thorough union with the Kingdom of Greece.

The Legislative Assembly of the Seven Islands voted unanimously an address to the Queen, praying that they might annex themselves to the Greeks of the mainland. Mr. Gladstone's visit was, in fact, a totally unsuccessful scheme for those who fondly desired that the Protectorate of England should be everlasting, and that the islanders should be brought to submit themselves to it and reconcile themselves with it. It may be taken for granted that Sir Edward Bulwer Lytton was not one of those who believed in the possibility of prevailing on the Greek islands to hold themselves aloof from the Greek Kingdom. No doubt, when he selected a man like Mr. Gladstone for the mission to the Ionian Islands, he foresaw well enough that the occasion would be availed of by the islanders to make such a demonstration as would convince the dullest Philistine in Westminster Palace that the hearts of the Greek islanders were unconquerably set on a union with the Kingdom of Greece. The people

of the islands received Gladstone with all the
enthusiasm and devotion which they believed due
to one who was at heart in favor of their national
aspirations.   They cheered him, and crowded
round him, and cried "Zeto" for him, not as the
Lord High Commissioner Extraordinary of an
English Tory Government, but simply as Gladstone the Philhellene.   His tour through the
islands and in the mainland was simply a trium-
phal progress.   His path was strewed with flowers.

Up to the last he maintained his assurances
that the only object he was commissioned to
attempt to accomplish was to make the Protectorate of England acceptable to the Ionian Islands,
and not to release the islanders from the Protectorate which had been imposed on England as well
as on the islands by the united counsels of the
Great Powers of Europe.   The islanders listened
and applauded, but all the same they insisted on
regarding Mr. Gladstone's mission as the foreshad-
owing of their national aspirations, of their union
with their countrymen in the Kingdom of Greece.
So indeed it proved to be before very long.   The
one material and practical result of Mr. Gladstone's
mission to the Ionian Islands was to make it
clear to even the dullest among us here at home
that there was no way of satisfying the Ionian
Islanders but by allowing them to unite them-

selves with Greece. We could easily, of course,
crush them by superior strength, but until we
had extinguished the life of the last Greek
islander we could not extinguish the just and
natural passion for union with parent Greece.
Mr. Gladstone, of course, got a great deal of
abuse from the Tory press in England, and was
accused of having stimulated and fomented the
desire of the islanders for a release from the
British Protectorate. The most hasty perusal of
Mr. Gladstone's speeches must have shown that
he was most cautious not to do anything of the
kind. In no way whatever did he exceed the
strict terms of his mission to the islands, but in
any case some of the London newspapers wrote
as if the Ionian Islands had been bound from all
time to a grateful devotion to England. They
wrote as if England had called the islands into
being, and as if any wish to get free from English control were as ingrate and graceless an
act as the conduct of Regan and Goneril, the
daughters of King Lear.

There was an attempt made for a while to maintain the Protectorate, but events soon settled the
question. The opportunity came a few years after.
The Greeks of the Kingdom got sick of the stupid
rule of their dull and heavy sovereign, King Otho.
They simply bundled him out of Athens, bag and

baggage.   Then came the question what to do
next.   The Greeks themselves had probably had
quite enough to do with kings for their time,
although they had had only one sovereign.   But
the Great Pow-
ers of Europe,
and perhaps
more especially
England, pressed
upon them that
they had really
better have a
king, for the mere
look of the thing.

There was at
that time no re-
public in Europe
but the Republic
of Switzerland,
and Greece did
not feel strong
enough to hold

GEORGE I. (GEORGIOS I.) KING OF GREECE
(Unknown photo.)

out against the pressure.   The Greeks invited Prince
Alfred of England, afterwards Duke of Edinburgh,
and still more lately Duke of Saxe-Coburg-Gotha,
and in fact they elected and proclaimed him King.
But there was a clear understanding in European
statesmanship that no prince of any of the great

reigning families should be appointed as a sovereign over Greece. It was not in the least degree probable that an English prince would have accepted or would have been allowed to accept any such responsible and precarious position.

The Government of the Emperor Napoleon III. promptly managed to put in a practical objection to the proposal by delicately pointing out that if any of the Great Powers were to be allowed to appoint one of its princes to the throne of Greece, France had a prince of her own Imperial house quite disengaged, who might have a claim at least as good as another. The allusion was, of course, to the "unemployed Cæsar," as Monsieur Edmond About described him, the late Prince Napoleon, the Emperor's cousin, a man of extraordinary intellect, culture, and capacity, a statesman and a brilliant orator, by far the most gifted of the Napoleon family since that family's great founder, but who with all his gifts came to nothing in the end.

The sovereign and government of England would not in any case have allowed Prince Alfred to accept the crown of Greece, even if the Prince himself had had the slightest ambition that way. But in any case the significant remark of the French Government would have settled the question. "Punch" worked a capital comic cartoon out of the offer made to the sailor lad Prince Alfred.

Then some one started the suggestion that a prince of the House of Denmark should be made King of the Greeks, and the suggestion was accepted. The House of Denmark, it is hardly necessary to say, is brought by marriage bonds into close relationship with the royal family of England. The Prince of Wales is married to a Princess of the House of Denmark. The second son of the King of Denmark was offered the crown of Greece, and accepted it and became King — not of Greece; the Greeks, like the French of later monarchical times, were very particular about the title — but King of the Hellenes. Meanwhile the English Government had undergone a change, and Lord John Russell had come into office as Foreign Secretary under Lord Palmerston as Prime Minister and with Mr. Gladstone as Chancellor of the Exchequer. The occasion seemed propitious to the new Government to allow the Ionian Islanders to carry out their long-cherished wish. Lord John Russell obtained the consent of the great continental powers to the handing over of the islands to the Kingdom of Greece and its new sovereign. A great deal of anger was expressed, of course, in some of the Tory newspapers, and Lord John Russell's action was denounced as though he had hauled down the flag of England from one of the Empire's most ancient and cherished possessions

EARL RUSSELL (LORD JOHN RUSSELL)

in cowardly deference to the demand of some great foreign power. As I have already pointed out, England had never conquered the Ionian Islands, had never annexed them, had never set up any claim whatever to their ownership, and had merely

accepted, out of motives of public policy, the uncomfortable and troublesome charge which had
been imposed upon her by the other great States
of Europe. Some years passed between Mr. Gladstone's visit and the cession of the Ionian Islands
to the Greek Kingdom, but the one event was the
direct consequence of the other. But for Mr. Gladstone's visit the Liberal Government and the English people generally would never have known how
resolute, how passionate, how unconquerable, was the
desire of the Ionian Islanders to be in union with
the people of the Kingdom of Greece. The object-
lesson which, as I remarked before, is always needed
in political affairs was supplied by the reports and
descriptions of Mr. Gladstone's progress through the
seven islands. Not one Englishman in fifty thousand cared before that visit three straws about the
condition or the feelings of the Ionian Islands. The
ordinary Englishman hardly knew who the islanders
were, or where they lived, or what was the matter
with them. He saw now and then in his daily
paper some brief announcement that the Lord High
Commissioner had dissolved another Parliament
at Corfu. The announcement did not affect him
with any manner of interest. Very likely he did
not know where Corfu was, and in case he did,
would not have cared. But the condition of things
became very different when one of the foremost

English statesmen, perhaps the most picturesque statesman of his time, was sent out to inquire into the alleged grievances of the Ionian Islanders, and when the papers every day began to contain long descriptions of his movements and full reports of all the addresses delivered to him and all the replies which he returned. Then the minds of many men woke up at once to the reality of the state of things, and to the fact that there was in the far-off Levant a race of men over whom England had no right of conquest or rulership whatever, whom she was simply taking charge of to oblige the other great European powers, and who were filled with a passion to be united politically with their kindred in Greece. By the time that the Greek revolution had been accomplished, the English public was quite prepared for the proposal of Lord John Russell. With a large number of that public the mere sentimental consideration that the brother of the Princess of Wales was to be the new King of the Hellenes settled the matter altogether. The vast majority, therefore, of the English people entirely approved the withdrawal of the British Protectorate, and the annexation of the islands to the Greek Kingdom.

CHAPTER XVIII

Mr. Gladstone soon came into power again as Chancellor of the Exchequer. This was in 1860, a time indeed of storm and stress for the whole civilized world. Louis Napoleon had completed his campaign in Lombardy, and every one saw that the Lombardy campaign was only the beginning of new disturbances in Italy. The peace of Villafranca had been patched up by the Emperor because he thought that he had got all he wanted for his prestige. Italian officers broke their sword-blades across the marble tables of cafés in Milan when they heard that Victor Emanuel and Count Cavour had consented to the terms of peace. England had a new war in China put upon her. From the United States came the first words that told the world of a great civil war about to break out. John Brown had made his momentous raid into Harper's Ferry for the purpose of running off negro slaves, and he had been tried, convicted, and executed, and his soul, as the popular ballad truly said, was "marching on." Abra-

ham Lincoln had been chosen by the National
Republican Convention at Chicago as candidate
for the Presidency of the United States, and we
on this side of the Atlantic were beginning to
understand what that meant. England was har-
assed just then by the outbreak of a number of
strikes, illustrating in action the immemorial conflict between capital and labor. There was something approaching to a panic among the English
people with regard to the attitude of Louis Napoleon. We had gone very cordially and cheeringly
with him into the Crimean War, but now it suddenly came to the minds of people that we had
better make up our minds to prepare for what
Mr. Disraeli sarcastically called "a midnight foray
from our imperial ally." "True," said Tennyson
in a poem, "that we have a faithful ally, but only
the devil knows what he means." Let an English
statesman look where he would, he saw but storm-
clouds and portents of alarm.

It was at just that moment that Mr. Gladstone as Chancellor of the Exchequer seemed to
have made up his mind to go in for the broad,
bold course of financial reform, of the lightening
of taxation as far as possible everywhere, and
especially of the diminution or the complete removal of the odious taxes on popular education.
One of Mr. Gladstone's first achievements was

the establishment of a Commercial Treaty between England and France, by virtue of which the lighter French wines were to be admitted with a small duty into England for popular consumption, and English manufactured goods were to

RICHARD COBDEN
(From an old engraving)

be admitted into France at a corresponding diminution of impost. The idea of such a commercial treaty belonged in the first instance to Mr. Bright, but was put into shape by Mr. Cobden. Mr. Gladstone gave it his warm and practical support, and Lord Palmerston had no particular objection; did not care very much either way. Mr. Cobden went over to Paris backed up by all the influence Mr. Gladstone could give to him, and entered into negotiations with the Emperor Napoleon the Third. The Emperor was naturally very willing to be on friendly terms with England, although if it had been necessary for the support of his dynasty to make war against England he would have done so without scruple. So he readily entered into terms with Mr. Cobden. Cobden had the powerful support of Monsieur Michel Chevalier, a famous political economist of that time, and also of the Emperor's cousin, Prince Napoleon, whom Cobden afterwards described to me as on the whole the best-informed man he had ever met. The Commercial Treaty was passed; we got light clarets to drink instead of fiery ports and ardent sherries; and the French people got all sorts of comfortable garments of English manufacture.

Mr. Gladstone was denounced a great deal for the part he had taken in adopting Cobden's policy as to the Treaty of Commerce. He was sometimes talked of in the House of Commons as if he had given the French invading armies a safe landing-place on the shores of England. He took all these attacks with a sort of amused good humor. One thing was certain: he always gave back in ridicule a great deal more than he got in denunciation. The declaimer who had the courage to attack him in Parliament was soon, to use a very colloquial expression, sorry he spoke. That was a splendid session of Parliament for Mr. Gladstone and his policy. He and Bright fought the battle all to themselves. Mr. Cobden was for the greater

part of the time still in Paris; nor, although a most
persuasive and convincing speaker, could he possibly be compared as a Parliamentary orator with
Mr. Gladstone or Mr. Bright.   Disraeli led the
opposition, but he neither knew nor cared much
about the whole subject, and in any case his position was naturally very trying when he had to
reply to Bright and be replied to by Gladstone.
It is not pleasant to be set between two such
millstones.   The grinding process is apt to be
severe.

Still more important for Mr. Gladstone's career
and for the development of education in Great
Britain and Ireland was his measure for the abolition of the duty on paper.   One has to go back
a little in order to explain what this duty on
paper really was.   The duty on paper has been
described as the last remnant of an ancient system of finance which tended to the severe repres-
sion of popular journalism.   First of all there was
a stamp duty, which was imposed with the avowed
object of preventing the growth of seditious newspapers — that is to say, of newspapers advocating
any manner of popular reform.   In the early part
of the century the stamp duty amounted to four-
pence on every single copy of a newspaper issued.
Later on it was reduced, and in 1836 it was
brought down to a tax of a penny, represented

by the red stamp of the Government on every copy. Then there was a tax of sixpence on every advertisement in the newspaper. The editor of a great London morning journal has told me that he can well remember the time when a Government official came down to the office of the paper somewhere after midnight every day before the paper had gone to press, insisted on seeing an early copy, and then proceeded to mark with pencil what he considered to be advertisements. Of course, about the regular trading announcements there could be no manner of doubt. When Messrs. Brown proclaimed that they had a lot of new silk dresses from Paris to dispose of, or Messrs. Jones informed the gratified public that they had imported a stock of the finest wines from Bordeaux or Burgundy at the cheapest prices, there could be no sort of a question as to the genuineness of the advertisement. One might say that there ought to be no tax upon advertisements at all, but, admitting the existence of such a tax, and the right of Parliament to impose it, there could be no question as to the application in these particular instances. My friend the editor assured me, however, that the Government officials were most arbitrary in their definition as to what constituted an advertisement and was therefore liable to the tax. A harmless line appeared in the corner of the paper announcing that Mr. Robinson, M.P., was about to address his constituents in the ensuing week. That is an advertisement, the Government official declared. No, it is only a piece of news, the editor pleaded. " News me no news," the official replied, and he marked it down with a sixpenny tax. The latest of all these imposts was the heavy duty on the paper material itself. This was really an enormous imposition; and let it be clearly understood that the distinct purpose of that and all other imposts was to make it difficult for anybody but a capitalist of great means to produce a newspaper at all. No journal could come into existence until it had satisfied the authorities that it was able to provide the amount of capital necessary to meet all this enormous taxation. As I have said already, the distinct and avowed object of the taxation was to prevent the issue of cheap newspapers. At this time the first organized movement for the publication of cheap newspapers was beginning to be made in England. The city of Liverpool, the place of Mr. Gladstone's birth, led the effort by starting the first penny daily paper ever published in Great Britain. Lancashire, Mr. Gladstone's county, was then and always since has been in the front of every great movement of social reform. London soon took up the scheme of cheap daily newspapers. The "Daily Telegraph" and the "Morning Star" were started as penny daily papers. The "Daily Telegraph" is at this hour probably the most prosperous and popular daily paper in Great Britain. But the effect of the duty on the paper material was still an almost crushing obstruction to cheap journalism. It soon became evident that with this heavy imposition it was almost impossible that a penny daily paper could pay its way. There had for some time been an important agitation going on for the abolition of all repressive taxation on popular education. Charles Dickens took a leading part in the movement, and had even gone so far as to come into conflict with the legal authorities of the country because he persisted in publishing a weekly journal which contained actual news as well as literature. Mr. Gladstone saw that the time had come for giving life and strength to the new ideas. He became impressed with the fact that there was no way more efficacious of spreading popular education than by the multiplying of cheap newspapers which brought the daily story of the world home to the huts and the garrets of the poor. Up to that time it was quite common for a number of persons to club together and subscribe for a daily paper, which they read by turns. The usual understanding was that the subscriber who got

the paper last should be entitled to keep it in
his possession. At that time, as an English writer
has observed, it was the creed of many that cheap
newspapers meant the establishment of a daily
propaganda of socialism, communism, red republicanism, blasphemy, bad spelling, and general
immorality.

Mr. Gladstone took quite the other view of the
question. He had full faith in the intelligence of
his countrymen and of the English-speaking peo-
ples in general to keep the cheapest newspaper
press within the limits of common sense and decency. He had no faith whatever in the good
working of a restrictive money-fine to keep down
enterprise in the issue of cheap newspapers. The
newspaper was, according to his belief, one of the
most powerful influences towards the spread of
national education, and he soon made up his mind
to abolish the last tax which stood in its way.

In his financial scheme of 1860 he announced
that the Government had resolved to abolish the
duty on paper. It is hardly necessary to say that
such a proposition met with the strongest opposition from both sides of the House. It became a
mere question of what we call vested interests.
There were many influential manufacturers of
paper in the House of Commons, and these all
joined in an organized opposition to any scheme

W. E. GLADSTONE

(From a photograph by Vincent Brooks Day & Son)

which threw open the business of newspaper publishing to free and common competition. Naturally, the well-established and high-priced journals
objected to the idea of a penny "rag" being enabled to compete with a sixpenny daily journal.
Therefore the battle was fiercely fought out in
the House of Commons and in the daily press,
and Mr. Gladstone became, naturally, the object
of much fierce denunciation. According to many
of his critics, the result of his policy could only
be the overthrow of the altar and the throne, the
aristocratic system and the whole moral creed, of
the nation. The vested interests in the House
of Commons were then, as they are even still, very
strong, and one vested interest was generally found
ready to stand by another. In the early part of
the session Mr. Gladstone was very unwell, and
his financial statement had to be put off for some
days. When he did come to make his statement,
the force of his marvellous eloquence and reasoning power compelled the House of Commons to
pass the provision for the abolition of the paper
duty. But at each stage of the measure the
majorities in favor of the abolition fell and fell.
The second reading was carried by a majority of
fifty-three; the third reading was carried by a
majority of only nine. This naturally gave new
courage to the House of Lords, and in the Heredi-

Q

tary Chamber a motion was made and carried by a large majority to reject altogether Mr. Gladstone's bill for the repeal of the duty on paper.

This action on the part of the House of Lords brought on a constitutional crisis as serious as any that has happened in our time. The House of Lords, it should be understood, has no power to impose taxation on the people of England. But if the House of Lords has no power to initiate taxation on the people, it was fairly and justly contended by Mr. Gladstone and Mr. Bright that neither can the House of Lords have any right to reimpose on the English people any tax which the House of Commons has seen fit to take off. This is, indeed, the evident common sense of the matter. If the House of Lords could have the constitutional right to reimpose a tax which had been taken off by the Representative Chamber — that is, the taxing Chamber — there could be no reason whatever why the House of Lords should not have the right to initiate taxation of its own free will. Nobody even among the Tory leaders of the House of Lords ventured to contend that the Hereditary Chamber had any right to initiate taxation, but it was plausibly argued that when a certain scheme of taxation came before the peers, the peers had a perfect right to modify the scheme in any way that they thought fit.

The question then came down to a very narrow issue. The repeal of the paper duty was put off for one session; but the public out-of-doors, having full faith in the leadership of Mr. Gladstone, were not much excited by what Mr. Gladstone well called the "gigantic innovation" on the part of the Hereditary Chamber. There were meetings held, to be sure, all over the country, and the action of the House of Lords was strongly and justly denounced. But the general feeling was one of perfect conviction that Mr. Gladstone would put the whole thing right, and therefore there was no popular disturbance whatever. I remember the time well. I was even then in the thick of political life, and I can say with certainty that only the strong faith in Mr. Gladstone's capacity as a leader prevented something not unlike a national convulsion. The Liberals had little faith in Lord Palmerston. Lord Palmerston's sympathies went a good deal with the Tories and against the Radicals. Mr. Gladstone absolutely condemned the conduct of the House of Lords. Lord Palmerston only proposed a series of mild resolutions reaffirming the rights of the House of Commons with regard to national taxation. Then for the first time it became clear to all the world that Mr. Gladstone was bidding his final farewell not merely to the Tory party but

to the party of the Whigs — that is to say, the
lagging and backward section of the Liberals.
His final declaration on the subject was yet to
come, but it may already be anticipated by some
consideration of the conditions under which the
House of Lords was still stimulated into setting
up its will against that of the House of Commons.

I have said that the majorities in favor of
Mr. Gladstone's measure dwindled at each stage,
and at last came down to a poor superiority of
nine. The fact is that at that time the House
of Commons was only constitutionally and techni-
cally representative of the majority of the people.
The franchise was so high and so limited that it
excluded the whole mass of the working classes.
There was not at that time a single man in the
House of Commons who represented, or was entitled to speak for, the laboring population of
the three kingdoms. The great Reform Bill introduced by Lord Grey and Lord John Russell
thirty years before, and carried after a two years'
struggle, had admitted what men called the middle
classes of England to the right of voting for the
election of a member to the House of Commons.
But the working classes and the poor had been
wholly left out of the measure. It remained for
men like Lord John Russell and Mr. Gladstone
and Mr. Bright to initiate later on the movement

which admitted the workingmen and the poor to a share in the representation of the country.

Therefore the House of Commons, to which Mr. Gladstone submitted his scheme for the abolition of the duty on paper, took but a languid interest in the matter when the instantaneous spell of his eloquence was over. Most of the members, or nearly all of them, could very well afford to pay sixpence for their daily paper, and they were not responsible for their votes to any of the class who most especially wanted cheap newspapers. The peers, therefore, naturally took courage. They felt little doubt that the majority of the House of Commons would be rather obliged to them than otherwise for the course they had taken in resisting Mr. Gladstone's reform. But the country kept quiet, as I have said, because it had full faith in Mr. Gladstone's determination, and because it was quite certain that the peers would not resist him for very long.

As a matter of fact, Mr. Gladstone's scheme was passed into law in the very next session. The peers did not attempt any further resistance. If anything could have proved more clearly than another the utter worthlessness of the existence of the House of Lords, it would have been proved by its action with regard to the paper duties. For the House of Lords said in one session that to

make paper cheap would be to flood the country
with abominable newspapers, spreading everywhere
the doctrines of anarchy and profligacy, and in
the very next session it said in effect, " Well, if
Mr. Gladstone and the House of Commons want
this iniquitous measure, of course they must have
it. If they really want to ruin the country, we
must only let them ruin the country, and make
no further work about it." A story went at the
time that Lord Palmerston sent up a message to
the House of Lords to give them advice as to
their conduct with regard to the repeal of the
duties on paper. I do not venture to vouch for
the truth of the story, but, if it was not true, I
think, at least, it ought to have been true. Lord
Palmerston, it was said, sent up a message to the
House of Lords to say that the rejection of Mr.
Gladstone's scheme was a very good joke for
once, but they really must not try it another time.
The peers would seem to have acted promptly
upon this suggestion. They did not try the joke
another time. The duty on paper was repealed,
and the three kingdoms got their cheap newspapers in abundance. It is almost needless to
say that not one of the penny papers that started
into existence all over this country advocated
any doctrine of anarchy or profligacy or disorder.
Better-conducted papers do not exist in any coun-

try in the world than the cheap journals which
Mr. Gladstone by his policy helped into existence.
With one single exception, there are only penny
and half-penny daily papers in Great Britain and
Ireland now. There is not one of these cheap
papers that is not far superior in its array of news
and in the style of its writing to any of those high-
priced journals existing thirty years ago because
of the legislation which Mr. Gladstone abolished.

No other man could have done the work so
well as he did. Cobden could not have done it,
Bright could not have accomplished it. For
neither of these men was in office, and neither
had the command of the House of Commons
which was possessed by Mr. Gladstone. Likewise, it has to be said that neither of them could
have had the same influence over Lord Palmerston which Mr. Gladstone was enabled to exert.
Palmerston did not really care three straws about
the repeal of the taxes upon education, or, indeed,
about any other popular reform. But then his
heart was not set so much the other way as to
induce him to enter into a struggle for power
with Mr. Gladstone. Palmerston knew perfectly
well that Gladstone was the coming man, and
that if he were to set himself in opposition to
Mr. Gladstone, or make any serious attempt at
restraint of Mr. Gladstone, the national will of

the country would put the younger man in the more commanding place. There is a story of a philosopher who said of himself that he would just as soon be dead as alive. Being asked why, then, he did not kill himself, he made the very reasonable and consistent answer that he would just as soon be alive as dead. Lord Palmerston's views as to popular reform were of much the same nature. He would just as soon have no popular reform as any. But if pressed upon the subject, he soon found out that he would just as soon have any popular reform as none whatever.

Such a man had no chance against the ever-growing energy and earnestness of Mr. Gladstone. His very style of speaking in the House, easy and colloquial, humorous, full of shrewd hits, and occasionally enlivened by a somewhat cheap cynicism, was in curious contrast with the impassioned and majestic flow of Mr. Gladstone's convinced and convicting eloquence. The two men never really came into antagonism at all. But they represented two distinct influences, and had Lord Palmerston been a younger man it is quite likely that the influences might have come into collision at one time or another. Lord Palmerston's chief interest was in foreign affairs, and there, curiously enough, his policy was rather revolutionary in its tendency. Mr. Gladstone was almost always

in sympathy with every foreign cause that represented freedom and advancement, but his dearest
interests were with the happiness and with the
improvement of the people of his own two islands.
So far as home affairs were concerned, Lord Palmerston's great idea was to put off any sort of trouble,
to let things slide, to keep away as long as possible
any effort at reforming things which perhaps after
all could do just as well without reform, and, generally speaking, not to make any bother.   Mr.
Gladstone's whole soul was with political and
social reform.   He saw with the eye of genius
and of philanthropy that these countries were
oppressed by what must be called class legislation, and his whole soul was aflame to give help
to those who could not help themselves.   Lord
Palmerston, though he lived to a good old age,
did not live long enough to come to any serious
extent in the way of Mr. Gladstone's progress.
Indeed, about the time of Gladstone's scheme for
the abolition of the paper duties it became a common saying among the followers of Mr. Cobden
and Mr. Bright that Radicals must wait quietly
until Palmerston's disappearance, and that then
Gladstone would come to the front and would do
the work which the country wanted.   Up to this
time Mr. Gladstone had not spoken out distinctly
on the great question of the Parliamentary fran-

chise. But people already saw that that would be his next work of reform, and that he was destined to be the leader of the people in England. From the days when Macaulay had described him as the hope of the stern and unbending Tories, what a distance he had already traversed! He was now the great hope of the Radical advocates of reform and progress. Cobden and Bright now began to call him the leader of the English democracy.

In his early college days Mr. Gladstone developed a strong passion for riding. I do not know whether he ever cared to ride to hounds or not; but he certainly loved riding for its own sake, quite apart from the fascination of hunting; and he became a rider of marvellous skill and courage.

Often have I seen him, in my younger days, galloping over the fields around Chester—close to the Welsh frontier, within which stands Hawarden Castle. The famous American horse-tamer, Rarey, when he was in England, spoke of Mr. Gladstone as one of the finest and boldest riders he had ever seen—and Rarey was a man who, on such subjects, quite knew what he was talking about. Years after, when Mr. Gladstone was Chancellor of the Exchequer, he was taking his usual ride in the park —Hyde Park—on a very spirited and even wild young horse. The horse plunged and ran away—

got off the ordinary track of riders and came along a spread of turf divided by rails and gateways. The horse made for one of the little gateways — of light and slender iron — and went straight over it. Mr. Gladstone was apparently quite determined to have the better of that horse. The moment the horse had leaped the gate the rider turned him round and put him at the gate again. Again he topped it, and again his master turned him and made him go at it once more, and surmount it yet another time. So it went on until the horse was fairly but very harmlessly conquered, and the rider was the supreme victor of the day. It is hardly necessary for me to say that this little incident was watched by many curious eyes, and that it found its way into the papers. I happened to be in London at the time, and was deeply interested. I saw auguries in it, and I do not think my prophetic inspirations were altogether disappointed by the result. It would take a very reckless horse or a very reckless political opponent to get the better of Mr. Gladstone. He has made his party face many a stiff fence since the far-off days of that little event in Hyde Park.

CHAPTER XIX

THE AMERICAN CIVIL WAR

I HAVE already mentioned the fact that the great Civil War in America had broken out. The war created a curious difference of opinion in this country. What is commonly called "society" was almost altogether in favor of the South. The English democracy and working classes generally were entirely in favor of the North. Some of our educated men were divided in opinion. Carlyle, who perhaps could hardly be called, on that question, an educated man, was rabidly in favor of the South, or, rather, was rabidly opposed to the North. He knew nothing whatever about the matter, and used to boast that he never read American newspapers. On the other hand, John Stuart Mill, probably the most purely intellectual Englishman of his time, was heart and soul with the cause of the North. Cobden and Bright were, of course, leaders of public opinion on the side of the North. Harriet Martineau, probably the cleverest woman who ever wrote for an English newspaper, advocated

the cause of the North day after day. Lord
Palmerston, in his heedless, unthinking way, had

JOHN STUART MILL.
(From a photograph by the London Stereoscopic Co.)

talked some jocularities after the battle of Bull
Run which were offensive to the minds of all
Americans who supported the cause of the North.
Lord Palmerston, however, although Prime Min-

ister, was always regarded as an irresponsible sort
of person, who could not be expected to refrain
from his joke, no matter whom the joke might
offend.   But a profound sensation was created in
the Northern States when Mr. Gladstone unluckily
committed himself to a sort of declaration in favor
of the South.   Speaking at a public meeting at
Newcastle-on-Tyne on the seventh of October, 1862,
he gave it as his conviction that Jefferson Davis
" had made an army, had made a navy, and, more
than that, had made a nation."   This declaration
was received in America with feelings of the
most profound disappointment.   It produced
something like consternation among the English
Radicals who were proud to follow Mr. Gladstone.   The pity of it was that he should have
spoken on the subject at all before he had made
himself thoroughly acquainted with it.   The pity
of it was that he should have taken no account
of the opinions of men like Cobden, who knew
the American States well, like Bright, and like
Stuart Mill.   However, we must take Mr. Gladstone as Nature made him, impetuous, earnest,
full of emotion, and quick of speech.   " If I were
always cool in council," says Schiller's hero, " I
should not be William Tell."   If Gladstone were
always cool in council he would not be the great
orator, philanthropist, and reformer that we know

him to be. Five years later on Mr. Gladstone
made a frank and ample admission of his mistake. " I must confess," he said, " that I was
wrong; that I took too much upon myself in
expressing such an opinion. Yet the motive was
not bad. My sympathies were then — where they
had long before been, where they are now — with
the whole American people. I, probably, like
many Europeans, did not understand the nature
and the working of the American Union. I had
imbibed conscientiously, if erroneously, an opinion
that twenty or twenty-four millions of the North
would be happier, and would be stronger — of
course, assuming that they would hold together
— without the South than with it, and also that
the negroes would be much nearer to emancipation under a Southern government than under the
old system of the Union, which had not at that
date been abandoned, and which always appeared
to me to place the whole power of the North at
the command of the slaveholding interests of the
South. As far as regards the special or separate
interest of England in the matter, I, differing
from many others, had always contended that it
was best for our interest that the Union should
be kept entire." It is only fair to remember that
many of the strongest abolitionists of the North
had for years been growing into the conviction

that if the South did not secede from the North,
the North would have to secede from the South.
It was perfectly true, as Mr. Gladstone said, that
the whole power of the North had been for a
long time at the command of the slaveholding
people of the South. The election of Abraham
Lincoln to the Presidency was the first signal
that that time had gone by.

Mr. Gladstone's attention, however, was closely
occupied by domestic affairs and by his work as
Chancellor of the Exchequer. He had not travelled in America as had Cobden and Harriet Martineau, nor had he, like Stuart Mill, the leisure to
make himself master of the study of American
politics and life. Anyhow, the mistake was amply
atoned for. It was a mistake which hurt the
best admirers of Mr. Gladstone in England even
more than it hurt his best admirers in the Northern States of America, and it was fully atoned
for by more than one admission of error and
expression of regret. Nobody could have doubted
for a moment that Mr. Gladstone's wishes thoroughly went for the prosperity and the progress
of the great American Republic.

In 1865 the Parliament which had begun six
years before came to its natural end. Mr. Gladstone presented himself again as a candidate to
the electors of Oxford University. Times had

changed, however, since his latest election. He
was becoming more and more an advanced reformer. He had expressed himself in the House
of Commons to the effect that the present position of the State Church in Ireland was unsatis-
factory. The Irish Church, as he frankly admitted,
ministered only to one-eighth or one-ninth of the
whole Irish population. This speech created a
profound sensation among his Oxford constituents.
To many of the University dons it seemed like
flat blasphemy. When the voting closed, Mr.
Gladstone was at the bottom of the poll. He
issued a parting address in which he said: " After
an arduous connection of eighteen years, I bid
you respectfully farewell. My earnest purpose to
serve you, my many faults and shortcomings, the
incidents of the political relation between the University and myself, established in 1847, so often
questioned in vain, and now at length finally dissolved, I leave to the judgment of the future. It
is one imperative duty, and one alone, which in-
duces me to trouble you with these few parting
words — the duty of expressing my profound and
lasting gratitude for indulgence as generous, and
for support as warm and enthusiastic in itself,
and as honorable from the character and distinc-
tions of those who have given it, as has, in my
belief, ever been accorded by any constituency to

R

any representative." To the Bishop of Oxford, who wrote him a most sympathetic letter, Gladstone sent a reply in which occurs the following passage: "Do not join with others in praising

me because I am not angry, only sorry, and that deeply. For my revenge, which I do not desire, but would baffle if I could, all lies in that little word 'future' in my address, which I wrote with a consciousness that it is deeply charged with meaning, and

SAMUEL WILBERFORCE, 1805-1873

that that which shall come will come. There have been two great deaths or transmigrations of spirit in my political existence — one very slow, the breaking of ties with my original party; and the other very short and sharp, the breaking of the tie with Oxford. There will probably be a third, and no more." This expression of Mr. Gladstone's aroused some alarm in the mind of the Bishop of Oxford. He asked for some explanation of its meaning. "You are not a Radical," the Bishop wrote, "and yet you may, by political exigencies, if you submit to be second, be led into heading a Radical party until its fully developed aims assault all that you most value in our country, and it, the Radical party, turns upon you and rends you." Mr. Gladstone's rejoinder, full as it is of gratitude and sympathy, was not likely to have quite cleared up the doubts of the Bishop of Oxford. Mr. Gladstone was not, however, left actually out in the cold by the decision of the Oxford electors. Some of his friends in South Lancashire had provided against such a possibility by nominating him as a candidate for that northern constituency. At a general election a man may be nominated for several constituencies, and, if he be elected for more than one, he has only to choose which place he will sit for. Mr. Gladstone was elected for South Lancashire, but he came last on the list of the three representatives. The two others were strong local Tories —obscure men, comparatively.

Lord Palmerston had said, or was believed to have said, to a friend, that Gladstone was a dangerous man, and had best be kept in Oxford. "In Oxford," went on Lord Palmerston's phrase, "he is muzzled, but send him elsewhere he will run wild." In one of the spirited speeches which Gladstone made to the electors of South Lancashire he referred good-humoredly to Palmerston's remark.

"At last, my friends," he said, "I am come among you; and I am come, to use an expression which has become very famous and is not likely to be forgotten, I am come unmuzzled." The general elections gave to the Government a slight majority, and Mr. Gladstone resumed his old office as Chancellor of the Exchequer. Everybody thoroughly understood the difference between his position as member for South Lancashire and member for Oxford University. We shall presently find that South Lancashire Toryism became too strong for him, and that he had to seek for a more liberal and progressive constituency. The Bishop of Oxford saw probably by this time that his fears about the possibility of Gladstone drifting on into genuine Radicalism were by no means unlikely to be justified. More than once after his election for South Lancashire he had to go on for new constituencies — for constituents who were marching with the movement of his mind.

In truth, Mr. Gladstone's mere acceptance of office under Lord Palmerston marked a new stage in his political career. He had definitively broken away from the Tory party. While he still remained an independent member, he had given, up to the last, some votes now and then in support of the Tory Government where he believed that they were acting on a rightful principle. But even then he had voted with them only when it seemed to him that their action, however inspired, was tending towards a policy of Liberal reform. Now it was becoming every day more and more plain that Mr. Gladstone was growing out of the dusk of Toryism into the dawn of Liberalism. When he consented to take office under Lord Palmerston, it was proclaimed to every one that he had given up the last of his old traditions. Lord Palmerston, to be sure, was not much of a Liberal; he was not, indeed, much of anything except a Prime Minister and a very clever leader of the House of Commons. But Mr. Gladstone simply accepted Lord Palmerston as everybody else did. He regarded him as the man inevitable for the moment, the man who could, when occasion required, put on a decent show of leading the Liberals, and at the same time could to a certain extent propitiate and even manage the Tories. Mr. Gladstone's sympathies were very cordially given to Lord John Russell, now Foreign Secretary, who was a sincere and a thorough Liberal reformer. Lord John Russell and Mr.

Gladstone worked together most cordially. They were both strongly in favor of some measure of reform which should admit the mass of the people to the franchise. They both strongly disliked Lord Palmerston's bumptious and aggressive tone in foreign politics. They both disliked Lord Palmerston's plans for a vast expenditure on fortifications and on what Mr. Disraeli called "bloated armaments" as a protection against possible or problematical invasion. Lord Palmerston, it is well known, was never drawn towards Mr. Gladstone, and was sometimes heedlessly outspoken in his disparagement of his great colleague.

CHAPTER XX

MR. GLADSTONE at last declared himself a convinced and definite supporter of the popular suffrage. The declaration came about in a sudden and
unexpected sort of way. Wednesday in the House
of Commons is one of the days which is considered
to be the property of the private members until
that period of the session comes when the Government, whatever it may be, having muddled away
the time at its disposal, finds itself compelled by
the necessities of the case to absorb all the sittings
of the House. On Wednesday, the eleventh of
April, 1864, a bill was brought in by a private member for the extension of the franchise in boroughs.
On such occasions it is usual for members of the
Government to keep quiet and take no conspicuous
part either way. Some Minister usually rises and
utters a few careful and commonplace words, com-
mitting the Government to nothing in particular.

On this occasion Mr. Gladstone struck into the
debate, and even with vehemence. He contended
that the burden of proof rested, not upon those

who claimed for the working classes the right to
the franchise, but on those who denied that right.
" We are told," Mr. Gladstone said, " that the working classes do not agitate for the suffrage, but is it
well that we should wait until they do agitate? In
my opinion, agitation by the working classes upon
any political subject whatever ought not to be
made a condition previous to any Parliamentary
movement, but, on the contrary, is to be deprecated,
and, if possible, prevented by wise and provident
measures." " An agitation by the working classes,"
he pointed out, "is not like an agitation by the
classes above them having leisure. The agitation
of the classes having leisure is easily conducted.
Every hour of their time has not a money value;
their wives and children are not dependent on the
application of those hours of labor. But when a
workingman finds himself in such a condition that
he must abandon that daily labor on which he is
strictly dependent for his daily bread, it is only because then, in railway language, the danger-signal
is turned on, and because he feels a strong necessity for action, and a distrust in the rulers who have
driven him to that necessity. The present state of
things, I rejoice to say, does not indicate that distrust; but, if we admit that, we must not allege the
absence of agitation on the part of the working
classes as a reason why the Parliament of England

and the public mind of England should be indis-
posed to entertain the discussion of this question."
In the course of his speech Mr. Gladstone asked
whether the working classes "are not our own flesh
and blood?"   This speech naturally created a
great sensation.   Some of Mr. Gladstone's own
colleagues seemed to be nearly frightened out of
their lives.   The Conservative newspapers wrote of
it as if it were a modern reproduction of Rousseau's
doctrine of the social contract.   The measure
which Mr. Gladstone advocated was not carried at
that time, and nobody had the least expectation
that it was likely to be carried.   But everybody
knew perfectly well that the lowering of the suffrage to admit the working classes had become a
matter of certainty when once that speech had
been spoken.

Then at last it was plain to every one that Mr.
Gladstone had absolutely broken away from all the
traditions of his early Parliamentary career.   He
had put himself at the head of the free-trade movement.   He had put himself at the head of the
movement for the repeal of taxes upon knowledge.
Now he was putting himself at the head of the
movement for the extension of the right of voting
so as to admit the working classes and the poor
generally to the exercise of a vote as to the persons whom they considered best fitted to represent

them.   From that moment it was merely a question
of time, of sessions, when the principle of popular
representation should be carried into law and into
practice.

Two years later the Government of which Mr.
Gladstone was the leader in the House of Commons brought in a bill to extend the franchise so
far as to make what I may call the better condi-
tioned of the working classes free to exercise a
vote at an election.   One great difficulty had been
removed out of the way of any movement for the
extension of the suffrage.   Lord Palmerston was
dead.   Every one knew that so long as Palmerston
lived he would be sure to throw cold water on any
proposal to give a vote to the working classes.
His influence in the negative sense was immense,
and it was thoroughly understood, as I have said,
by men like John Bright, that no good measure
of suffrage reform had a real chance in the House
of Commons while Palmerston was still leader of
the Government.   But now Palmerston was gone.
That strange career which had fostered every
revolution abroad and discouraged every genuine
reform at home had come to an end.   It would
not be easy to get readers at this day to understand what an influence was exercised over the
House of Commons, and over the English public
generally, by the easy-going, careless, contemptu-

ous ways of Lord Palmerston.   He was able to
infuse a sort of natural cynicism into the well-to-do
classes of English life which made them think it
ridiculous to take serious trouble about any questions of political reform.   He represented exactly
the mind of the sort of man who, in domestic

HENRY J. TEMPLE, VISCOUNT PALMERSTON
(From an old woodcut)

affairs at least, cared nothing about anybody.
When domestic politics went against Lord Palmerston, he made some great outburst in foreign
affairs, and then the man in the streets threw up
his hat for him and shrieked aloud that Palmerston was the one who could make the foreign
tyrants shake in their shoes.   It is not likely that

there will ever again arise in English politics a
man of the type of Lord Palmerston.   He was not
a Tory; he laughed at Toryism and its old-fashioned prejudices; but he did not care one straw
for any really liberal measure.   The enthusiasm of
Gladstone was unintelligible to him.   He could
not understand why a man like Gladstone should
concern himself in the least about the question
whether the working classes ought or ought not
to have any share in the suffrage.   He was a
genial, kindly hearted man, who would have liked
people to be as happy as possible, but it was not
in his nature to think that people were any the
happier for having votes.   He went through the
world gay and careless so far as domestic affairs
were concerned, and only stirred to enthusiasm
when some foreign question arose, on which he
was much more likely to be wrong than right.

As I have said, there was a sort of truce to the
question of suffrage reform while Palmerston lived.
Now that he was out of the field, Earl Russell and
Mr. Gladstone resolved to bring in a bill for the
extension and the expansion of the suffrage.   It
was not really a very sweeping measure of reform.
Looking back now at its introduction, one can
only wonder how so tentative and limited a measure could have been expected to satisfy the demands of the English democracy.   One has to

ask in amazement what would have been thought
of such a measure in Canada or in the Australian
colonies.   Still, it was a distinct advance for the
time, and it had the qualified approval and the full
practical support of John Bright, who now, since
the death of Richard Cobden, was left the great
leader of the popular reform movement in England.   The measure, although made as moderate
and as limited as even timorous reformers could
have desired, did not pass through the House of
Commons.   Then, as much more lately, Mr. Gladstone found himself confronted by a formidable
secession from the ranks of his own party.   A
number of Liberals declared against his Reform
Bill and supported the Tories in their opposition
to it.   The opposition was a phenomenon which
occurs again and again in the history of an English Liberal Ministry.   Some of the followers of
the Ministry are always sure to think that the
leaders are going too far in the way toward demo-
cratic institutions, and they lose heart or turn
back, or even join the opponents of all Liberalism.

This happened in 1832, when Lord Grey and
Lord John Russell brought in their Reform Bill.
It happened when Lord John Russell brought in his
Reform Bill in 1860.   It happened in 1866, when
Lord Russell as Prime Minister in the House of
Lords, and Mr. Gladstone as leader of the House

of Commons, brought in their Reform Bill; and
it was to happen again, as we shall see, when,
twenty years later, Mr. Gladstone brought in his
measure of Home Rule for Ireland.   In 1866 the
Reform Bill was not Liberal enough to arouse any
great passion of enthusiasm in the country, and
yet it was too liberal for the faint-hearted members
of the Radical party.   It would be needless now
to go into any details of the measure or any criticism of them, and, indeed, details of that great
controversy have rather a personal than a political
interest.   Mr. Gladstone, Mr. Bright, and Mr. Disraeli were seen at their very best in that memorable fight, but, of course, every one knew that
these men would do their best in such a strife.

The honors of the debate were really carried off
by Mr. Robert Lowe, who died years after in
obscurity as Lord Sherbrooke.   Robert Lowe had
won distinction in New South Wales, where he
had become a prominent politician.   He came
over to settle in London, and, being a man of
great literary gifts, he obtained a position as leader-
writer for the "Times."   He found a seat in the
House of Commons, and was commonly regarded as
a man likely to make a name in Parliamentary debate.   For a long time, however, he gave no distinct proof of any capacity that way.   His opportunity came with Mr. Gladstone's Reform Bill of 1866.

Lowe had somehow acquired the more narrow-minded literary man's hatred of all popular reform. With him culture ranked as the first and foremost of everything. The idea of a man being allowed to vote at an election who could not read Greek and Latin was revolting to his soul. He was not really a great Greek and Latin scholar. He did not know Greek nearly as well as Gladstone did or as John Stuart Mill did; but he prided himself more on his classical knowledge than was the way of Gladstone or Stuart Mill.

He had a contempt, which he did not even pretend to conceal, for the working classes and the poor generally. Therefore he threw his whole soul into an impassioned opposition to Gladstone's mild and moderate measure of reform. He had a marvellous literary gift of phrase-making, of paradox, of sarcasm, and of illustration. He had read much in many literatures; he had apparently a wonderful memory, and whenever an idea occurred to him some quotation floated with it, double — swan and shadow. He was certainly the comet of a season; he dazzled and startled the whole House of Commons. I heard almost all those great debates, and I remember them well. I know that Gladstone was at his best, that Bright was at his best, that Disraeli was at his best, but I cannot help acknowledging that the chief interest was absorbed by Mr.

Lowe. Many things were against him. He had
a very bad voice and a wretched articulation; his
sight was miserably short, and if he had any notes
he found it almost impossible to read them; he had
to compete with three men whose voices and articulation were magnificent; and yet he held his own.
I was greatly interested in the whole struggle, and
in the part which Mr. Lowe took in it. I came to
know him very well later on, and found him, as
many people said they did not find him, a genial
and agreeable companion. But his success in
those reform debates of 1866 and 1867 was a wonder and a puzzle to me. I could not dispute the
success, but it astonished me quite as much as did
the success of Sir Bulwer Lytton in the former
days which I have described. I could not question
the wonderful freshness of Lowe's phrase-making,
and the aptness of his illustrations. Still, I could
not understand, and I cannot understand now, how
he came to carry off the honors of debate from
Gladstone, from Disraeli, and from Bright. The
one thing certain to my mind is that he did it.

It will not settle the question to say that the
House of Commons was apathetic about reform, and
was only too glad to hear somebody put the arguments against reform in sparkling and brilliant sentences. All that was done as well as it needed to be
done by Mr. Disraeli until the following year, when

he became a reforming statesman himself. Yet not even Mr. Disraeli aroused the enthusiasm of the Tories themselves nearly so much as Mr. Lowe did during the season of which he blazed the comet.

The Reform Bill broke down under two influences —the influence of those who were opposed to all reform, and the influence of those who complained that by that bill they were not getting reform enough. The measure had to be given up, and Earl Russell and Mr. Gladstone resigned office. Mr. Gladstone, in his closing speech on the bill, rose to a height of eloquence which he had never exceeded before and has not surpassed since. Mr. Disraeli had been unwise enough to remind Mr. Gladstone, in the course of the debate, that he, Gladstone, had spoken against the Reform Bill of 1832 in the Oxford Union Debating Society. Mr. Disraeli, it should be brought to the memory of the reader, as I have, I think, brought it to his memory already, had begun life as an extreme Radical reformer. " The right honorable gentleman," said Mr. Gladstone, " secure in the recollection of his own consistency, has taunted me with the errors of my boyhood. When he addressed the honorable member for Westminster [Mr. Stuart Mill], he showed his magnanimity by declaring that he would not take the philosopher to task for what he wrote twenty-five years ago. But when he caught one

s

who, thirty-six years ago, just emerged from boyhood and still an undergraduate at Oxford, had
expressed an opinion adverse to the Reform Bill of
1832, of which he had so long and bitterly repented,
then the right honorable gentleman could not resist
the temptation.   He, a Parliamentary leader of
twenty years' standing, is so ignorant of the House
of Commons that he positively thought that he got
a Parliamentary advantage by exhibiting me as an
opponent of the Reform Bill of 1832.   It is true,
I deeply regret it, but I was bred under the shadow
of the great name of Canning and under the
shadow of the yet more venerable name of Burke.
My youthful mind and imagination were impressed
just the same as the mature mind of the right honorable gentleman is now impressed.   I had conceived that fear and alarm of the first Reform Bill
in my undergraduate days at Oxford which the
right honorable gentleman now feels.   My position,
sir, in regard to the Liberal party is in all points
the opposite of Earl Russell's.   I have none of the
claims he possesses.   I came among you an out-
cast from those with whom I associated, driven
from them, I admit, by no arbitrary act, but by the
slow and resistless forces of conviction.   I came
among you, to make use of the legal phraseology,
in formâ pauperis.   You received me with kindness, with indulgence, generosity, and, I may even

say, with some measure of confidence. The relation between us has assumed such a form that you
can never be my debtors, but that I must forever
be your debtor." In the closing sentences of his
speech Mr. Gladstone said: "You cannot fight
against the future. Time is on our side. The
great social forces which move onwards in their
might and majesty, and which the tumult of our
debates does not for a moment impede or disturb
—those great social forces are against you. They
are marshalled on our side, and the banner which
we now carry in this fight, though perhaps at this
moment it may droop over our sinking heads, yet
soon again will float in the eye of heaven, and
it will be borne by the firm hands of the united
people of the three kingdoms, perhaps not to an
easy, but to a certain, and a not far distant, victory."

This was one of the greatest speeches Gladstone
has ever made, and the frank explanation of his
conversion to Liberal principles put his antagonist,
Mr. Disraeli, hopelessly in the wrong. The Re-
form Bill was defeated by means of the alliance
between Mr. Lowe and the Tories; and Lord
Russell and Mr. Gladstone resigned office. Lord
Derby and Mr. Disraeli came back to power.
Now, what had happened in the meantime? Mr.
Disraeli and Mr. Lowe had opposed the Reform
Bill of Russell and Gladstone on the distinct

ground that a lowering of the suffrage was the sur-
render of the Government of England into the
hands of the ignorant, the improvident, and the
reckless.   That was the case distinctly set up over
and over again by Mr. Disraeli and Mr. Lowe,
and on those grounds the Reform Bill was lost.
The moment Lord Derby and Mr. Disraeli came
back to power, it was made known that they
intended to introduce a Reform Bill of their own.

The Houses of Parliament met on the 5th of
February, 1867, and the Queen's speech announced
that the attention of Parliament would again be
called to the question of the representation of the
people.   Mr. Disraeli himself explained afterwards
very fully in a speech why he had thus come round.
He told the public that he had spent the recess in
educating his party up to the level of a liberal
suffrage.   Apparently his conviction was that a
new Reform Bill had to come somehow or other,
and he did not see why he should not introduce
it as well as anybody else.   It must give the stranger some subject for odd reflections on English
politics when he reads of an English statesman
who turned out of office a greater English statesman because he had introduced a measure for
lowering the Parliamentary suffrage, and, having
got into office by that means, at once set about
to reduce the suffrage still lower than his prede-

cessor had attempted to do. This is exactly what happened.

Mr. Disraeli brought in a scheme of reform which, though in its beginnings it seemed moderate enough, led to the resignation of three of his most important colleagues, who naturally thought the introduction of any Reform Bill was an abandonment of the proclaimed Tory sentiments of the year before. The late Lord Shaftesbury said in a letter, " It seems to me monstrous that a body of men who resisted Mr. Gladstone's bill as an extreme measure with such great pertinacity should accept the power he retired from, and six months after introduce a bill many degrees nearer than his to universal suffrage, and establish beyond all contradiction the principle they so fiercely combated of giving a predominant interest to any class." Robert Lowe well described the situation. " What was a conflict last year," he said, " is a race now." Mr. Disraeli, as he accepted the support of the secessionist Liberals in opposing Mr. Gladstone's Reform Bill, accepted now the alliance of the extreme Radicals in the extension and the expansion of his own measure. The result was that the bill became practically a measure of household suffrage, and went in the popular direction far beyond the limits which Mr. Gladstone had endeavored to go. Mr. Disraeli.

of course, did not care in the least for any principle of consistency. In his heart he was probably still a Radical Reformer, but, as I have
suggested before, he took up with the Tories because there was not much competitive talent in
their ranks and he had a good chance of securing a leading place. No doubt in his soul and
sense he despised the stupidity of the men who
could really believe that a household suffrage
meant the ruin of England. So he allowed himself to be led by the Radical party of the House
of Commons, and he surpassed Mr. Gladstone and
Mr. Bright in his measure for the extension of
the suffrage.

Robert Lowe found himself in a peculiar position during the progress of Disraeli's Reform
Bill.   In the former session he had to fight
against Gladstone and Bright, and was supported
by Disraeli; in the session of 1867 he had to
fight against Gladstone, Bright, and Disraeli. He
stuck to his professed principles — to do him
justice. He had proclaimed himself an opponent
of a popular suffrage, and he kept up his opposition to the end. He had a perfect contempt for
the poor and the working class and "the people
who live in these small houses." He fought with
wonderful pertinacity and skill all through the
long debates of 1867. His cause, of course, was

lost.   It could not be otherwise when the Liberals and the Tories were alike determined to

ROBERT LOWE
(From a photograph by Maull & Fox)

carry a measure of reform.   But he fought with the desperate tenacity of a brilliant gladiator.   To this day I never could quite understand the secret of his personal success.   The question of his posi-

tion as a Parliamentary debater has been settled
long since.   Nobody now would think of describing Robert Lowe as an orator belonging to the
class of Gladstone or Bright or Disraeli.   His
very defects of voice and articulation would of
themselves have almost of necessity excluded him
from such a place.   Part of his success, I think,
was found in the fact that he was a brilliant literary man and leader-writer, addressing a political
assembly in a style to which that assembly was
not accustomed.   It was as if we could imagine
Junius making a speech in the peculiar style of
Junius the writer.   Anyhow, the success was certain, and the most conspicuous figure of those
two sessions of debate was not Bright, not Gladstone, not Disraeli, but Robert Lowe.   The remainder of Lowe's career was nothing.   He published a volume of verses.   He was made a peer,
and he died in comparative obscurity.   He was
a man who had, I believe, made many enemies
by his bitterness of tongue and his sarcastic ways.
I can only repeat for myself that I have the most
pleasing and genial recollections of my acquaint-
anceship with him, and that although we had
hardly any political opinions in common, and he
never even professed to have any sympathy with
my national cause, I always found him kindly,
friendly, and personally sympathetic.

At the close of 1867, Earl Russell, the Lord
John Russell of former years, announced his determination to retire finally from active political life and from the leadership of the Liberal
party in the House of Lords.   Lord Russell distinctly pointed to Mr. Gladstone as the future
Liberal Prime Minister.   Not many weeks after,
it was announced to the public that Lord Derby,
owing to his failing health, had given up the
Premiership, and that Mr. Disraeli had become
Prime Minister.   So the two great political rivals
were started in a new sort of rivalry.   Mr. Disraeli was Prime Minister of England, and it was
perfectly certain that should his party be turned
out of office Mr. Gladstone would be his successor.
The event came about sooner than any one in
England could have expected.

CHAPTER XXI

"GLADSTONE is down in the dust," said a cheery and elated Tory, one who would have been cheery under all conditions, but was elated now — that is to say, just after the passing of Disraeli's Reform Bill. "Dizzy has jockeyed him out of the leadership of the democrats, and we sha'n't hear of him as Prime Minister in our time." Alas! how easily things go wrong! The prediction was falsified very soon after its utterance. The crisis arose on a motion made in the House of Commons by an Irish member condemning the existence of the Irish State Church. About the Irish State Church I need not say much. It was a Church established and endowed by the State, and its teachings were utterly rejected by five-sixths of the Irish people.

That is almost enough to proclaim its absurdity and its injustice.

The Irish member who brought forward the motion, Mr. John Francis Maguire, long since

266

dead, a great personal friend of my own, a man whose high character and genuine abilities were recognized on both sides of the House, described the State Church as "a scandalous and a monstrous anomaly." It had been described in even harsher terms before by great English Protestants like Sydney Smith. Sydney Smith said, in his amusing fashion, a blending of humor and common sense, that "there is no abuse like it in all Europe, in all Asia, in all the discovered parts of Africa, and in all we have heard of Timbuctoo."

Mr. Bright spoke in the course of the debate, and his speech at once stamped the question as one of the most serious importance. He condemned the Irish State Church as strongly as Mr. Maguire had done. He admitted that grave difficulties of detail were yet in the way of a satisfactory arrangement, but in solemn and thrilling tones he reminded the House that "to the upright there ariseth light in the darkness." On the fourth night of the debate, however, it was that the reality and the gravity of the subject were impressed upon every mind. For on that fourth night of debate Mr. Gladstone spoke up and declared that, in his conviction, the time had come when the Irish Church as an institution maintained by the State must cease to exist. There was only one opinion then in the mind of every reasonable man in the House, and that was that the days of the Irish State Church were over, that Gladstone had pronounced its doom.

One immediate and very impressive effect of Mr. Gladstone's speech was that Mr. Maguire at once withdrew his motion. Only too gladly he left the whole subject in the care of the one man living who had most power to carry the movement against the Irish Church to a full success. A few days after the debate on Mr. Maguire's motion Mr. Gladstone gave notice of a series of resolutions condemning the existence of the Irish State Church. On the thirtieth of March, 1868, Mr. Gladstone proposed his resolutions. It must be observed that Mr. Gladstone was a supporter of the English State Church. But then every argument in favor of the English State Church was an argument against the Irish State Church. I am not going to enter here into any of the arguments for or against the maintenance of any State Church anywhere. But the claim made by Mr. Gladstone, and all those who thought with him, was that it represented the great majority of the English people and that it had a spiritual work to do which was sympathized with and accepted by that great majority.

This, the one strong defence of the English State Church, is the very strongest condemnation of

the Irish State Church.   As it was said at the
time, "the more strongly an Englishman was inclined to support his own Church, the more anxious he ought to have been to repudiate the
claim of the Irish Church to a similar position.
The State Church in Ireland was like a mildewed
ear blasting its wholesome brother.   If the two
institutions had to stand or fall together, there
could be but one end to the difficulty: both must
fall."   Mr. Gladstone carried his resolutions by
a large majority, and Mr. Disraeli announced
that the Government would dissolve and appeal
to the country.   We have seen already that, on
more than one momentous occasion, Mr. Gladstone took the opportunity of some motion made
by a private member to announce a great determination of his own.   It was so in regard to the
lowering of the franchise; it was so in regard to a
former question touching the arrangements of the
Irish State Church.   Nothing can give a better
idea of the position which Mr. Gladstone had established in public estimation than the fact that from
the moment he proclaimed his conviction the
country saw that there could be only one result.

The general election came on, and the Liberals
returned to power.   Mr. Gladstone himself was
defeated in his Lancashire constituency.   This
was, as I have already shown, almost a matter of

certainty, but he had been put up for Greenwich, a very Radical constituency, and there he was elected. Now, in the case of the Irish State Church, as in the other instances to which I have made allusion, Mr. Gladstone's announcement of his policy was sudden, but it could hardly have been unexpected by most people. Even in this short volume I have given evidence enough to show that Mr. Gladstone had been losing for a long time all faith in the spiritual ministry of the Irish State Church. A man may be a perfect devotee of the principle of a State Church, and yet may be conscientiously unable to accept the idea that a certain institution is a State Church merely because it is authoritatively allowed to call itself a State Church, and to pocket the money of the State. Most people, therefore, must have fully understood that when Mr. Gladstone had made up his mind on a certain principle, that principle was very likely to be expressed in strong political action. Mr. Gladstone himself had given out his ideas as to the method with which Ireland ought to be governed. He adopted the principle announced long ago by Charles James Fox, that Ireland ought to be governed according to Irish ideas, and that, to quote the words of Fox, "the more Ireland is under Irish government, the more she will be bound to English interests." Mr. Glad-

stone prepared for his new task on this principle.
He made it known that, according to his opinion,
the three great troubles of Ireland — "the three
great branches of the upas-tree " — were the State
Church, the land-tenure system, and the system of
national education. He formed his new Cabinet
with a view to this career of reform — to the hewing down of these three branches. Mr. Bright,
for the first time, accepted political office. It
should be said that Mr. Disraeli acted with good
sense and dignity when the result of the elections
became known. He resigned office at once, without waiting, according to the usual practice, for
a formal vote of the House of Commons to tell
him that he had no longer the confidence of the
country. I need not go into the events of the
session at any length. Enough to say that
the Government carried its proposals that the
Irish Church should cease to exist as a State-
supported establishment, and should pass into the
condition of a free episcopal church. The first
great reform was accomplished in Ireland.

Nor did Mr. Gladstone wait long to set about
the second reform. He turned his attention at
once to the Irish land system. We have heard
a good deal since that time of the Irish land system, and it is not too much to say that as it
then existed it has been condemned by every civ-

JOHN BRIGHT IN LATER LIFE

(From a photograph by Mackintosh & Co., Kelso, Scotland)

ilized nation in the world. Ireland is almost altogether an agricultural country. The demand for
land was in most cases a demand for the first
necessity of life, and the Irish landlords had it
almost all their own way, except in the province

of Ulster, and could make any terms they liked. It was merely a question of "pay whatever the landlord asks, or go out of the farm and starve."

The landlord let to a tenant his farm in what was described by Mr. Bright as prairie condition. The tenant hired the land in its raw, native state. By his own incessant labor and the labor of his whole family he succeeded in converting some patch of worthless bog into a farm capable of growing food for his family. Then the landlord claimed the right to raise the rent because of the improvements which the tenant himself had made. The tenant complained, and the landlord simply turned him out and let at a higher price the land to another bidder. In the province of Ulster things were somewhat different. Over the greater part of Ulster the system of what was called tenant-right prevailed. This system was, indeed, the growth of a custom merely, but it had gradually come to acquire something like the force of a law. In fact, the Ulster population are a sturdy, half-Scottish race, and in Ulster there are a great many manufactures to fall back upon, and it would not have been possible to compel the people of Ulster to put up with the land-tenure system — that is to say, the utter supremacy of the landlord — which the southern and western populations had to endure

T

The principle of tenant-right was that a tenant should be allowed to remain in possession of his holding so long as he paid the rent agreed upon, and that he should be entitled, when he gave up the land, to compensation for the value of any yet unexhausted improvements which he had himself made.   If in the meantime he was anxious to give up the farm, he was free to do what a man who has a long lease of a tenancy in England may do—he might sell to any bidder, whom the landlord was willing to accept as a tenant, the right to become his successor in the specified occupation of the holding.   Put in few words, the reform which Mr. Gladstone proposed to make was to declare the tenant-right custom in Ulster the universal law in Ireland.   Mr. George Russell observes that when on a former occasion agrarian reformers had urged the extension of the tenant-right system as a legal institution to Ireland, with the view of allaying Irish discontent, Lord Palmerston merely declared that tenant-right was land-lord's wrong, and "this imbecile jest," as Mr. Russell rightly calls it, had been meekly accepted as closing the controversy.   Mr. Gladstone proposed to do exactly that which Lord Palmerston had ridiculed as impossible, unlawful, and unjust. From the very condition of things it is plain that land is entitled to come under the authority and

arrangement of the State, just as well as every
other form of business. There is, indeed, more
reason that it should come under that authority
than almost any other form of enterprise or work.
Land cannot be increased in its extent by any
power of man. The whole agricultural area of
Ireland might be submerged in Lake Michigan
and hardly noticed there. If, therefore, you leave
the landlord in such a country absolute master
over his tenantry, to do with them what he will, it
is plain that you leave him master of their means
of living and of their lives. The more industrious
in such a case the tenant was, the more hard-
working, the more skilful, the more successful, the
worse it was with him — for all that he had done
only gave the landlord a better chance of letting
the land to a new tenant at a higher price.

There was great talk then about freedom of
contract and about the right of the landlord to
enter into a bargain with his tenant uncontrolled
by any interference of the State. During the
process of such arguments, to which I listened
for many years, I was often reminded of the
chapters in " Monte Cristo" by Alexandre Dumas
the elder, which described the capture of a Paris
millionaire banker by an Italian brigand. The
millionaire grows hungry and asks for something
to eat. The brigand tells the millionaire he can

have anything he likes within reason — fowls,
mutton, wine, fruit, pastry, and so forth, but they
must be paid for. The millionaire says he should
like a fowl with some wine. He is told that he
can have them, but the brigand puts on them
some enormous and unapproachable price. The
millionaire storms, the brigand is calm. "You
can take them or leave them, my dear sir," he
says; "there is no compulsion; here there is perfect freedom of contract." This was exactly the
freedom of contract which the Irish tenant-farmer
enjoyed under the landlord system. He was not
compelled to pay an increased rent because of
the improvements his own skill and labor had
made, but if he did not pay he had to pack off
out of the land, and was perfectly free to go into
the workhouse. The real question was whether
there was anything so sacred in the property right
of the Irish landlord as to exempt him from that
legislative control which is always interfering with
the property right of the mine-owner, the mill-
owner, the railway company, the factory-owner, the
shopkeeper, the right of the master over his ap-
prentice, the mistress over the hire and treatment
of her servants, the theatrical manager over the
conditions under which his theatre is worked.
Many people talked at the time as if Mr. Gladstone's proposal contained some startling innova-

tion, something new and audacious in the making
of laws. What Mr. Gladstone proposed to do was
simply to affirm the principle that the Irish landlord
must submit himself to the same right of State intervention and control in his dealings with others which
was established and acknowledged by every other
class and every other member of the community.

Mr. Gladstone applied himself to his task with
an energy and a pertinacity which can only not
be called surprising because one naturally looks
for wonders of that kind from Mr. Gladstone.
Nothing, we should have thought, could have
been less congenial with Mr. Gladstone's training
and tastes and habitudes than the study of such
a question, so dry, so intricate, so localized, so
foreign to all his previous interests, as that of
the Irish land system. We have seen that, until
lately, he had hardly turned his attention to Irish
questions at all. The position of the Irish State
Church would naturally have aroused his interest,
because it was part of the subject which had
always occupied his attention; and when once he
had made up his mind as to the failure of the
Irish State Church system, he could have no difficulty whatever in explaining to any audience the
reason which convinced him that this ought not
to be and that that ought to be. The whole subject of churches in their various forms had been

dear and familiar to him from his earliest days.
But to the question of Irish land-tenure he had
up to his mature years never given any attention
at all. He must have gone to the study of that
Irish land-tenure question as one goes to the study
of a foreign language, yet he made himself completely its master in what for any other man would
have been an incredibly short space of time. His
explanation of his bill to the House of Commons
was a perfect masterpiece of clearness, of ampli-
tude, and of detail. There was something positively artistic in the symmetry with which Mr.
Gladstone arranged his outlines and his details.
To the ordinary observer it might have seemed
that such a measure must be necessarily all made
up of details, and that it would be impossible to
convey any clear idea of an outline and a form
through their mass and their complexity. But
Mr. Gladstone drew his outline with the firm
hand of a master, so that every one fully compre-
hended what it meant to describe, and then he
touched in all the details, laying light, firm hand
on each, and giving to each its place, significance,
and proportion. I have often spoken with some
of the Irish law-officers who helped Mr. Gladstone
with that measure, men intimately acquainted with
every fact of the Irish land-tenure system, and
they were agreed in expressing their wonder at

the accuracy and completeness with which he had made himself its master. The bill was carried through both Houses of Parliament, not, of course, without a struggle, but, on the whole, with less force of resistance than might have been expected. It did not quite succeed in its object. It was a first and an experimental measure, and no first and experimental measure ever does quite succeed in its object. It has had to be amended and expanded over and over again. It has been amended and expanded by Tory as well as by Liberal governments. The whole question of Irish land-tenure is even still a subject under the consideration of Parliament, and the very session in which I am writing has had a new Irish land bill brought in by a Tory administration. But Mr. Gladstone's land bill of 1870 introduced a new principle, which no one since has ever attempted to abolish. That new principle was that the Irish tenant was entitled to some share and property in the improvements which he himself had made in his farm. It was, therefore, in the best sense of the word, a revolutionary measure. It created a new principle, and that principle has since been settled. It did not go nearly far enough in the right direction, but it showed the direction in which legislation ought to go, and it was on that account the opening of a new era for Ireland.

CHAPTER XXII

THESE early years of Mr. Gladstone's administration were years of tremendous energy in reform.
It almost takes one's breath away to recall the
many splendid reforming enterprises on which
Mr. Gladstone ventured with a courage that
seemed never to be daunted. He set himself to
work to establish a great system of national education for England. Strange to say, up to that
time there had been no public system of elementary education in England. The State had doled
out a miserable grant to the help of private
charity, for the teaching of the children of the
poor. England was behind many of the countries
of the civilized world in this respect. She was
far behind Prussia and most of the German
States, she was far behind nearly all, if not all,
of the States of the American Union. This, in
fact, was the first time when the principle was
set up that the State ought to provide for and
enforce a popular elementary education. I do not
propose to go into the details of this measure,

and, for one reason, because it was not put into form by Mr. Gladstone's own personal inspiration. There were, indeed, some parts of it which did not commend themselves altogether to his feelings or his judgment. But he adopted it as, on the whole, the best scheme that then had a chance of success. It, too, like the Irish land measure, has been the subject of much controversy and many schemes of alteration and improvement. But, like the Irish Land Bill also, it made a new departure and established a new principle.

A measure was carried in 1871 to substitute the ballot for open voting in the elections for the House of Commons. Mr. Gladstone had at one time been opposed to the ballot, as, indeed, most other public men in England had been. It is a curious fact that Mr. Gladstone began as an opponent of the ballot, and afterwards became convinced by practical experience and observation that the secret vote, on the whole, was far better than the open system; while Mr. John Stuart Mill, who began as an advocate of the ballot, had ended as its opponent. The bill went through both Houses, and was carried into law. Not the faintest idea now exists in the mind of any English public man of proposing to repeal the measure. The immemorial British fashion of recording one's vote in public, and thereby leaving the tenant at the mercy of his landlord, the small shopkeeper at the mercy of the local magnate, the factory-worker at the mercy of the factory-owner, is almost forgotten now in this country. Educated young people of the present generation would probably find it hard to believe that such a system, with all its glaring and monstrous abuses, could ever have existed in a civilized country.

Another great abuse which Mr. Gladstone abolished was the system of purchase of commissions in the army — the system under which a young man with money bought himself an officer's commission, and bought, step by step, his subsequent stages of promotion. So far as I remember, no such system was known in the army of any other great and civilized State. Mr. Gladstone was determined on abolishing it, and as he found that the House of Lords was determined to stand in the way, he abolished it himself by what I may call a constitutional *coup d'état.* It came about in this manner. Purchase in the army was allowed and established by the warrant of the sovereign alone. The whole practice was therefore dependent upon royal regulation. It was in the power of the sovereign at any moment to say that the purchase of commissions should cease. Now, the House of Commons, the Representative

VICTORIA, QUEEN OF GREAT BRITAIN AND IRELAND AND EMPRESS OF INDIA

Assembly, had, under Mr. Gladstone's inspiration, pronounced against the purchase system. The House of Lords still held out in its favor. Mr. Gladstone, therefore, acting on his constitutional authority as Prime Minister, advised the Queen to cancel the royal warrant which authorized the buying and selling of commissions in the army.

The Queen, who is the first and only constitutional sovereign who ever sat on the throne of England, acted on the advice of her Prime Minister. A new royal warrant was at once issued, declaring that all purchase or sale of commissions in the army must come to an end. This step, taken by Mr. Gladstone, raised a storm of controversy in the country. Even some of his own followers, some of the most advanced Radicals in Parliament, were strongly against it. There could be no doubt that the exercise of the royal power in abolishing the purchase system was perfectly constitutional. The question raised was whether the Prime Minister was justified in thus cutting short a great Parliamentary controversy by the sudden interposition of the royal prerogative. There can be no doubt that Mr. Gladstone's course was a bold one, bold even to the extent of audacity. Probably if he had been content to wait, the reform would have been carried in the following session. It is certain that the abolition

of purchase in the army and the principle of promotion there by merit has come to be accepted
now by the universal public opinion of England.

There again is a reform introduced by Mr. Gladstone which nobody in his senses would think of
trying to repeal. But this is just what people
were saying who condemned the advice which
brought about the intervention of the royal prerogative. "Why not wait?" they said. "The abolition of purchase is certain to come now that the
House of Commons and public opinion have
declared against the practice. Why give any
excuse for the argument that the Prime Minister
has cut short public controversy on a great public
question by a course of action which is absolutely
without precedent?" There is a great deal to
be urged in favor of this argument. I said so
at the time; I put my opinions on record more
lately; and I am ready to say the same thing
now. But, at present, the purchase system having been abolished forever, one's chief interest is
in the action of Mr. Gladstone himself. It was
a splendid instance of political intrepidity. It
carried a great reform. It was not in violation
of any constitutional principle. On the contrary,
it still further emphasized the duty of the sovereign to act on the advice of the minister; and
it won a great battle.

CHAPTER XXIII

I HAVE already mentioned the fact that Mr. Gladstone had likened the three principal defects in the
system of governing Ireland to the three branches
of the upas-tree, and had shown how these defects
belonged to the State Church system, the land
system, and the system of university education.
The time had now come, according to Mr. Gladstone's view, for dealing with the question of university education in Ireland. Ireland had two
universities, that of Dublin — Trinity College, as
it is commonly called — which bestowed its honors on the members of the Protestant Church .
only; and the Queen's University, a lately created
institution, which was founded on a purely secular
principle and was therefore condemned by the
heads of the Catholic Church. Here, then, there
was, in a country the vast majority of whose people
were Roman Catholics, one university which would
not accept the Catholics on equal terms with their
fellow-subjects, and which, indeed, imposed in an
indirect and negative way penalties on them for

being Roman Catholics, and another university which the Roman Catholic as such could not recognize or accept. There was no other university in the country. The Catholics had long been loud and earnest in their demands for a chartered Catholic university. The argument employed by most of the English statesmen was that to grant any State aid to a Catholic university would be to endow a sectarian institution out of the national funds. The Catholics made answer that the University of Dublin was in fact a State-endowed institution, and that the Queen's University was set up by a grant from the State.

Mr. Gladstone made a brave effort to settle the question. His proposal was to make the University of Dublin the one national university in Ireland, and to make it a teaching as well as an examining body. Trinity College, Dublin, the Queen's Colleges of Cork and Belfast, the existing Catholic University — an institution which had no charter, but was supported altogether by private funds — these bodies were to become affiliated members of the new university. The money to sustain the university was to come in proportionate allotments from the revenues of Trinity College, a very wealthy institution; from the consolidated fund, the fees of students, and the surplus of Irish ecclesiastical property. Trinity College and each of the other affiliated colleges would be allowed to frame schemes for its own government. Thus, therefore, Mr. Gladstone proposed to establish in Ireland one central university to which existing colleges and colleges to exist hereafter might affiliate themselves and in the governing of which they would have a share, while each college could make what laws it pleased for its own constitution, and might be denominational or undenominational as it thought fit. The Legislature would give an open career and fair play to all alike, and in order to make the university equally applicable to every sect it would not teach the disputed branches of knowledge or allow its examinations for prizes to include any of these disputed questions. The colleges could act for themselves with regard to the teaching of theology, moral philosophy, and modern history. The central university would maintain a neutral ground so far as these subjects were concerned, and would have nothing to do with them.

That is a description of the scheme quite full enough for the readers of to-day. With regard to the provision which excluded theology, moral philosophy, and modern history, it may be borne in mind that Stuart Mill had long been endeavoring to convince the world that the teaching of history is not one of the functions of a national university, and had better be left to private education. I only

mention this fact in passing because some of the
severest attacks made on Mr. Gladstone's bill by
what are called cultured people were made on the
ground that he excluded those great subjects from
the teaching of the proposed Irish university.   It
is, therefore, only fair to observe that a man of the
culture and intellect of Stuart Mill had preached
the doctrine before Mr. Gladstone adopted it, and
tried to put it into practice.   There is a great deal
to be said for the views of Mr. Gladstone and Mr.
Mill; but it is not necessary for me to go into the
subject here.   In the debate on the whole question,
Mr. Disraeli, especially, scoffed at the notion of a
university which was not to be "universal" in its
teaching.   Mr. Disraeli, who, as far as education
was concerned, was far below the level of Gladstone
and Mill, had evidently got it into his head that
a university was so called because it taught everything that could possibly be learned in the universe.   The scheme had a great deal to recommend
it if philosophic compromise could be made the
principle of communities and of parties; but it had
one fatal defect — it pleased nobody.   Nearly all
the different parties in the State found fault with it.
The English Nonconformists cried out against the
measure which proposed to endow a distinctly
Catholic university out of national funds.   The
Irish Protestants were furious at the proposed

breaking up of the long-established university system in Dublin.   The Catholics declared that it did
not in any sense meet the justice of their claims as
regards the Catholic university.   It soon became
certain that a large number of the Protestant Nonconformist Members of Parliament were determined
to oppose it.   Mr. Disraeli's speech during the
closing debate was full of brilliancy and triumphant
sarcasm.   He knew what the end was to be, and he
exulted in the already certain defeat of his great
opponent.   Mr. Gladstone's speech in reply was
dignified, serene, and even pathetic.   It was the
speech of one who could bear anticipated defeat
without bitterness, without despondency, "rather in
the independence of a quiet than the disdain of a
despairing heart," if I may quote some almost forgotten words of Bulwer Lytton.   I listened to that
speech of Mr. Gladstone's with an absorbed interest.   So, indeed, must every one have done who
had the privilege to hear it.   Especially touching
were the few sentences in which Mr. Gladstone
expressed his regret for his inevitable severance
on that occasion from the Irish National Members
with whom he had worked so happily and so successfully on the bill for the abolition of the Irish
Church and the Land Tenure scheme for Ireland.
The division and the defeat came.   It was not, indeed, a great defeat.   The measure was thrown out

U

by a majority of only three.   But, as Mercutio says
of his wound, "'t is not so deep as a well, nor so wide
as a church door, but 't is enough — 't will serve."

Mr. Gladstone, of course, resigned office at once,
and Mr. Disraeli was sent for by the Queen.   Mr.
Disraeli, however, prudently declined to accept
office under such conditions.   He pointed, not
unreasonably, to the fact that on most questions
there would be a majority against him; and he
drew, in a subsequent speech, an amusing picture
of the troubles imposed on a Prime Minister who
has on various great public questions a majority of
the House of Commons against him.   Of course, it
might be said that he could have dissolved Parliament and called for the judgment of the country
at a general election.   But, as he once more not
unreasonably put it, How could he appeal to the
constituencies against a decision of the House of
Commons which had his thorough approval?   Disraeli, in fact, knew quite well that the time was not
opportune for him, and he also knew that the opportune time was coming soon.   He held to his resolve; he declined to undertake office, and there
was nothing for it but that Mr. Gladstone should
return, not indeed to power, but to office.   There
is a vast difference between being in office and
being in power, as Mr. Disraeli had pointed out
in the amusing speech to which I have lately al-

luded.   Mr. Gladstone came back, not to power,
but to office.   It must have been a painful thing
for him to continue still to be Prime Minister
under such conditions.   He came back to office

OSBORNE HOUSE, ISLE OF WIGHT
(From a photograph by Frith & Co., Reigate, England)

very unwillingly, as everybody knew.   He was
tired of the whole business.   He had good reason to feel disappointed.   His health had been
severely injured by the excessive strain of the
work to which he had devoted himself with an
unsparing and almost reckless self-sacrifice.   He
knew well, every one must have known, that, com-

ing back to office under such conditions, he must come back with a diminished and a discredited influence. Any outside observer could have seen all that. It must have been borne keenly into Mr. Gladstone's knowledge. A man with a less magnanimous nature than Mr. Gladstone might have refused point-blank to undertake so thank-less, so disheartening, and so futile a task. But that was not Gladstone's way. Sensitive and highly strung as he was by nature, he was always able to subject his own personal feelings to the public good. He came back to office seeing, as everybody must have seen, that the end was near.

In truth, the force of reforming energy had spent itself for a time. In English political life there is a law of action and reaction so palpable in its working that almost any intelligent observer might undertake to issue a weather prophecy about its movements. Mr. Gladstone had come into power on the crest of the third wave, as boatmen say, and with that impulse had accomplished a magnificent series of reforms in legislation. Now, however, the force was spent. The outer public had grown tired of mere reform. Great political questions in England are not always decided by the men who take a real and active interest in them. The fate of a great administration is often decided by men whose general inclination is to be let alone unless when something is in the air which has a special attraction for them.   They murmur to their own souls that they are rather tired of reforming measures; that they are rather tired of Gladstone and his energy; and when election comes they either stay at home and do not vote at all or they vote against the energetic and wearisome administration.   It must have been clear to Mr. Gladstone that a turn in the tide had come.   Still, he had no inclination to embarrass public life and Parliament by refusing to return to office, although well knowing that he was only to be a stop-gap there.   With what Burke would have called a "proud humility," he bowed his head and entered the Prime Minister's room again.   During his short career of renewed office he enabled the late Mr. Fawcett to carry a measure for the abolition of religious tests in the University of Dublin.   He did the best he could do just then for that cause of university education in Ireland which he had so generously undertaken; as he could not bring in a great reform, he brought in one of a minor degree, but still on the way to a complete scheme. Better a small reform than nothing, he thought. His nature was always a curious compound of the thinker, perhaps even of the dreamer, and of the worker.

CHAPTER XXIV

THE ALABAMA QUESTION

I NEED not go into the internal troubles which, according to public conjecture, helped towards the speedy overthrow of the Liberal party. There was some talk of dissensions, talk likely enough to be true, among the members of the Liberal Cabinet. Election after election here and there, as vacancies were made, began to be lost to the Liberals. It was plain that the full tide of reaction was in force.

The Alabama question had undoubtedly created some trouble for Mr. Gladstone's Government. It has always seemed to me that one of the best and bravest things Mr. Gladstone ever did was his acceptance, and I might even say his enforcement, of the principle of arbitration with regard to that question. The Treaty of Washington, arranged in May, 1871, prevented, in all human probability, the breaking off of diplomatic relationship, and possibly even the outbreak of a war between England and the United States. The American Government had done what any

Englishman with any brains in his head would have known they would do, and were entitled to do — they insisted on a settlement of the claims arising out of the damage done by the Alabama and other cruisers of the Southern States which had been built in English dock-yards and had sailed from English ports and were sometimes to a great extent manned by English sailors.

Up to a certain point the English statesmen had rather paltered with the question; they had expressed themselves willing to go into arbitration as to any individual claims for personal damage done which a few Englishmen might have to present on the one side of the quarrel and a few Americans on the other side. But this was not by any means what the American statesmen required, and what, as everybody now believes, they were entitled to expect. Their claim was made as a nation injured by another nation. Such a claim was not to be met by merely admitting a willingness to pay for any personal damages that this or that American citizen might have sustained. Mr. Gladstone's Government, under his direct inspiration, finally agreed to accept the most ample and complete terms for the discussion of the whole controversy. They declared themselves willing to treat the subject in dispute as a national and not merely an individual lawsuit.

A commission was sent out to Washington which was to hold conference with an American commission, and to enter upon all the different subjects of dispute still unsettled between England and the United States. Of these subjects the principal were the Alabama question, the San Juan boundary, and the Canadian Fishery question. The Dominion of Canada was represented on this commission. Of the English commissioners, one is still alive, the Marquis of Ripon. Lord Iddesleigh, who was then Sir Stafford Northcote, and Mr. Mountague Bernard, Professor of International Law at the University of Oxford, are dead. Sir John A. Macdonald, who represented Canada, is also dead. I was in the United States during the whole time while that tribunal held its sittings, and I need hardly say how deep was the interest with which I endeavored to follow its proceedings. The result we all know.

Out of the Washington treaty came the Geneva award. It was welcomed with satisfaction by all reasonable men on both sides of the Atlantic. But with a certain class of persons in England it did not tend to make the Liberal administration popular. Especially it did not tend to make Mr. Gladstone popular with these people. Mr. Disraeli, in the debate on the address on the opening of the session in 1872, denounced, not exactly the Alabama treaty itself, but the formal paragraph in the Queen's speech explaining it. He insisted that some of the claims admitted for ar-

STAFFORD HENRY NORTHCOTE, EARL OF IDDESLEIGH
(From a photograph by London Stereoscopic Co.)

bitration amounted to the sort of tribute that might be exacted from a conquered people.

Mr. Gladstone made in reply a speech of admirable good temper and sound sense and eloquence. He pointed out that most of Mr. Disraeli's arguments applied only to what were called the indirect or constructive claims, which claims had never been really supported or sanctioned by American statesmanship.

Mr. Gladstone's speech was, in substance, an

THE CITY HALL AT GENEVA

(As seen from the Promenade de la Treille. The main façade faces the Rue de l'Hôtel de Ville. The windows of the hall since known as "The Alabama Chamber" are those opening out on the Promenade)

appeal to the patriotism and the good feeling of the English-speaking people on both sides of the Atlantic.   All the same it is quite certain that his popularity in England was diminished by the mere fact that he had accepted an arbitration which told heavily against England.   "We have

caved in to the United States," or, indeed, "to
the Yankees," was the common phrase used in
certain English clubs, dining-rooms, and smoking-
rooms. One of Mr. Gladstone's own colleagues,
Mr. Lowe, entered on an elaborate defence of
the treaty, which was more likely to increase than
to diminish its unpopularity among certain classes
of Englishmen. Mr. Lowe went on to argue
that we had at least saved a great deal of money
by the arrangement. He was at the pains to
point out that, whether we were right or whether
we were wrong, it cost us much less to pay up
the claims than it would have cost us to lose or
even to win in a warlike struggle with the United
States. If any line of argument might have
turned sensible and reasonable Englishmen against
the treaty, it would have been such a line of argument as this. It exactly sustained the doctrines
the Tories always preached about what was then
called the Manchester school, the school of Cobden and of Bright, that the men of that school
cared nothing for the honor of their country,
but only balanced the expense of maintaining it
against the cheapness of sacrificing it. No really
thoughtful Tory could ever have believed that
Mr. Gladstone felt or encouraged such sentiments. As a matter of fact, neither Mr. Cobden
nor Mr. Bright ever expressed or encouraged or

felt them. But Cobden and Bright had undoubtedly said things now and again which an unscrupulous enemy might twist into an expression of
disregard for the national honor. Nothing ever
said by Mr. Gladstone could be perverted into
any such meaning. Yet, all the same, the result
of the Alabama treaty was to put him into the
position, among the minds of the vulgar, of one
who had, in homely phrase, "knuckled down to
the Yankees."

CHAPTER XXV

THE TIDE TURNS

PARLIAMENT had been summoned for February the fifth, 1874, with the important words "for the despatch of business." It is perhaps hardly necessary to tell most of my readers that during the recess Parliament is summoned nominally from time to time, not with any practical purpose of bringing it back to work, but in order that it may be constitutionally liable to be recalled to work if any sudden emergency should arise. But when the words are added "for the despatch of business," that always means that Parliament is summoned for actual work on that particular day. Parliament, then, was summoned for February the fifth, 1874, for the despatch of business. On the night of January the twenty-third, 1874, an amazing report began to spread abroad among certain limited circles of political men in London. I remember that night well; perhaps I may be allowed to describe it in words of my own which were published a few years after the occasion: " Men were mysteriously beckoned away from dinner-tables and

drawing-rooms and club-rooms. Agitated messengers hurried to ministerial doors seeking for information. There was commotion in the newspaper
offices. The telegraph was set in constant action.
Next morning all the world read the news in the
papers. Mr. Gladstone had suddenly made up his
mind to dissolve Parliament, and seek for a restoration of the authority of the Liberal Government
by an appeal to the people."

Mr. Gladstone explained the reason for his decision in an address to his constituents. He
declared that he could no longer put up with the
difficulty of seeming to have the authority he had
received in 1868 now sunk " below the point necessary for the due defence and prosecution of the
public interests," and that, therefore, he proposed
to appeal to the constituencies by a dissolution of
Parliament, in the hope of thus obtaining a popular
approval of his general policy. Should he be successful in that endeavor, he undertook that, if restored to power, he would introduce a series of
financial reforms which would include the complete
abolition of the income tax. Now I think there
can be no mistake as to the general impression
produced by the publication of Mr. Gladstone's
address, and by the dissolution of Parliament.
The grumbling was especially widespread among
his own followers and his own party. The time

of the Parliament had nearly run out, and there were many Liberals who had little hope of being returned again to the House of Commons. Such men were most unwilling to lose even a year of Parliamentary existence. They could not understand Mr. Gladstone's motive, and they looked upon themselves as positively ill treated. "Why didn't he think about us?" they muttered among themselves. "We have voted with him very faithfully, and he might have had a little more consideration for us." Such men as these could not understand the motive of Mr. Gladstone. To him it seemed ignoble that a Prime Minister should remain in office one hour after he had found reason to believe that he no longer possessed the confidence of the majority of the people. To him a seat in Parliament was a matter of utter insignificance unless it enabled a man to do some good for his constituents and for the country. He might almost have spoken the eloquent words of Burke in the immortal speech at Bristol; and, indeed, there are many striking points of resemblance between the character of Burke and the character of Gladstone. "It is certainly," said Burke, "not pleasing to be put out of the public service. But I wish to be a member of Parliament to have my share of doing good and resisting evil. It would, therefore, be absurd to renounce my objects in

order to retain my seat. I deceive myself, indeed,
most grossly if I had not much rather pass the
remainder of my life hidden in the recesses of
the deepest obscurity, feeding my mind even with
the visions and imaginations of such things, than
to be placed on the most splendid throne of the
universe tantalized with a denial of the practice
of all which can make the greatest situation any
other than the greatest curse."

Mr. Gladstone flung himself into the contest
with all his characteristic earnestness and energy.
He had not usually been what we call an open-air
orator. But on this occasion he went down to
Greenwich and addressed enormous popular meetings held on Blackheath. It was there that I for
the first time heard Mr. Gladstone as an open-air
orator addressing a monster meeting. There are
in this country, at all events, three distinct kinds
of political eloquence. There is the eloquence of
the House of Commons. There is the eloquence
of the platform indoors at one of the great gather-
ings in St. James's Hall, for instance; and then
there is the eloquence addressed to the monster
meeting in the open air. These, as I have said,
are quite distinct forms of oratory, and the man is
indeed seldom to be met with who can make a
success with all three. Many a speaker who can
hold the House of Commons in breathless interest

during a long oration is found ineffective in St.
James's Hall, and would be hopeless at an open-air
meeting. On the other hand, many a powerful
platform speaker who can carry his audience with
him is found wholly unsuited to the peculiar style
and atmosphere of the House of Commons. I
confess that I had some doubt whether Mr. Gladstone, with all his powers of voice, would be able
to suit himself exactly to the task of addressing
a great open-air meeting. His warmest admirers
must admit that he has a somewhat dangerous gift
of over-refining, and over-refining would never do
for a monster meeting. The speaker must strike
strong, direct, resounding, echoing blows. But
Mr. Gladstone had not got three sentences of his
speech out before I felt certain that he would
prove himself just as much at home with the
Blackheath meeting as with St. James's Hall or
with the House of Commons. His voice swelled
and rang out to the uttermost verge of the vast
crowd, and no listener had any occasion to trouble
himself for one moment by a fear lest he should
miss something of what the great orator was
saying.

I never admired Mr. Gladstone more than I
did during those days when he fought so splen-
didly against impending fate. The fate was impending, however, all the same. When the

x

elections were over, it was found that the Conservative party had a majority of about fifty, and
that even the calculation of that majority was
made on an assumption far too favorable to the
Liberals, for it assumed that every Irish Home
Ruler might be counted as a Liberal. In fact,
the great reforming ministry was down in the
dust. The Liberal statesmen had tried too much,
had done too much, had spent their force in too
many splendid efforts and enterprises, and the
time came at last when the spirit of Conservative
reaction prevailed over them. Mr. Gladstone followed the example set by Mr. Disraeli in 1868,
and at once resigned office. This was by far
the best course to take. It had been the custom
on former occasions that a Ministry defeated at
a general election should return to office and
wait until the reopening of Parliament and until
the majority of the House of Commons had, after
a long debate, declared its want of confidence in
them. All this would have been, under such
conditions, but a mere waste of time. Mr. Disraeli was right in setting the example. Mr. Gladstone was right in following it. The Queen
invited Mr. Disraeli to form a Conservative administration, and he was not long in settling
down into office.

Then came another surprise and shock for the

Liberals in all parts of the country. Mr. Gladstone suddenly announced, in a letter to Lord Granville, dated March 12, 1874, that "for a variety of reasons personal to myself, I could not contemplate any unlimited extension of active

BUCKINGHAM PALACE
(From a photograph by Valentine, Dundee, Scotland)

political service, and I am anxious that it should be clearly understood by those friends with whom I have acted in the direction of affairs that at my age I must reserve my entire freedom to divest myself of all the responsibilities of leadership at no distant time. The need of rest will prevent me

from giving more than an occasional attendance
in the House of Commons during the present
session. I should be desirous shortly before the
commencement of the session of 1875 to consider
whether there would be advantage in my placing
my services for a time at the disposal of the Liberal party, or whether I should then claim exemp-
tion from the duties I have hitherto discharged.
If, however, there should be reasonable grounds
for believing that, instead of the course which I
have sketched, it would be preferable, in view of
the party generally, for me to assume at once
the place of an independent member, I should
willingly adopt the latter alternative." This
letter brought back to the minds of some of us
a passage in that speech of Burke's from which
I have already quoted. "Gentlemen," said Burke,
"I have had my day. I can never sufficiently
express my gratitude to you for having set me
in a place wherein I could lend the slightest help
to great and laudable designs. If I have had
my share in any measure giving quiet to private
property and private conscience, if by my vote
I have aided in securing to families the best
possession, peace, if I have joined in reconciling
kings to their subjects and subjects to their
prince, if I have assisted to loosen the foreign
holdings of the citizen and taught him to look

for his protection to the laws of his country, and for his comfort to the good will of his country-men, if I have thus taken my part with the best of men in the best of their actions, I can shut the book. I might wish to read a page or two more, but this is enough for my measure — I have not lived in vain." Can it, then, be true that Mr. Gladstone, in the words of Burke, has had his day? He was much older even at that time than Burke was when he thus expressed his readi-ness to close the book. But it had never occurred to any of us to regard Mr. Gladstone as an old man, or even as within measurable distance of old age. To us he was the very embodiment of strength and spirit and indomitable energy.

The news sent a thrill of surprise all over the country, and a shock of utter amazement and dis-turbance through the whole Liberal party. There can be no doubt that for some time many of Mr. Gladstone's most devoted followers were complain-ing bitterly of the course he had taken. Mr. Glad-stone pleaded his advancing years; but, it was asked, were not the years of Mr. Disraeli still more advanced, and had Mr. Disraeli said one word about seeking retirement? was he not, on the contrary, entering with alacrity on a great new chapter of his political career? Men gloomed darkly and whispered sadly about the

manner in which the party was to be left to
cureless ruin. Let it be understood that many
of the bitterest of these utterances came out of
the very devotion to Mr. Gladstone and confidence in his leadership which were felt by the
vast majority of his followers. Why does he leave
us? How can we exist without him? That was
the manner in which the questions shaped themselves. It did, indeed, seem at one time as if the
whole Liberal organization had received a blow
from which in our time it never could recover.
The very commotion which his threatened retirement created among the best of his own followers
was but another tribute to his political genius,
another form of proclaiming to the world that
in the belief of the Liberal party he was the one
man indispensable to the Liberal cause.

CHAPTER XXVI

Mr. GLADSTONE seemed resolved to shake himself free, for the time at least, from the responsibilities of political leadership. On the thirteenth of January, 1875, he addressed another letter to Lord Granville, in which he explained that the time, he thought, had arrived when he ought to revert to the subject of his letter of the twelfth of March in the former year. " Before determining," said Mr. Gladstone, " whether I should offer to assume the charge, which might extend over a length of time, I have reviewed with all the care in my power a number of considerations, both public and private, of which a portion, and these not by any means insignificant, were not in existence at the date of that letter. The result has been that I see no public advantage in my continuing to act as the leader of the Liberal party, and that, at the age of sixty-five, and after forty-two years of a laborious public life, I think myself entitled to retire on the present opportunity. This retirement is dictated to me by my personal views as to the best method

of spending the closing years of my life. I need
hardly say that my conduct in Parliament will
continue to be governed by the principles on
which I have heretofore acted; and whatever arrangements may be made for the treatment of
general business, and for the advantage or convenience of the Liberal party, they will have my
cordial support. I should, perhaps, add that I am
at present, and mean for a short time to be,
engaged on a special matter that occupies me
closely."

The "special matter" turned out to be chiefly
an attack on "The Vatican Decrees in their bearing on Civil Allegiance," in the form of a pamphlet
which had an immense circulation and caused a
very angry controversy. The pamphlet was the
outcome of various articles written by Mr. Gladstone on the question of Ritualism and the popular
dread, which he did not share, that the ritualistic
clergy could, if they would, carry the Church of
England over to Rome. The publication of the
pamphlet on the Vatican Decrees in their bearing
on civil allegiance caused disappointment and consternation among the Roman Catholics in England, Ireland, and the Empire at large. The long
friendship between Mr. Gladstone and the late
Cardinal Manning was chilled for a time in the
blasts of this debate.

HENRY EDWARD, CARDINAL MANNING

(Elliott & Fry, London)

Perhaps it would have been better if Mr. Gladstone had left the whole matter alone. But Mr. Gladstone could not help himself; he had to follow his star. His mind refused to give itself absolutely up to any one study of life forever. Great as he was in the House of Commons, his vast energies needed some other field of activity now and then. It was not like the case of Mr. Disraeli, who, when he had an interval of rest from the cares of office, sat down and threw off a three-volume novel. Mr. Disraeli was not burning to write the novel. He had written novels before. He could wait very placidly until a suitable opportunity came for adding to their number. But Mr. Gladstone had eminently what the heroines of modern fiction are fond of calling a complex character. When he had spent a certain time over politics and political reform, and when he had either carried or failed to carry some great measure, then it appeared to him, or it appeared to be borne in upon him, that there was something else waiting at his hand that he could do and which he ought to endeavor to do with all his might. Thus it seemed to have been borne in upon him, at the time that he had made up his mind to resign the leadership of the Liberal party, that the state of the Church of England required his immediate attention.

Probably the Public Worship Regulation Bill,

brought into the House of Lords, and coming thence down to the House of Commons, inspired Mr. Gladstone with the idea that he ought to interpose on behalf of the Church of England. Mr. Gladstone emerged for a moment from his retirement to oppose the bill. I need not go into the question raised by the introduction of this measure, which has no interest for us now otherwise than as a subject affecting the internal discipline of the State Church. But undoubtedly these theological debates led him on to the publication of his pamphlet against the Vatican Decrees. I need not revive this old controversy. It belongs now to ancient history. Its interest for me, and I fancy for most of my readers, will mainly be found in the fact that it illustrated the irrepressible, indomitable eagerness of Mr. Gladstone's mind to take a kind of rest, after it had stretched itself out in one direction, by stretching itself out in another.

However, Mr. Gladstone held to his resolve not to retain the leadership of the Liberal party in the House of Commons. He stood by his plea for immunity founded on the right of his sixty-five years. People were not slow to observe that if Lord Palmerston had retired from public life or had died at the age of sixty-five, England would never have known the fulness of his power as a Parliamentary debater. Some of us, no doubt, re-

membered also that if Count von Moltke had gone
into private life or had died at the age of sixty-
five, the world would never have known that he
had the capacity to be the greatest soldier since
the days of Napoleon and Wellington. But Mr.
Gladstone persevered in his resolve, and at last it
became actually necessary that the Liberal party
should choose his successor.

The choice was not easy, although it was very
narrow. By far the greatest orator and the greatest influence in the party after Mr. Gladstone, an
orator who sometimes even surpassed Mr. Gladstone himself, was John Bright. But every one
knew that John Bright would not accept the office of leader. With all his capacity for hard
work at a spell, there was a great deal of the
indolent man about him. He told me himself
that his pet ambition in life was an unconquerable desire to be doing nothing. This desire,
unconquerable though he called it, he managed
to trample in the dust whenever public service
was required of him for any good purpose. But
it was certain that he had no taste for the management of a party, and that he would not become the
Liberal leader.

Mr. Robert Lowe, afterward Lord Sherbrooke,
was, as we have seen already, a man of great ability,
a brilliant debater, endowed with high intellect and

furnished with high culture, a man of eloquence and epigram and paradox, with an almost fatal gift of sarcasm, and hopeless as a possible leader of the Liberal party.   The choice was limited

WILLIAM EDWARD FORSTER
(From a photograph by Elliott & Fry, London)

practically to the late Mr. W. E. Forster and to Lord Harting- ton, at present the Duke of Devonshire. Mr. Forster was a Yorkshire man, with all York- shire's rugged- ness of ability, a strong man, but not concilia- tory, a man who put his head down and went straight at anything that came in his way.   And so the choice fell upon Lord Hartington.

Now between Mr. Gladstone and Lord Harting- ton there was a whole vast field of difference.   The Liberal party, although it saw nothing better to do, never realized so thoroughly the extent of its loss as when it found that Lord Hartington was

to be its leader.   Let me not do injustice to Lord
Hartington.   He was a man of ability and of absolute political integrity.   There was nothing whatever to win him away from political integrity.   He
had a great position, he was heir to vast wealth and
to a dukedom.   But he had not in his nature one
single gleam of enthusiasm.   It would have been
impossible for him to inspire enthusiasm in others.
No ray of imagination brightened his slow, solid,
some people even said stolid, common sense.   The
hearts of some of the more advanced Liberals sank
within them when they found that they had come
from Mr. Gladstone to Lord Hartington.

But there was nothing else to be done, and
Lord Hartington was elected leader of the Liberal
party.   Without any disparagement to Lord Hartington, it may be said that the light seemed suddenly to have gone out.   The Liberal party became
for the time colorless and lifeless to the ordinary
observer.   Mr. Gladstone himself, in one of his
Homeric studies, points out the supreme light of
interest which always follows the movements of
Achilles.   When Achilles is off the stage, the
scene is comparatively dark.   So it was with Mr.
Gladstone himself and the House of Commons.
Everything seemed lacking in interest.   Lord
Hartington did his very best.   He strove hard
to make himself a good debater, and to a certain

extent he succeeded. He had to struggle against
the heaviest and worst manner that it is almost
possible to conceive in the case of a man with
any gift of speech at all. His voice was harsh
and heavy. His manner was stolid, and he had
no real oratorical capacity or even inclination. He
was perfectly well aware of his own defects, and
was to a great extent embarrassed by a contin-
ual over-consciousness of the vast difference in
debating power between him and his superb
predecessor. But he set himself to work with a
thoroughly British doggedness of determination,
and in the end he hammered himself, if I may
use such an expression, into a really good Parliamentary debater. For myself, I may say that I
watched Lord Hartington's career at the time,
and I conceived a decided admiration for his
dogged resolve to do the best he could.

But of course the whole condition of things
was changed so far as public interest was concerned. There were, for the time at least, no
more great debates. Disraeli had no longer an
opponent fit to cross swords with him. Bright
took little part in public affairs. The Tories for
the most part had it all their own way. Lord
Hartington could and did improve his own style
of Parliamentary speaking, but the truth soon became only too apparent that he could not lead

a Liberal party. Men who had come lately into
the House were crying "Forward!" while Lord
Hartington was crying "Back!" It was known
to every one that Lord Hartington had no real
sympathy with the objects and the aspirations of
the newer Liberal party. He was, of course, an
aristocrat by birth and training and association,
and he had not one gleam of the imagination or
the enthusiasm which has sent many a born and
bred aristocrat into the ranks of some great popular
movement. He was perfectly willing that justice
should be done to every reasonable and temperate
claim on behalf of the people, but he could not
look forward, and he apparently could not believe
in anything but a grudging concession of portion
after portion of some popular claim. He differed
only from the high old-fashioned Tories in the
fact that he was not willing to put his foot down
and say, Nothing shall ever be done in the way of
change.

There was always in Mr. Disraeli, and there
was for a time in the late Lord Randolph
Churchill, a strong inclination for the cause of
the English working democracy, and for an endeavor to take the lead in that way and convert
the workingman into a Tory democrat. But Lord
Hartington cared for nothing of all this, and did
not want to convert anybody into anything. He

was perfectly content to let things rest as they were, with the half-reserved admission that if any change should have to be made it ought to come

SPENCER COMPTON CAVENDISH, EIGHTH DUKE
OF DEVONSHIRE
(From a photograph by the London Stereoscopic Co.)

by little and little and at distant intervals of time. Many people thought him haughty, believed him to set high account upon his rank and to look down with contempt upon all his social inferiors. For myself, I do not believe that Lord Hartington ever troubled himself about his rank

or thought about his rank. He had always been the son of a Duke and heir to a dukedom, and he was just as well accustomed to it as he was accustomed to being a man. But he was shy, reserved, and awkward in manner, and this was what made people think him distant and haughty. In any case it can be easily understood what an immense difference there was between such a man as this and the leader whom the Liberal party had just lost.

Mr. Gladstone appeared now and again in the House of Commons and took part in a debate. Every time he spoke only served to impress the Liberal party more and more with the greatness of the loss it had sustained. Mr. Disraeli meantime was playing a showy and an ambitious part. He was athirst for influence in foreign affairs and even for intervention in foreign affairs. He had it for a time all his own way. Mr. Lowe stood up to him once or twice, and held his own very pluckily and manfully. But Mr. Lowe was only an isolated gladiator, and Mr. Disraeli was the master of many legions. Therefore Mr. Disraeli ran the country into all manner of enterprises abroad. He brought up again a so-called imperial principle, which was to restore the policy and the system of Elizabethan days; and in fact the foreign policy of Great Britain went, if I may use so vulgar an expression, "on the rampage."

Where, all the time, was Mr. Gladstone? the Liberals kept asking. He was engaged in polemical controversy with Cardinal Newman and Cardinal Manning. One general conclusion was adopted on both sides of the House: that Mr.

Y

Gladstone never meant to lead a political party again. It was urged, and with great show of reason, that a man with his knowledge of affairs would never have got into antagonism with all the Roman Catholic subjects of the Queen and all Roman Catholic sovereigns and princes and people everywhere if he had the remotest intention of assuming again such a part in public life as might lead once more to his becoming Prime Minister. People did not reflect that all through his career he had a positive passion for theological study and for theological controversy.

In his youth, as we have seen, he was anxious to become a clergyman, and if he had done so he would have become, in all human probability, one of the greatest Churchmen England has ever known. Down to his latest days, whenever he had a chance, he always sought relief from politics in classical study or in theological dispute. At this particular period of his career Mr. Gladstone no doubt sincerely believed that his political work was over. There seemed nothing particular for him to do, and according to all appearance the reign of the Tories was likely to be long. He had always a contempt, hardly even disguised, for Disraeli's flashy foreign policy, but he probably thought that at this time there was no great harm to be done, and, at any rate, not much to be accomplished by formal opposition. But those who believed that Mr. Gladstone had buried his whole existence in a controversy conducted, so to speak, in the Roman catacombs, soon found how completely they had misunderstood the man and failed to take due account of the possibilities of the time.

CHAPTER XXVII

ACHILLES RECALLED

THE moment was soon to come when Mr. Gladstone was to be seen in the front of the fight again. Like Achilles, he was soon to come with a rush forth from his tent and lead on the battle. It was the irony of fate, indeed. Who brought him out of his tent? Was it an appeal from Lord Hartington or from Mr. Bright? Nothing of the kind. Neither Lord Hartington nor Mr. Bright brought back Mr. Gladstone to political leadership. Mr. Disraeli did it himself. Mr. Disraeli, all unconscious of what he was doing, brought back to the battle the great swordsman with whom he was never quite able to compete. Mr. Disraeli's speeches and his action on the Bulgarian question summoned Mr. Gladstone in a moment away from his theological studies, and, before England well knew what was happening, he was there again to the front, the practical, although not yet the nominal, leader of the Liberal party.

In the meantime the Government of Mr. Disraeli

THE HOUSES OF PARLIAMENT

was not doing particularly well so far as domestic affairs were concerned. The Tory statesman had nothing striking to offer to the country. If Mr. Gladstone had tried to do too much, it seemed as if Mr. Disraeli were inclined to do too little. He appeared to prefer in domestic affairs to cling to the policy, supposed to be safe, of letting things alone. But this is seldom safe in England. People soon get tired of a Government which does little or nothing in domestic affairs. They want to have a sense of being kept alive by their rulers. It may seem strange, but to me it is perfectly certain that the outsider class who quarrelled with Mr. Gladstone because he was always giving them a surprise soon began to grumble at Mr. Disraeli because he was giving them no surprise at all. Besides, it must be owned that he had suddenly got into stormy waters in foreign affairs. It was a time of trouble with Russia and with Turkey, and Mr. Disraeli was disposed to go much farther with what we may call the Jingo policy than some of his own colleagues were willing to do. Probably, too, he was growing tired of a long Parliamentary career. He had had almost every success to which he could have aspired. The long day's task was all but done. On the eleventh of August, 1876, he spoke for the last time in the House of Commons, and then he

passed into the House of Lords as Lord Beaconsfield.   He crowned his career by accepting for
himself the title which was at one time offered to
a far greater man, Edmund Burke, and which
Burke had declined on the ground that splendid
titles were then of little value to him.   I heard
Mr. Disraeli's last speech in the House of Commons, as I heard later on his last speech in the
House of Lords.   Each was a memorable occasion.   The first was the closing of a great political career.   The last was the closing of a great
personal ambition.

Let me go back, however, to Mr. Gladstone's
reappearance in the front of the political field.
The circumstance that brought about this sudden event was the conduct of the Turkish Government in the province of Bulgaria.   Bulgaria
was probably one of the worst-governed places in
the world.   The Turkish Government ruled by
its pashas, and its pashas made life intolerable
for the people in Bulgaria.   An insurrection broke
out there, and the Sultan sent large numbers of
Bashi-Bazouks and other irregular troops to put
down the rising.   They did put it down, and
with a vengeance.   Their idea, if they can be supposed to have had any idea, seems to have been
to make a desert and call it peace.   There was
simply a battue or massacre of Bulgarians.   Re-

ports began to filter into Constantinople of the
wholesale slaughter of men, women, and children.
The correspondent of the London "Daily News"
in Constantinople inquired into these reports and
found them only too true. The "Daily News"
afterward sent out its brilliant Irish-American
correspondent, the late Mr. MacGahan, to the
scene of the slaughter, and Mr. MacGahan was
able to verify with his own eyes the terrible truth
of the reports. It had been contended by the
friends of the Ottoman Government in England
that there had been an armed insurrection, and
that the insurgents were conquered in fair and
open conflict. Mr. MacGahan saw with his own
eyes whole villages whose streets, otherwise deserted, were covered with the bodies of slaughtered
women and children.

Mr. Disraeli was singularly unhappy in his way
of dealing at first with the terrible stories which
came from the correspondent of the "Daily News"
at Constantinople. No doubt he did not believe
in them. But he took no trouble to make any
inquiries. His worst enemy could not suppose that
he was a man indifferent to human suffering, or
that if he thought there was anything in the stories
he would have made fun of them. But he appears
to have assumed at once that there could be nothing serious in any statement made by the foreign

correspondent of a London Liberal newspaper.
Therefore, when questioned in the House of Commons on the subject, he treated the whole matter
in his most audacious vein of persiflage and sarcasm. He described the reports as "coffee-house
babble." He made fun of the massacres, and
was especially sportive about the tortures. Oriental races, he boldly declared, were not in the
habit of applying themselves to torture; they
generally, he insisted, "terminated their connection with culprits in a more expeditious manner."
Now, Mr. Disraeli in his earlier days had been
in European Turkey and in Asia Minor. Being
an Oriental himself by extraction and by sympathy, he must have read some books about Oriental
history. He must have known, too, that the torture of enemies was very commonly practised
among Oriental races. Yet he stood up in the
House of Commons and had the fatuity — it can
be called nothing less — to insist that torture was
hardly known in the East, and the bad taste to
make jokes about the stories that were told of
outraged and mutilated women.

A tremendous effect was produced upon the
whole country by the narratives of Mr. MacGahan
and by the reports of Mr. Baring, the English
consul, who was sent out especially to Bulgaria
to make inquiries, and whose official reports bore

out only too well the investigations and the con-
clusions of the special correspondent of the "Daily
News." Mr. Bright effectively described the agitation which arose in England as an uprising of
the English people. So it was, but where was
the leader? Where, to quote the words of Walter
Scott, "was Roderick then — one blast of Roderick's bugle-horn were worth ten thousand men"?

Roderick, that is Gladstone, came to the front
and sounded a tremendous note upon his bugle-
horn. He put himself in front of the agitation,
and forgot for the time his polemics and his critical essays. He threw his whole soul into the
movement against the Ottoman Government in
Bulgaria. He made speeches and brought forward motions in the House of Commons. He
addressed meetings all over the country. He was
the principal orator at a great meeting held in
St. James's Hall in London, one of the most
enthusiastic meetings it has ever been my fortune
to attend, and where he made one of the most
powerful and impassioned and at the same time
convincing speeches I have ever heard even from
his lips. Even Mr. Carlyle came forth from his
seclusion and from his usual indifference to political movements of any kind, in order to send a letter
to the promoters of the meeting in St. James's Hall
to declare his conviction that the expulsion of the

Turks from Europe, though a somewhat drastic measure, was yet the only hopeful remedy for the oppression and the miseries inflicted by the Ottoman Government on its subject populations in the southeast of Europe.

As I listened to the speeches at that meeting, my memory carried me back to distant days when, as a very young man, I had heard John Henry Newman deliver his famous lectures on the Eastern Question. That was just before the outbreak of the Crimean War, and what Newman told us, and told us vainly, would be the only outcome of the war is accepted now as gospel truth by every party and by every public man in England. I remember one thrilling sentence in which Newman declared that the Turk had just as much right to his dominion in Europe as the pirate has to the sea which he sails over and ravages.

Mr. Gladstone issued his famous pamphlet called " Bulgarian Horrors and the Question of the East." In the pamphlet he declared that the only way to secure any lasting good for the Christian population of Turkey was to turn the Turkish officials out, "bag and baggage." The words were seized upon by some of Mr. Gladstone's political opponents. These persons professed or pretended to believe that Mr. Gladstone was calling out for the actual physical expulsion of all the Turks, men, women, and children, out of Europe, and the admission of Russians in their stead. What Mr. Gladstone meant was, of course, obvious and clear. He meant that the Turkish Government as a government should cease to reign in Europe. It will come to that in the end. It will have to come to that before very long. If Mr. Gladstone had been to the front of the battle in 1895 and 1896, as he was in 1876, civilization probably would not have been horrified and disgraced by the prolonged massacres of Christians in Armenia.

In 1876, however, Mr. Gladstone's movement was completely successful. It ended — I am hurrying over familiar historical details — in the setting up of Bulgaria as a practically independent province under the nominal suzerainty of the Sultan. It is now a well-ordered and a prosperous State. Many events conspired to bring about its practical independence, but I know of no influence which had a greater power that way than the position taken up by Mr. Gladstone as the leader of the agitation in England.

Mr. Disraeli soon after passed through to the House of Lords. Mr. Gladstone was compelled by the force of events to resume his position as leader of the Liberal party. He was compelled, indeed, to do more than that. The Conservative Government was fast breaking down. Mr. Gladstone

again and again challenged the Tories, who had
had six years of office, to appeal to the country by
dissolution and a general election, and thus make it
certain whether the constituencies were or were
not in favor of their policy.   The Tories knew that
a general election must come on within another
twelve months in any case.   So they took heart of
grace, and announced a dissolution of Parliament.

The result of the general election was that the
Conservatives were for the time utterly overthrown.
They were routed, horse, foot, and artillery.   It
was a complete catastrophe.   When the votes at
the elections were counted up, it was found that the
Tory party was nowhere.   The Liberals came back
with a majority of more than one hundred and
twenty.   No Liberal statesmen had ever before
been backed up by so splendid a following.   There
was a moment of official delay, of unavoidable hesitation, of formal anxiety and suspense.   For whom
was the Queen to send?   On whom was she to
impose the task and the responsibility of forming a
new administration?   Mr. Gladstone was merely,
in the official sense, an ordinary Liberal Member of
the House of Commons.   Lord Hartington was
the leader of the Opposition in the House of Commons, and Lord Granville was the leader in the
House of Lords.   The Queen sent in the first
instance for Lord Granville, and afterward for Lord

Hartington. But, of course, Lord Granville and Lord Hartington perfectly well knew that neither of them had led the Liberal party to victory. One name, if we may so put it, came out of the Liberal polling-booth, and that was the name of Mr. Gladstone. Lord Granville and Lord Hartington alike declared that on Mr. Gladstone's shoulders alone could rest the responsibility of forming a new administration. "They both as-

GRANVILLE GEORGE LEVESON-GOWER, SECOND
EARL GRANVILLE

(From a photograph by the London Stereoscopic Co.)

sured the Queen," says Mr. George Russell, "that the victory was Mr. Gladstone's, that the Liberal party would be satisfied with no other leader, and that he was the inevitable Prime Minister. They returned to London in the afternoon and called on Mr. Gladstone in Harley Street. He was expecting them and the message which they brought, and he

went down to Windsor without a moment's delay.
That evening he kissed hands, and returned to
London as Prime Minister for the second time.
Truly his enemies had been made his footstool."
Mr. Disraeli's Eastern policy and Mr. Disraeli's
speeches on the Bulgarian question had forced Mr.
Gladstone to the front, and made him Prime Minis-
ter once again.

CHAPTER XXVIII

Mr. Gladstone, however, had troubles enough before him to embarrass the work of any ordinary man. He had no longer Mr. Disraeli to oppose him, but his natural impulses compelled him to take up a course of action which was attended by difficulties insuperable for the time at least. He had now become member for Midlothian in Scotland. Mr. Gladstone, in his new administration, took upon himself the double functions of Prime Minister and Chancellor of the Exchequer.

I need not go through the list of the administration, but shall merely mention that Mr. Bright, Mr. Chamberlain, and Sir Charles Dilke accepted office. The ministry seemed to every observer immensely strong, and the majority at Mr. Gladstone's back was overwhelming. Yet it must be owned that the years of this Government ended for the most part in disappointment and in disaster. Why was this? It was simply because Mr. Gladstone was Mr. Gladstone and could not be anybody else. He could not be Lord Mel-

bourne, for example, whose single appeal was,
"Why can't you let things alone?" He could
not be Lord Palmerston, who was perfectly content so long as he could humor and propitiate
and cajole the majority in the House of Commons. He could not even be Lord John Russell,
who, although a man of a zeal and earnestness
much more like to his own, could nevertheless
express sometimes his willingness to "rest and
be thankful" for what had already been gained.
Mr. Gladstone was, but only in his own high,
unselfish way, like Johnson's Charles of Sweden,
who thought nothing gained while aught remained
to be done. To become the head of a government was for him only to be put into a place
where he must at once occupy himself in trying,
at any trouble and any pain, to improve the condition of his fellow-subjects. So the moment he
was settled into office he began to turn his
thoughts to new and great measures of reform.

Many events had directed his attention to the
condition of Ireland. The state of the Irish
tenant-farmer appeared to him to call for immediate remedy. I have already spoken of the
Land Bill for Ireland which he carried through
in 1870. That bill had established a great principle by making it certain that the tenant as well
as the landlord owned something in the land

which the tenant's own labor had converted from a swamp into a productive farm.

The Land Bill of 1870 was, however, only an experiment, and Mr. Gladstone determined to advance upon it and improve it. Against him he had, of course, in such an attempt, the whole strength of the landlord party in Ireland, the whole strength of the Tory landlords in England, who most mistakenly imagined that their interests were bound up with those of Irish landlordism, and the whole strength of the House of Lords. Mr. Gladstone consented, as a temporary measure, to the introduction of a bill which, pending expected legislation, should in the meantime secure to any evicted Irish tenant compensation for any improvements effected in his farm by his own industry and his own skill. The House of Lords threw out the bill. The effect upon Ireland was disastrous. The Irish peasants could not be supposed to study and to understand all the constitutional difficulties that stood in the way of Mr. Gladstone's scheme of reform. What they saw was that the House of Lords — the House of landlords — was able to control Mr. Gladstone, and that there was no hope from English statesmanship.

I do not want to go minutely into the history of that most melancholy time; but something

z

has to be said about it in order to tell aright the story of Mr. Gladstone's political life. The Irish peasant classes were in despair. Agrarian outrage became frequent in Ireland, and Mr. Gladstone's Government believed it necessary to adopt new coercive legislation. The whole thing had got into the old vicious circle again. The legislative refusal of the tenants' rights caused agrarian disturbance, agrarian disturbance gave an occasion for coercion, further coercion led only to new disturbance, and so on *da capo*. I remember speaking in the House of Commons some time during the earlier period of Mr. Gladstone's administration, and declaring my conviction that the action of the House of Lords in rejecting the Compensation for Disturbance Bill was the fountain and origin of all the agrarian trouble then going on in Ireland. I shall never forget how Mr. Gladstone, seated on the Treasury bench, leaning across the table, with flashing eyes and earnest gestures, called " Hear! Hear! Hear!" to my declaration.

Mr. Gladstone was between two terrible difficulties at the time, the difficulty with the House of Lords and the difficulty with the Irish people. The Compensation for Disturbance Bill was purely a temporary measure. It merely required that the evicting landlord should stay his hand

until a complete measure of land reform had been
introduced, or should compensate the evicted
tenant for the improvements which that tenant
himself had made in the landlord's property. It
may be asked why did not the Irish peasantry
wait in patience until the full measure of land
reform had been prepared and introduced. The
Irish peasantry are a very intelligent peasantry.
They saw that the House of Lords had strength
enough to reject Mr. Gladstone's small and temporary measure, and they asked what chance
was there for the passing of his scheme of permanent land reform. Over and over again has
a tenant-farmer said to me: "We don't blame
Mr. Gladstone; but we know only too well that
the House of Lords will never let him do anything for the good of Ireland." So there grew up
in the minds and hearts of the Irish people a
feeling of utter disbelief that anything good could
ever come for them out of even the best-inten-
tioned English statesmanship. Agrarian outrages
are, under such conditions, the natural, the inevitable result of popular despair.

In the meantime a new state of things had
arisen in Irish politics. The Home Rule movement had taken a fresh, an energetic, and even
an aggressive form. It was now led by a man
of genius, the greatest Irish leader who had ever

been known since the time of Daniel O'Connell.
Mr. Parnell was then a very young man, but he
had made himself thoroughly master of the situation both in
England and in
Ireland. He
had an absolute
and unlimited
belief in the
power of consti-
tutional agita-
tion in a consti-
tutional coun-
try. At no time
from first to last
did he give the
slightest coun-
tenance to any
acts of violence.
But he had
made up his
mind to use the

CHARLES STEWART PARNELL
(From a photograph by Mr. Wm. Lawrence, Dublin)

House of Commons as the platform of Irish agitation, and to unite Home Rule and Land Reform as
inseparable elements in the new campaign. His
policy was to insist on a full hearing for these
great Irish questions in the House of Commons,
and, furthermore, — and herein lay ·the great

secret of his success, — to insist that if the House
of Commons would not listen to the story of
Irish grievances, it should do no business at all.
This was the whole purpose of obstruction as Mr.
Parnell meant it and planned it.   He was confi-
dent that if we but got a fair hearing we should
make good the justice of our national claims, and
his policy was to say to the House of Commons,
" If you will not listen to us, then neither shall
you listen to any one else."

The vigorous assertion of such a policy put, of
course, a great difficulty in Mr. Parnell's way, and
at this time Mr. Gladstone was only beginning
to study the whole question of Home Rule for
Ireland.   But I know that even then Mr. Gladstone felt a certain sympathy with Mr. Parnell's
motives and a considerable admiration for his
courage and his capacity.   The two forces, however, were certain to come into collision sooner
or later.   The Irish people began to be, for the
time, disappointed with Mr. Gladstone.   They had
regarded him as the one statesman who was destined to do justice to their cause.   They found
only new coercion bills and the supremacy of the
House of Lords.   Mr. Gladstone, on the other
hand, was, I suppose, somewhat disappointed with
the representatives of the Irish people.   Perhaps
he thought that they might have trusted him

more and waited with less impatience for favorable opportunities. They, on their part, found their country drifting into total disorganization, and saw no way of putting heart into the people and of preventing the spread of further outrage than by letting Ireland see that she had a band of men who could stand up for her claims in the House of Commons and who could, on her behalf, resist in constitutional fashion the authority and the power of any English government.

Thus after a while things got from bad to worse, and Mr. Gladstone was persuaded by some of his official colleagues into allowing the introduction and passing of a measure empowering the authorities in Dublin Castle to arrest and imprison for an indefinite time any one they pleased and whom they believed to be "reasonably suspected" of dangerous purposes. No charge was necessary, no trial or conviction was necessary; the man was "reasonably suspected" of an intention to do something or other making for disturbance and he was forthwith locked up in prison. Mr. Parnell himself, Mr. Dillon, Mr. Sexton, and nearly all the leaders of the Irish National movement were put into prison cells. In every town and village all over Ireland the principal promoters of the national movement were locked up in jail.

Mr. Gladstone's heart had never been in this business. He had only accepted such a policy because his advisers in the Irish Government told him that unless armed with such exceptional powers they could not undertake to be responsible for the maintenance of order in Ireland. Mr. Gladstone therefore consented reluctantly to let this new development of coercion go on for the present. Probably he could have done nothing else; a man not on the spot and not personally acquainted with the conditions of Ireland could hardly have refused to act on the advice of the Irish Government. But I am not speaking lightly or without knowledge when I say that Mr. Gladstone himself never had much faith in the efficacy of such a coercion measure as that which was now administered in Ireland.

We all remember Burke's famous saying, that he did not know how to draw up an indictment against a whole nation. More difficult, assuredly, it must be to put a whole nation into jail. The authorities in Dublin Castle did not put into jail just the very set of men whom it would have been for the welfare of the country to incarcerate. They put into prison men like Mr. Parnell, Mr. Dillon, Mr. Sexton, and all manner of other men whose private characters and whose public conduct alike showed them to be incapable of any sympathy with crime or outrage of any kind, and they left out of prison the murderous gang who were even then planning the assassination of certain obnoxious officials in Dublin Castle.

JOHN DILLON
(From a photograph by Russell & Sons)

In the meantime Mr. Gladstone thought it right to release Mr. Parnell and most of his friends from prison. This resolve led to the resignation of the late Mr. Forster, who was then Chief Secretary to the Lord Lieutenant of Ireland and who was the principal author of the new coercion scheme. Mr. Forster had gone over to Ireland animated with the purest and sincerest feelings of kindness toward the Irish people. He had, indeed, proved that kindness many years before by his personal exertions in Ireland to relieve distress at the time of the great Irish famine. But he was a man of a strong will and at the same time of a sensitive nature. He appears to have got into his mind that, as Ireland had reason to know him for her friend, she ought to have been content to receive any measures from his hand because of his good intentions. Populations, however, do not do things in that way, and the Irish people declined to keep quiet under the imprisonment of their leaders and of nearly all the representative Nationalists in the country. Then Mr. Forster became angry with the Irish people, and the Irish people became angry with Mr. Forster, and when Mr. Gladstone insisted on releasing Mr. Parnell, Mr. Forster threw up his office. Then it soon became apparent that he had imprisoned the wrong men; at all events that he had certainly not imprisoned the right men.

The assassin gang of whom I have spoken, and who at several times tried without success to murder Mr. Forster himself, succeeded in murdering the Chief Secretary, Lord Frederick Cavendish, and Mr. Thomas Burke, a Dublin Castle official, in the Phœnix Park. No crime more shocking has startled the public conscience of our day. A wild outcry was raised in England by many people against Mr. Parnell and his followers, who were openly accused of having had something to do with the instigation of the murders. Mr. Gladstone never gave way in the least before this outcry or changed the course of his pacific policy. Mr. Parnell wrote to him a frank

LORD FREDERICK CAVENDISH
(From a photograph by the London Stereoscopic Co.)

and friendly letter, offering, if Mr. Gladstone wished it, to retire from Parliament and public life altogether in order that Mr. Gladstone's policy should not be endangered in England by association with so unpopular a name. Of course Mr. Gladstone declined to accept such a sacrifice, and strongly advised Mr. Parnell to stick to his post, which Parnell did.

The men who plotted the Phœnix Park murders had for one of their motives the desire to bring discredit upon every constitutional movement. One effect of the crime was just the opposite of that which they intended. I date the beginning of a really friendly understanding between Mr. Gladstone and the Irish National party, between the Irish National party and the English democracy, from the time when it became apparent that the leaders of popular opinion in Ireland regarded the criminal and the murderer as the worst enemies of the National cause. It is but justice to say that the English people generally displayed thorough good sense and manliness throughout the whole crisis. Not one in every ten believed for a moment that Mr. Parnell and the Irish National party had any manner of sympathy with crime. Even among those, the minority, who did proclaim such belief, there came a sort of reaction. Something, however, had to be done to prevent the possibility of further crimes like those of the Phœnix Park. A new coercion measure, rigorous indeed and bitterly resented by the Irish representatives, but still directed against a movement of crime and not meant for the incarceration of everybody without trial, or even without charge, was pushed through both Houses of Parliament.

The Liberal Government in the meantime got into trouble about their occupation of Egypt. There was an uprising in Egypt against the Khedive under the leadership of Arabi Pasha. And

the English Government took the side of the
Khedive, and the English fleet bombarded Alexandria.   Mr. Bright resigned office rather than
have anything to do with a war policy in Egypt.
Mr. George Russell says with truth that the great
majority of Liberals accepted with reluctance, but
without resistance, a line of action which wore
"an unpleasant and close resemblance to the
antics of Lord Beaconsfield."   Indeed, the main
weakness of Mr. Gladstone's position was in the
fact that he had accepted a responsibility in
Egypt which he would never have created for
himself.   He had to accept it; he could not help
himself.   A great statesman, to whom the country looks for the carrying of many reforms, is not
free to refuse to take office and to endeavor to
realize those reforms merely because he has at
the same time to inherit some responsibility for
a policy which he did not himself initiate.   But
the trouble came all the heavier upon Mr. Gladstone inasmuch as he could have had no heart
for the task which was imposed upon him by the
Egyptian policy of his predecessors.   The trial, too,
came hard upon Mr. Gladstone's most devoted followers.   Nothing, says Mr. Russell, but absolute
confidence in Mr. Gladstone's political rectitude
and tried love of peace could have secured even
this qualified and negative sanction from his party.

The heroic career and striking personality of General Gordon had fascinated the public imagination, and the circumstances of his untimely death awoke an outburst of indignation against those who were or seemed to be responsible for it. In truth, the Government in England is held responsible for everything that happens during its time of office. Disraeli laid it down as a law that no administration could possibly survive three bad harvests. The Coercion Acts told against Mr. Gladstone's government in Ireland, the crimes in the Phœnix Park told against it in England, the Egyptian policy and the bombardment of Alexandria weakened Gladstone's influence with English Liberals, and the death of General Gordon roused against him the anger of the person who is commonly described, and not ineffectively described, as " the man in the streets." The man in the streets, of course, held Mr. Gladstone responsible for Gordon's death, Mr. Gladstone being just about as much responsible for it as the man in the streets himself. Why did he not rescue Gordon? demanded the man in the streets. Why did not the rescuing expedition reach Khartoum in time? The question of distance and difficulty never troubled the judgment of the man in the streets. His idea probably was that it was about as easy to send an

expedition to Khartoum as to send troops to
Chatham. The man in the streets, however, had,
as he always has, a good deal to do with the
direction of public opinion. Decidedly the events
in Egypt told heavily against the popularity of
Mr. Gladstone's administration. So keen and, I
may say, so cruel were Mr. Gladstone's political
enemies that it was made a charge against him
that he was seen in a London theatre applaud-
ing with evident delight a popular comedy on
the very evening when he must have known of
Gordon's death. The fact was that when Mr.
Gladstone visited the theatre no account whatever of Gordon's wholly unexpected death had
reached London. The story is only worth telling because it illustrates the kind of ignoble and
credulous rancor which political animosity can
still stir up in the minds of otherwise intelligent
and honorable Englishmen.

CHAPTER XXIX

The Egyptian difficulty was not the only foreign trouble which Mr. Gladstone inherited from his predecessors. The war with the Boers broke out. The English Government seems to have been deceived into the belief that the Transvaal Republic had become anxious to be taken under the direct protection of England. Sir Theophilus Shepstone, says the author of "England under Gladstone, 1880–1885," was sent out to investigate the situation. "He seems to have entirely misunderstood the condition of things, and to have taken the frightened desires of a few Boers as the honest sentiment of the whole Boer nation. In an evil hour he hoisted the English flag in the Transvaal and declared the little republic a portion of the territory of the British crown. As a matter of fact, the majority of the Boers were a fierce, independent people, very jealous of their liberty, and without the least desire to come under the rule to escape which they had wandered so far from the earliest settlements of their race."

Mr. Gladstone again and again denounced the Conservative policy which had brought about the temporary annexation of the Transvaal. The people of the Transvaal soon proved that they were not anxious to be under the government of England. They rose in revolt, if it ought to be properly called revolt, and they defeated the English troops more than once. Mr. Gladstone had in the meantime succeeded to power. Many Englishmen, and even some of those who generally supported Mr. Gladstone, were strongly of opinion that we ought not to come to terms with the Boers until we had inflicted on them some crushing defeat. Mr. Gladstone was not of that opinion. He thought we were wrong in annexing the Transvaal Republic, and he could not believe, as a statesman and a Christian, that we ought not to make peace with the Boers and give them back their Republic without first massacring enough of them to satisfy our heroic sense of honor. Nobody doubts that England could have conquered the Boers, could have sent out troops enough to extirpate the whole male population of the Transvaal Republic. Mr. Gladstone did not see honor, or credit, or glory, or Christianity in any such performance. He sent out

W. E. GLADSTONE.

(From the painting by E. Hader)

of the bravest soldiers and one of the most successful generals in the English service, Sir Evelyn Wood, with the express purpose of coming to honorable terms of peace with the Boers.

Peace was established on fair and honorable conditions. The Transvaal Republic was restored, with a British Protectorate against foreign nations and foreign invasion, and with a British High Commission, but with the entire local and national self-government for which the Boers, to do them justice, had fought so well. Mr. Gladstone, of course, was denounced by all the Jingoes of England. They raged against him because he had allowed the curtain of this drama to fall upon what they called the triumph of the Boers. Mr. Gladstone went on his course unheeding. He had asked of his own mind and heart and conscience what was the right thing to do and he had done it. It was a brave act. But it was an act only in keeping with the whole of Mr. Gladstone's career.

The one great domestic work of the administration this time was the passing of the Franchise Bill, which was a just and necessary sequel to the successive extensions of the voting power among the people. This measure was worked to a certain extent in conjunction with the Tory party. It became a measure of redistribution as well as

of extended suffrage. In other words, the whole
scheme of the constituencies was recast. Many
small boroughs, miserably small boroughs, ceased
to have separate representation in Parliament and
became merged into the population of the counties. Large counties were distributed into several
divisions. The measure was carried in the manner to which I have already alluded by the
co-operation of both parties, a mode of procedure
which might well be commended in almost every
case where the two parties are agreed as to the
general necessity of a measure. Mr. Gladstone,
Lord Hartington, and Sir Charles Dilke went
into a kind of joint committee with Lord Salisbury and the late Sir Stafford Northcote, and the
details of the scheme were easily arranged.

The work of the House of Commons was never
more trying than during this particular Parliament.
Mr. Lucy, in his clever sketch of Mr. Gladstone,
from which I have already quoted more than once,
says that "for comparatively young men on the
Treasury Bench the physical ordeal was trying.
Mr. Gladstone, with his threescore years and ten
upon his back, bore more than his full burden of
the day's work. He was in his place early and
late, his so-called 'dinner-hour' sometimes not ex-
ceeding thirty minutes. It was no uncommon
thing to find him at his post between two and

three in the morning after a turbulent night." Then Mr. Lucy tells us that toward the close of the session of 1884, Mr. Gladstone broke down. "The illness, which took the form of fever with congestion of the lung, was serious enough to alarm the nation profoundly. Downing Street was crowded with anxious callers." Mr. Gladstone, however, triumphed over all physical troubles. His friend, Sir Donald Currie, took him for a trip round the coasts in the steamer

SIR CHARLES DILKE
(From a photograph by Elliott & Fry)

Grantully Castle. Sea and meadow and forest and open air were always Mr. Gladstone's best medicine, and he soon came back prepared to carry on the work of the session with renewed energy. But it began to be gradually more and more evident that the administration had spent its force. Defeat came suddenly and almost unexpectedly on a clause in the Government's annual financial scheme. The House immediately adjourned, and next day Mr. Gladstone announced, not in so many words, but in the peculiar phraseology adopted in English Parliamentary life, that the Government had resigned office. The words he actually used were, " That, in consequence of a decision arrived at by the House, the Government had thought fit to submit a dutiful communication to Her Majesty." Of course everybody perfectly well understood the meaning of that. The Liberals were out of office once more. They had fallen victims partly to the inherited policy of their predecessors and partly to their conscientious desire to do justice to the people of Ireland, and yet their inability to see their way to any course which could really satisfy the people of Ireland. They went so far in one direction as to infuriate all the Tories and to discourage and alienate many feeble Liberals. But they did not go far enough in that direction to satisfy Ireland.

Lord Salisbury was invited to form an administration, and after some hesitation, caused by the difficulties of the time, he had to consent to do so. Lord Randolph Churchill joined the new ministry as Secretary of State for India. The administration did not last long. On the 18th of November Parliament was dissolved, and the question then which everybody asked everybody else was, What is to be the result of the general elections? The vote at these elections was to be taken under the conditions of the new Reform Bill which Mr. Gladstone had so lately introduced. The result of the elections was to give the Tories only a nominal majority, and even that majority depended altogether on the support of the Irish members. Lord Salisbury had to go out of office after a very short and uncomfortable interval, and Mr. Gladstone returned to power once more.

In the meantime the question of Home Rule came up again. An anonymous paragraph appeared in the newspapers announcing, on no particular authority, that Mr. Gladstone had come back to office determined to deal liberally with the question of Home Rule. The paragraph created consternation among the Tories and even among many of Mr. Gladstone's own followers. It was met with a prompt denial by some of Mr. Gladstone's own colleagues in office. Mr. Gladstone himself preserved for a while an ominous silence.

CHAPTER XXX

HOME RULE

MR. GLADSTONE's political opponents have made much talk about the suddenness of his conversion to Home Rule. The imputation is that he became a convert to the principle of Home Rule at the moment when he found that Irish Nationalist members were returned to Parliament in numbers strong enough to hold the balance of power between the two great English parties, the Liberals and the Tories. I think I shall be able to show that the conversion was by no means rapid; that it was, on the contrary, of slow growth, and that it was not occasioned by the mere fact that the Irish Nationalist members were strong enough to make themselves of account to the government of either party.

So long ago as 1879, shortly after I first became a member of the House of Commons, Mr. Gladstone showed himself inclined, not indeed to favor, but to consider, the question of Home Rule. Through a friend of his and of mine, Mr. James Knowles, the editor of the "Nineteenth

Century," Mr. Gladstone suggested that I should write one or two articles for the "Ninteenth Century" on the subject of Home Rule. As I understood the matter at the time, Mr. Gladstone did not give the slightest indication that he was in favor of the principle of Home Rule, but was of opinion that the hour had come when a fair statement of the whole subject ought to be brought under the notice of the English public. I have no doubt that Mr. Gladstone suggested my name as the writer of the articles for the reason that I was well known to that English public as a writer of

MR. JUSTIN M'CARTHY, M.P., IN 1879
(London Stereoscopic Co.)

books, and that while I was, and always had been, a strong Nationalist in Irish politics, I should not be regarded by any one as a man madly anxious to injure the British Empire.

There were two points, as I then understood, on which Mr. Gladstone desired that information should be given to himself and to the public of England. One was the question whether a scheme

of Home Rule could be shaped which could give
Ireland the management of her domestic affairs
without disturbing the balance of Imperial control. The other question was whether the great
majority of the Irish people were really anxious
for the restoration of a National Parliament.

It has to be remembered that at this time the
Irish Nationalist members, properly so called, were
but a small minority of the Irish representation in
the House of Commons. Those were still the days
of the high franchise in Ireland as well as in England — only that the franchise was relatively much
higher in Ireland than it was in England. Therefore the majority of the Irish representatives were
of the landlord class or of the moneyed class.

I wrote the articles as suggested, and I do
not suppose they wrought any particular effect on
the British public. The only possible interest they
can have now for my readers, or for myself, lies
in the fact that they show Mr. Gladstone's willingness at that time to consider fairly the question
of Home Rule and to have that question brought
under the notice of the English people.

Years went on, and meantime Mr. Gladstone
and the Irish Nationalist members had drifted
much apart. The English Liberal Government
was trying once again to keep Ireland quiet
by means of coercion Acts. An English Liberal

Lord-Lieutenant of Ireland had declared publicly
in the House of Lords that something was gained
at all events by driving discontent beneath the
surface — a statement about as wild as that of
one who should say that something was gained
by stopping the smell of pestilential drains.

Somewhere about that time I happened to meet
Mr. Gladstone, as we were passing through one
of the division lobbies of the House of Commons
to give our votes. He touched me on the arm
and drew me into conversation with him. He
said to me, in somewhat emphatic tones, that he
could not understand why a mere handful of Irish
members, such as my immediate colleagues were,
should call themselves *par excellence* the Irish
Nationalist Party, while a much larger number
of Irish representatives, elected just as we were,
kept always assuring him that the Irish people
had no manner of sympathy with us or with our
Home Rule scheme. "How am I to know?" he
asked me. "These men far outnumber you and
your friends, and they are just as fairly elected
as you are." I said to him, "Mr. Gladstone, give
us a popular franchise in Ireland and we shall
soon let you know whether we represent the Irish
people or whether we do not." He said, "You
know very well that I have always been anxious
to give a popular suffrage to Ireland as well as

to England." I said to him, "Yes, I know all
that; I thoroughly appreciate your purpose; but
when you can give us that popular suffrage you
will soon know what are the opinions of the Irish
people."

Time went on, and Mr. Gladstone carried in
1884 his measure which I have just described,
reforming the suffrage and redistributing the seats
in Great Britain and in Ireland. The effect of
this change was to make the franchise in both
countries something approaching very nearly indeed to manhood suffrage. In Ireland the immediate result was the total disappearance of every
representative opposed to Home Rule, except for
a few Tories in Ulster and elsewhere, and the
representatives of Dublin University who are
elected by a purely collegiate vote. The whole
representation of Ireland was one hundred and
three members, and out of that the Home Rule
party returned eighty-three.

I had some opportunity of talking to Mr. Gladstone after the general election which made this
change, and he told me frankly that his question
was answered so far as the national desire of
Ireland was concerned. Of course he did not
tell me whether or how far his mind was working
round in the direction of Home Rule. I did not
ask him. I had no need to ask him. I knew

that the subject had been under his consideration for several years. I felt assured that he had been thinking it carefully over, and that the result of the general elections had convinced him of one fact, at all events, about which he had been doubtful before. I knew that deep in his mind for many years had lain a conviction that there is such a thing as nationality, and that a state made up of a cluster of nationalities can only exist in strength by consulting the wishes of each of these as to its domestic affairs.

It therefore did not come on me as the slightest surprise when, in 1885, it began to be publicly said that Mr. Gladstone was a convert to the cause of Home Rule. His political opponents, and, indeed, some of his political supporters at that time, went about expressing in open-mouthed wonder their opinions as to the suddenness of his conversion. To me there was nothing sudden about it. Even in my own limited and casual experience I had known that the conviction was slowly growing up in the mind of the great states-man. I am not now discussing the merits of Home Rule. That question will settle itself sooner or later. What I am anxious to do is to impress upon my readers that there is absolutely no truth in the story that Mr. Gladstone, having always been a convinced opponent of Home Rule, came

round to the principle all in a flash the moment
the Irish Nationalist members became strong
enough to hold the balance between rival English
parties. I think even the facts that I have mentioned ought to be enough to settle that question
for any impartial mind.

In his action toward Home Rule Mr. Gladstone
was perfectly consistent in the true sense of the
word. He had learned something to-day which
he did not know yesterday, and he felt bound to
act upon the knowledge. Unless it is inconsistent for a statesman to admit the value of new
information, it was not inconsistent on Mr. Gladstone's part to admit that when opportunity was
given, the Irish people had proved themselves in
favor of Home Rule, and to take account of the
information and act upon it. So far back as 1874
Mr. Gladstone had publicly said in the House of
Commons that if it could be proved that there
was on the part of Great Britain and of Ireland
any desire to form a scheme which should give
Ireland a Parliament of her own and relieve the
Imperial Parliament from the necessity of looking
after Irish domestic affairs, he did not think much
of the statesmanship which could not shape a
plan to suit such a purpose. He said that he
did not himself see his way, on the spur of the
moment, to form such a plan, but he could not

believe that the intellect of Parliament could fail to devise it. As he explained then, his difficulty was not so much about the forming of the plan as about, what I may call, the previous question; the question whether Ireland really desired a national Parliament and whether Great Britain would be willing to yield to such a desire.

Later still, Mr. Gladstone made another admission which showed, even more clearly, that if Ireland were strong and united in her claim for the management of her own domestic affairs, such a wish ought to be taken into account by the Imperial Parliament. I remember well that, at the time, this admission was seized upon by several London papers as an evidence that Mr. Gladstone was coming over to the cause of Home Rule.

In point of fact, he had done nothing more in either case than to admit that under certain conditions, which conditions he did not believe to exist, it might be necessary for statesmanship to open a new chapter in the relations between Great Britain and Ireland. I am fully convinced that at that time Mr. Gladstone did not believe that Home Rule was really called for by the people of Ireland and was of opinion that the agitation for it was purely factitious and would be transitory. When it became known that his mind was made up in favor of Home Rule the amazement of some

of his own followers knew no bounds.   Then,
and for long after, the great complaint made
against him by some of his colleagues, in office
and in opposition, was that he had not consulted
them.   That was a grievance urged in especial
by Mr. Chamberlain and which appears to have
rankled in his mind.

I believe the first colleague consulted was Mr.
John Morley, who immediately afterward was put
by Mr. Gladstone into the office of Chief Secretary to the Lord-Lieutenant, that is to say, of
Chief Secretary for Ireland, and to whom therefore Mr. Gladstone would naturally turn with a
communication of such nature.   I may say for
myself that the news, when it came distinctly out,
brought to me no manner of surprise.   I had
had reason to believe for many years that Mr.
Gladstone's convictions were growing more toward
a belief in the rightfulness and even the necessity
of a scheme of domestic self-government for Ireland.   I had seen how, year by year, Mr. Gladstone's
faith in coercion measures had been falling away.
I had seen how the heat of temper into which at
one time he was often betrayed when vexed by the
obstructive policy of the Irish representatives had
changed into an apparent understanding of their
purpose and even into a certain sympathy with it,
at all events, toleration for it.

It soon came out that Mr. Gladstone's mind was made up. Even the fact that at the general elections the Irish population, under the direction

JOHN MORLEY
(From a photograph by the London Stereoscopic Co.)

of their leaders, had voted against him, did not change his views. Time had given the answer to that question in one of the division lobbies so many years before: Why do you, a mere hand-

ful of men, call yourselves the representatives of
Ireland? His own Franchise Bill, among other
things, had enabled us to prove that we were the
representatives of Ireland. Mr. Gladstone knew
very well that when we voted against him at the
general elections it was because we had been set
on by the Tories to believe that Lord Salisbury
would give us Home Rule, and we were prepared
to take Home Rule from any hands, the first that
gave it to us.

Into the long controversy concerning promises
made to us by the Tories it would be futile now
to enter. Mr. Gladstone's first Home Rule Bill
had the immediate effect of creating a new party
in English political life. Up to this time there
had been, roughly speaking, only two great political parties, the Liberals and the Tories. The
Liberals had a certain division among themselves
in the fact that some were very progressive, even
as Liberals, and some were so cautious and inclined to hold back that they differed little from
the more enlightened of the Tories. Still, whenever any party question arose the Liberals usually, although not invariably, voted as one man
and the Conservatives invariably, or almost invariably, voted as one man.

But now arose a new party, made up of Liberals
who were opposed to Mr. Gladstone's whole policy

of Home Rule and who called themselves Unionists, that is to say, supporters of the Act of Union which abolished the Irish National Parliament at the beginning of the century. These men broke away from Mr. Gladstone and the Liberals and set up a party of their own. This party at the outset professed and promised to be absolutely independent, but after a while, naturally and almost inevitably, became absorbed into the ranks of the Tories; and, as we shall presently see, many of its leading members soon accepted places in the Tory administration.

The most influential of the Unionists was Lord Hartington, now the Duke of Devonshire. The most active and conspicuous was Mr. Chamberlain. I need not go through the list of other names. I do not regard Mr. Bright as a member of the Unionist party, because, although to the great surprise of some of us he opposed Mr. Gladstone's Home Rule policy, he never identified himself with any new political organization, and it is utterly impossible to think of his becoming a member of a Tory Government.

The secession of Lord Hartington surprised nobody. Lord Hartington had, as I have said already, never shown the slightest sympathy with genuine Liberalism or with any really progressive movement. Lord Hartington's great ambition in

life was apparently a desire to be let alone. Mr.
Chamberlain's action, on the other hand, surprised
almost everybody. He had come into political
life as an extreme Radical. He was regarded by
the old-fashioned Tories as a red republican, a
revolutionist, an anarchist, and I know not what
else. They feared him and hated him. He had
denounced the landlord class in England again
and again in bitter and in scathing words. He
was the uncompromising enemy of the House of
Lords. He was in cordial sympathy and alliance
with the members of the Irish National party.
He rose in the House of Commons once to pay a
tribute of praise to Mr. Parnell and to express
his regret that he had not paid such a tribute of
praise long before. He was one of the Commissioners, if I may use the expression, who arranged
the famous Kilmainham Treaty, as it was called,
between Mr. Gladstone's Government and Mr.
Parnell.

I had many opportunities of interchanging ideas
with Mr. Chamberlain at that time, and I never
understood that he was not in favor of Home
Rule. When Mr. Gladstone brought in his first
Home Rule measure there was some excuse for
Mr. Chamberlain's withdrawing from the Government. The first Home Rule measure proposed
to leave to Irishmen the management of their own

affairs in a Dublin Parliament and to have no
Irish representatives in the Imperial Parliament
at Westminster. The Irish National party were,
on the whole, quite willing to accept this proposal. They did not particularly want to be in
the Imperial Parliament, and they were glad to
get Home Rule on almost any terms.

But there were two strong objections to the
scheme. One of these, sustained by some English members of Parliament who were and are
as strong Home Rulers as I am, was that the
whole principle which associates taxation with
representation would be violated by setting up a
House of Commons which could tax Ireland without Ireland's consent. The other objection, which
was started mainly by Irishmen living in England,
was that if there were to be no Irish representatives in the Imperial Parliament, there would be
nobody in that Parliament to look after the interests of the two or three millions of Irishmen
living in Great Britain. Therefore there did seem
some reasonable show of principle in the opposition of Mr. Chamberlain and others to Mr. Gladstone's first scheme of Home Rule. That measure
was rejected by the House of Commons.

But when Mr. Gladstone, later on, gave in to
the pressure of the Liberal objections to his
scheme and in his second Home Rule Bill, after

his return to office in 1892 and the general elections of that year, provided that Ireland should
be still represented in the Imperial Parliament
for Imperial purposes, just as a State in the
American Union is represented in Washington
for Federal purposes, Mr. Chamberlain still continued to oppose the measure with all his might
and main.

Sir George Trevelyan was one of those who
had resigned his office in Mr. Gladstone's administration because he could not approve of the first
Home Rule Bill. Mr. Chamberlain and he then
made the same objection to the measure. But
when the main cause of objection was withdrawn
Sir George Trevelyan at once returned to his
allegiance to Mr. Gladstone and took office as a
supporter of the second Home Rule Bill.

Mr. Chamberlain could not be induced to follow his example, and persisted in leading a separate party in the House of Commons. His attitude
was perplexing to those who had acted with him
in former days. People of course interpreted it
in different ways. Some said that it was the
story of Disraeli over again. Disraeli began as
a Radical and almost a Socialist. The commonly accepted theory of his life is that he found
there were too many clever and rising men on
the Liberal side and he thought he had better

betake himself to the Tories, among whom there
was certainly no redundancy of youthful genius.
According to this suggestion, Mr. Chamberlain's
idea was that there was more chance for him on
the Tory side than there could be under the over-
mastering influence of Mr. Gladstone.

Mr. Chamberlain was dissatisfied, people insisted,
because Mr. Gladstone would persist in remaining
at the head of affairs. He was ambitious and
might have said, like Hamlet, whom he resem-
bled so little in most ways, "I lack advancement."
In one of his speeches about that time he made an
unlucky reference to the satisfaction it gave him
to be in the society of English gentlemen. Ill-
natured critics seized upon the phrase and twisted
it and turned it to all manner of applications.
One perverse critic quoted the saying of Becky
Sharp in "Vanity Fair" to George Osborne, by
whose family she had once been employed as gov-
erness and whom she now, having got to a higher
place, wished to annoy: "But O! Mr. George,
what a pleasure it is to find one's self in the society
of English gentlemen."

Naturally such criticism did not tend to make
Mr. Chamberlain any the better affected toward his
former friends and colleagues. He went steadily
along his new way. He became a defender of the
House of Lords. He became a champion of the

cause of the landlords. He opposed every Liberal measure. Finally, as his enemies put it, he had his reward. He became a member of a Tory Government. He became, as such, a colleague of Lord

JOSEPH CHAMBERLAIN
(From a photograph by Elliott & Fry)

Hartington, of the Lord Hartington whom, when leader of the Liberal party in the House of Commons, Mr. Chamberlain had denounced in the face of the whole House as too laggard and reactionary for his position and had contemptuously described as the "late" leader of the Liberal party.

Probably the Unionist party has no future before it. It is likely to become wholly absorbed in Toryism. There was no particular reason why Lord Hartington, the present Duke of Devonshire, should ever have had anything to do with Radicalism and Radical measures. He probably would have described himself as a Whig of the old school, if he had really taken the trouble to consider what the Whigs of the old school were. But he took his political position just as it came to him, and he was content for a long time to work under Mr. Gladstone with patience, if without enthusiasm. He did the work set for him to do steadily and loyally enough, although he showed himself more than once a little puzzled by Mr. Gladstone's interest in the cause of the Irish tenant. The Home Rule scheme was quite too much for him, and rather than be a Home Ruler he consented to become a Tory. When such a man once enters the Tory ranks there is no conceivable reason why he should ever emerge from them.

In Mr. Chamberlain's case it is not likely that, even if he wished to return to the Liberal party, the Liberal party could welcome him back. When the Home Rule question is settled, and it will be settled some time, let pessimists say what they may, there will be no further reason for the existence of any so-called Unionist party.

Mr. Gladstone meanwhile bore himself with characteristic courage and good feeling. He had lifted Mr. Chamberlain into power and Mr. Chamberlain had turned against him. That in itself would be nothing to find fault with. No man in public life is supposed to pledge himself to follow

any leader whithersoever the leader may go.   If
Mr. Chamberlain was conscientiously opposed to
Home Rule for Ireland, he was absolutely right in
withdrawing from Mr. Gladstone's Government
when Mr. Gladstone went in for Home Rule.   But
in this instance Mr. Chamberlain had set himself
against Mr. Gladstone with a bitterness and a
vehemence which scandalized many even of Mr.
Chamberlain's own friends and allies.

Mr. Gladstone was always magnanimous and
forgiving in his personal dealings with those who
had deserted him and had come to oppose him.   I
remember being present in the House of Commons
when a curious and a touching little scene took
place.   Mr. Austin Chamberlain, son of Mr. Joseph
Chamberlain, had made a speech in opposition to
some policy or other of Mr. Gladstone, who was
still Prime Minister.   Mr. Gladstone came to reply
on the whole debate, and he paused to make a
special comment upon Austin Chamberlain's
speech.   The elder Chamberlain leaned forward
in his seat with a look of something like irritated
expectancy.   Could it be that he thought Mr.
Gladstone was about to say something scornful or
severe of the young man's speech ?   Could it be
that he really fancied such was the sort of use
a political opponent would naturally make of such
an opportunity ?   Mr. Gladstone broke into a few

sentences of what was evidently the most sincere praise of young Chamberlain's speech, and he spoke in some touching words of the pleasure which it must give to the father of the speaker. Mr. Chamberlain seemed to me, I must say, to be deeply affected. He quite lost his composure for a moment; it was plain that he was deeply moved. Mr. Gladstone had not used the opportunity in the way that he had apparently expected, but for a very different and far more congenial purpose.

Now there was, of course, nothing particularly wonderful in the fact that a great statesman and orator should praise a speech delivered by the son of a prominent and a bitter political opponent. Austin Chamberlain's was really a brilliant speech, full of the happiest promise. But still the genuine warmth and the sincere gladness of Mr. Gladstone's panegyric, following on Mr. Chamberlain's attitude and expression of what I have called irritated expectancy and succeeded by Mr. Chamberlain's collapse into sincere apologetic emotion, made up for me a picture which I could not help regarding as an illustration of the ways of the two men. I may say that on no occasion have I ever known Mr. Gladstone to behave with anything but magnanimity and generosity, even to the bitterest of his political opponents.

It is so in public life, it is so in private life.

During the fiercest struggles with the Irish party
in the days of obstruction, Mr. Gladstone once per-
emptorily interfered with Mr. Forster, who was
then Irish Secretary, on behalf of one of the Irish
members who was cast into prison as what was
called a suspect. This Irish member was a medical man by profession, and he held a position on
one or two medical boards under the control of
Dublin Castle. Mr. Gladstone knew little or
nothing about this Irish member, and certainly
knew nothing about the fact that the medical man,
when he was put into prison, had also been deprived of his public appointments. A debate on
the subject was started by the Nationalist members,
and during the course of the debate Mr. Gladstone
came in and learned for the first time that this
double penalty had been inflicted on the Dublin
physician. His quick and eager sense of justice
revolted against the idea. Let it be clearly borne
in mind that the men who were cast into prison
under the Suspect Act, as I may call it, were not
convicted of any offence, were not charged with
any offence, nor was there any intention of making
any charge against them. They were simply suspected of being persons whose sympathy with the
National movement might render it dangerous for
them to be left at large while there was still trouble
in the air. Mr. Gladstone had clearly understood

that such men were put into prison for the safety of
the community and for their own safety as well;
that they were "interned," if I may use the expression, at the discretion of the authorities, but that
when they were allowed out of prison they were to
suffer no further privation or stigma. It was plain
to Mr. Gladstone's just and generous mind that this
Irish Nationalist member ought not to be deprived
of any public appointment which he had held before his imprisonment. He was a medical man
of high standing in his profession and had always
borne an honorable character in public and in
private. His only offence was that he was an
ardent Nationalist, and it was not even asserted
that an ardent Nationalist might not also be a skilful medical practitioner. All this came home to
Mr. Gladstone's mind while he sat listening to the
debate, the whole subject of which was new to him.
He remonstrated earnestly with Mr. Forster, who
was in certain moods a particularly obstinate man.
Mr. Gladstone's sense of justice, however, prevailed
over Mr. Forster's obstinacy, and the released pris-
oner was restored to his public appointments.

I could go on mentioning cases such as this to
illustrate the breadth of Mr. Gladstone's mind and
the total absence of any feeling of personal ill-will
in his dealings with his opponents. I have no
doubt that he continues to this day to be on terms

of personal friendship with Mr. Chamberlain.   Mr.
Disraeli at one time tried him a great deal, but
that was because Mr. Disraeli never seemed to Mr.
Gladstone to have anything serious in him, never
seemed to have any faith in one cause or another,
and appeared to be led and governed altogether by
political ambition.   Where the treasure is there the
heart will be, and the treasure in that case, Mr.
Gladstone doubtless believed, was mere political
success.   Therefore he sometimes appeared to me
to be rather hard on Disraeli — probably all the
more hard upon him because he saw Mr. Disraeli's
tremendous capacity for commanding admiration
and leading people astray.   Mr. Chamberlain, of
course, had no gifts which could compare in show
and splendor with those of Disraeli, but still he was
a keen, capable, and unsparing man, and at the
moment of great political crisis he contrived to stab
Mr. Gladstone in the back.   Yet I never heard Mr.
Gladstone, in public or private, say an unfair word
of Mr. Chamberlain.

CHAPTER XXXI

"THE LONG DAY'S TASK IS DONE"

I HAVE put, for convenience, my general account of the two Home Rule measures of Mr. Gladstone into a single chapter. The Home Rule measure of 1886 was defeated because of the secession of a number of Liberals who found, or professed to find, their strong objection to the Bill in the fact that it excluded Ireland from representation in the Parliament at Westminster. The second Home Rule measure was introduced to meet and amend that special objection. Ireland was to have a representation of eighty members in the Imperial House of Commons, that number being her exact representation in proportion to the population. But these Irish members were not to vote on any measure exclusively affecting Great Britain. By this alteration of his former measure Mr. Gladstone hoped to be able to get over two sets of objections. The first was the objection of those who complained of Ireland's being taxed by the Imperial Parliament without representation. The second was the objection of those who complained

that, whereas the English members could not interfere in the affairs of Ireland, Irish members
might come over to the Imperial Parliament and
interfere in the affairs of England.

In the interval between the rejection of the first
Home Rule measure by the House of Commons
and the introduction of the second scheme many
things had happened.   There had, for example,
been a great split in the Irish party which had led
to the deposition of Mr. Parnell from the leadership.   Many of the best friends in England of
Home Rule were afraid that the principle had,
for our time at least, received a death-blow.   Mr.
Gladstone was not of any such opinion.   When
he became Prime Minister for the fourth time he
at once resumed his policy of Home Rule.

On Monday, the fourteenth of February, 1893,
Mr. Gladstone introduced his bill "for the better
government of Ireland."   The Bill was met with
every possible method of obstruction.   Mr. Gladstone's energy, enthusiasm, and eloquence triumphed over all opposition.   The debates on the
various stages of the Bill spread over practically
the whole of the session.   The Bill at last was
carried through the House of Commons, and in
September was sent up to the House of Lords.
The House of Lords disposed of it after four
nights' debate, and rejected it by a majority of

more than ten to one. Mr. Gladstone might, on the whole, have been well content. The peers reject every great reform measure which comes before them for the first time. They never resist for long. They yield when they see that public opinion is determined.

Many of Mr. Gladstone's followers insisted then that he ought to have appealed to the country at once on the one question of Home Rule. Mr. Gladstone, no doubt, had good reasons for not appealing to the country once again just at that moment. But the strength of the Government was undoubtedly diminished by the defeat of the Home Rule Bill and by the inaction that followed that defeat. The Government got into conflict with the House of Lords on two or three measures of purely social and municipal interest. There did not seem force enough left in the House of Commons to thrust these measures on the Hereditary Chamber. In one instance Mr. Gladstone himself withdrew a bill because it seemed hopeless to press it on against the hostile action of the House of Lords. There was a sort of languor, almost a kind of despondency, spreading itself like dry-rot among the ranks of the Liberal party. A keen observer might well have seen that a crisis of some sort was near. A crisis was indeed near, much nearer than most of us then imagined.

The House of Commons adjourned on the twenty-first of September, 1893, for a very short recess. Mr. Gladstone, who had been unflagging in his attendance at all the sittings, determined that the House must meet again on the second of November. The House did so meet, and, with only a short interval of Christmas holidays, sat up to the fifth of March, 1894. Mr. Gladstone had been enjoying a short holiday at Biarritz, a favorite holiday place of his, and he came back to the House at the end of February.

During his absence persistent rumors had been going about in London to the effect that he had made up his mind to resign his office as Prime Minister. These assertions were contradicted now and again, in a guarded sort of way, by persons who professed to have Mr. Gladstone's authority for the contradictions. Meanwhile a good many of us were allowed to know that Mr. Gladstone's mind was, at all events, gradually and earnestly turning toward a decision for his early resignation. Yet the outer public somehow thought little of the rumors, and perhaps found it almost impossible to believe that there could be in our time a House of Commons without Mr. Gladstone.

Mr. Lucy has described the occasion, on the first of March, 1894, when Mr. Gladstone made his last speech at the table of the House of Commons in the capacity of Prime Minister. "While the House," says Mr. Lucy, "was crowded to its fullest capacity, it did not surely know what was

WILLIAM E. GLADSTONE
(From a photograph taken by Mr. John Moffat)

happening. The air was full of rumors, but the immediate effect of the speech was to discredit the supposition that resignation was imminent. That it had been decided upon and must take

2 C

place at an early date was accepted as inevitable.
There was, indeed, one passage forming the closing words of this memorable speech that, read by
the light of subsequent events, plainly indicated
Mr. Gladstone's position — that of a knight who
had laid down his well-worn sword, hung up his
dinted armor, content thereafter to look on the
lists where others strove. The House of Lords,
in accentuation of an attitude long assumed, had,
he said, within the last twelve months shown itself ready not to modify but to annihilate the
work of the House of Commons. 'In our judgment,' Mr. Gladstone said, slowly and emphatically,
'this state of things cannot continue.' After a
pause, necessitated by the vociferous cheering of
the Liberals, he added, 'For me, my duty termi-
nates with calling the attention of the House to the
fact that it really is impossible to set aside, that we
are considering a part, an essential and inseparable part, of a question enormously large, a question that has become profoundly acute, a question
that will command a settlement and must at an
early date receive that settlement from the highest authority.'" That question was, of course, the
jurisdiction of the House of Lords.

The matter immediately before the House of
Commons was not one of supreme importance,
but still it involved a conflict between the Repre-

sentative Chamber and the Hereditary Chamber. Mr. Gladstone's Home Rule scheme had been destroyed for the time by the action of the House of Lords, and his mind must have gone back to many a crisis when some great scheme of reform had been retarded in its movement by the same irresponsible authority. Observe that the House of Lords is not really capable of preventing any great measure from being carried in the end. It can only retard and obstruct, and it always gives way when pressure enough has been put on it to make it clear that the public are becoming impatient of its intervention. Even if one could believe that the whole country belonged to the peers and the landlords, there would still be no justification for the existence and operation of the House of Lords, inasmuch as the peers always give way when public indignation becomes too strong to be resisted.

Mr. Gladstone had fought against the House of Lords on many a momentous occasion of his public life. It was but fitting that he should take leave of public life with an announcement that the time had come when the country must pronounce a decisive opinion on the position of the House of Lords. Yet it was not understood in the House of Commons, at least by the majority of those who listened to him, that that was to be

Mr. Gladstone's last utterance in the assembly
where he had been conspicuous for so many years.
As Mr. Lucy puts it, "Looking on the upright
figure standing by the brass-bound box, watching
the mobile countenance, the free gestures, noting
the ardor with which the flag was waved, leading
to a new battlefield, it was impossible to associate
the thought of resignation with the Premier's
mood."

So indeed it happened that in the House of
Commons few were those who knew that that
was Mr. Gladstone's farewell to public life.   If
that had been known the excitement and emotion
in the House would have been something without
precedent or parallel in our times.

But there was nothing of a farewell tone about
the speech, nothing tragic, nothing even purposely
pathetic, and, as Mr. Lucy says, the flag seemed to
be waved leading to a new battlefield. Some of us,
of course, were in the secret, or at least were
vaguely forewarned of what we had to expect.
Shortly after Mr. Gladstone sat down I met Mr.
John Morley in one of the lobbies. "Is that,
then," I asked, "the very last speech?" "The
very last," was his reply. "I don't believe one
quarter of the men in the House understand it
so," I said. "No," he replied, "but it is so all the
same."

Another man, not Mr. Gladstone, would probably on such an occasion have made it plain that
he was giving his final farewell to the assembly

*Above all other present pur-
poses, vindicate the rights of
the House of Commons as the
organ of the nation; and re-
establish the Honour of England,
as well as consolidate the
strength of the Empire, by con-
ceding the just and Constitutional claims of Ireland*

W E Gladstone

July 5. 1895

MR. GLADSTONE'S HANDWRITING — FROM AN ADDRESS TO HIS ELECTORS

which he had charmed and over which he had
dominated by his eloquence for so many years.
Lord Chatham certainly would not have allowed
himself to pass out of public life without convey-

ing to all men the idea that he spoke in Parliament
for the last time.   But Mr. Gladstone, with all his
magnificent rhetorical gift and with all his dramatic instinct, had no thought of getting up a
scene, had no thought of any tableau to precede
the fall of the curtain.   He was no doubt thinking only of the duty which must soon devolve
upon the Representative Chamber — the duty of
putting some limitation on the intervention of the
House of Lords.   Engrossed with that thought,
and eager to stir the House of Commons to a
full sense of its responsibilities and its duties, he
not unnaturally conveyed the idea to the majority
of his audience that he was to lead a new campaign.

The mind of at least one of his listeners went
back to the day when, more than thirty years before, he had denounced the conduct of the House
of Lords, in preventing the repeal of the tax on
paper, as a "gigantic innovation," which the Representative Chamber was bound to resist.   As he
had taken upon himself the leadership of that
movement on the part of the House of Commons
in 1860, it was not unnatural that by the kindling
energy of his manner when he spoke in that March
of 1894, he should have led most people to believe
that he was ready for the battle again.   Certainly
there was nothing in his apparent physical energy,

in his voice, in his gesture, in his manner, to indicate that he found himself unfitted for any further
Parliamentary struggle.

More than twenty years before he had formally
resigned the leadership of the Liberal party on
the ground that he was outworn and could no
longer continue the fight. Yet on the first moment when a great public crisis aroused the
attention of the civilized world he had come
back, almost as a matter of course, to take his
place at the head of the struggle. It could not,
therefore, be wondered at if many men in the
House of Commons, seeing the extraordinary vitality of the Prime Minister, should have thought
that there was no greater reason why he should
give up political life at the age of eighty-four than
there had proved to be when for a short time he
forsook it at the age of sixty-four.

The truth is that we had all grown into the
way of regarding Mr. Gladstone as a sort of being
endowed with immortal youthfulness and vitality.
The outer public, even the majority of members
of the House of Commons, did not know that the
sight of those luminous eyes had been fading and
dimming and that the statesman's hearing power
had been giving way so much as to make official
work a serious trial to him. We heard his voice,
we noted his energy of movement and gesture,

we were delighted by his thrilling eloquence, and
we could not understand all in a moment why
he should wish to retire from the field of his
fame.

So, in the theatric sense, I should describe his
last speech as a dramatic failure.   Numbers of
men lounged out of the House when the speech
was over, not having the least idea that they were
never again to hear that voice in Parliamentary
debate.   Yet I for one do not regret that Mr.
Gladstone thus took his leave of political life.   I
am not sorry that there were no fireworks; that
there was no tableau; that there was no melo-
dramatic fall of the curtain.   The orator making
his closing speech was inspired by his subject
and was not thinking of himself.   One single
sentence interjected in the course of the speech
would have told every one of his hearers what was
coming and would have led to a demonstration
such as has probably never been known in the
House of Commons.   It did not suit with Mr.
Gladstone's tastes or inclinations to lead up to
any such demonstration, and therefore while he
warned the House of Commons as to its duties
and its responsibilities he said not a word about
himself and about his action in the future.   Parliamentary history lost something no doubt by the
manner of his exhortation, but I think the char-

acter of the man will be regarded as all the greater because at so supreme a moment he forgot that the noblest Parliamentary career of the Victorian era had come at last to its close.

On Monday, the fifth of March, 1894, I had what I may be allowed to call my last official interview with Mr. Gladstone. He wrote me a letter on the Saturday before, asking me to call and see him at twelve o'clock on Monday. He was still occupying his official chambers in Downing Street. He received me, as was his wont, with the greatest kindness and friendship. We talked over many things, the past, the present, and the future. He was full of brilliant talk, as he always could be when in the mood, and he wandered off away from the track of our subjects many times to bring in reminiscences of the past and of men whom he had known and of political storm and stress in which he had had a serious part to play. I could not but admire the wonderful elasticity of the mind which could thus, for a moment at least, shake itself quite free from the troubles of the present and the immediate future and find a relief and a refuge in even the casual memories and anecdotes of much earlier days. We talked, as was natural, a good deal about Home Rule. He expressed a wish, such as he had often expressed before, to see some of us Home Rulers at Hawarden Castle and to talk over political prospects in a friendly and confidential way. He referred again and again to Mr. Parnell, and spoke of him, as he ever had done,

THE OFFICIAL RESIDENCE ON DOWNING STREET
(From a photograph by Mr. Monger of London)

with kindness and with consideration.   Mr. Parnell's, he said, had been a really great career; one of the greatest in modern times, considering the limited materials with which he had to work; and

he expressed, as I had often heard him express
it before, his deep regret that such a career should
have come to so tragic a close. I remember well
that he found fault with one course of action taken
by the Irish members, still under Mr. Parnell's
leadership, while we were opposing one of Mr.
Gladstone's own coercion measures.

The story is interesting in so far as it illustrates the singular fairness and candor of the
great statesman. He found no fault whatever
with us for opposing to the very uttermost his
coercion policy. That he quite understood to be
a part of our national duty. What he did complain
of was that when an English Liberal member proposed an amendment, making a certain division of
the bill stronger and harsher than the Government
intended to make it, and when the Government
determined to oppose the amendment, we did not
come and vote with them in opposition to it. The
truth was that Mr. Parnell and a number of other
Irish members, including myself, had been sus-
pended, as the technical phrase went, from voting
in the House for a certain limited time because
of our renewed acts of obstruction, and, as we
could not vote, our colleagues naturally declined
to take any part in the division. Mr. Gladstone
talked with the most perfect good-humor about
the whole affair and only dwelt upon it as the one

sole incident in the long struggle about which
he thought he had a fair right to grumble at the
conduct of the Irish members. He expressed to
me over and over again his absolute conviction
that the cause of Home Rule for Ireland was destined to succeed and before very long. No measure, he said, of really national importance which
has passed by a safe majority through the House
of Commons can ever be long retarded by the
resistance of the House of Lords.

In words which, though really conversational,
were as impressive to me as human eloquence
could make them, he bade me tell my colleagues
that his heart was ever with the success of our
cause and that he prayed for that success and gave
it his blessing. I have not been often so much
moved as by those words. I took leave of Mr.
Gladstone as if I had been leaving some being
who belonged to a higher order of the world than
the commonplace existence of every day. I passed
out into St. James's Park, feeling as though even
the sunshine and the grass and the trees and the
lake were commonplace things after such a farewell. I had one regret, and I cherish it still. I
wish I had asked Mr. Gladstone to give me something from his desk or his table, — a pen or a pencil or a book or anything whatever, — just as a
mark and memory of the occasion. I have many

letters from him, and he has sent me several times some pamphlet which he has written or in which he has felt a special interest. But I should like to have got something from him in memory of that last official interview. The meeting was, to use Carlyle's expression, not easily to be forgotten in this world.

Since then I have not seen Mr. Gladstone. The House of Commons is nothing like the place that it was when he was there. The Irish people feel that they have lost in him a friend and a guide, whose place is never likely to be filled again in our time. I felt all that as I was taking leave of him on that memorable day. Since the time of Charles James Fox Ireland never had had a distinct and an avowed friend amongst the men who made up administrations or led oppositions in the English House of Commons until we came to the days of Mr. Gladstone. Nor had Fox himself obtained even the chance of making such a move on our behalf as was made and sustained by Mr. Gladstone. I do not ask all my readers to agree with my views about Home Rule, but I do ask them to take what I say as the sincere expression of Irish opinion with regard to the English statesman who risked everything — place, power, popularity, all that could make life dear to any ambitious man — for the sake of serving a country so poor and so

lowly that it could offer for such services no reward
whatever but the reward of gratitude. I was thinking of all this when I came out of the official residence in Downing Street and passed into St.
James's Park, and felt as if I had been looking on
at the fall of a dynasty.

CHAPTER XXXII

GLADSTONE'S BUSY LEISURE

THEN came a season of what would have seemed to be extraordinary energy and overwork for any other man, but which was only a season of rest for Mr. Gladstone. He turned his attention once again to theology. He wrote letters, essays, and even books on theological subjects, nor in the meantime did much escape him in politics or even in light literature. He allowed the outer world to know, although in becoming guarded fashion, his opinion on this or that measure which was under discussion in Parliament, or on this or that subject of political controversy outside Parliament. He did not volunteer these opinions. He certainly did not obtrude them on the public, but if he were asked for a few words of counsel or of guidance he gave them in a helpful, friendly, modest sort of way. He read books of passing interest, even novels, and he did not disdain to say what he thought of them if they contained anything worth thinking about at all. He seems to me like another Charles the Fifth sitting down in his cell in the convent of St. Yuste, withdrawn to all seeming from the outer world and its doings, and yet keeping himself closely informed of everything that was going on and taking the keenest interest in the movements of that political life from which he had withdrawn himself forever.

We in London followed all his goings and his comings, his writings and his sayings, with an attentiveness which never relaxed. He went to Biarritz, he went to the Riviera, he talked with French public men and Spanish public men, he received friends at Hawarden, he kept up his position there as an active promoter of every good local movement. We were all delighted to hear that his sight had grown better and that his hearing had grown better. He sometimes buried himself in books and would work on a stretch ten hours in the day. He made short voyages and appeared to enjoy them with a perfectly youthful activity for the reception of new impressions.

Perhaps I cannot better illustrate the variety of his occupations than by mentioning the book, apparently of the most solid importance, which he wrote on Bishop Butler and Bishop Butler's theology, and the article on Sheridan which he contributed to "The Nineteenth Century" in June, 1896. I am not qualified to say anything about

CATHERINE GLADSTONE

the work on Bishop Butler, but I know at least
that it created a great sensation in England and
that it was discussed and debated and replied to
by reviewers and writers without end. The article in "The Nineteenth Century" on Sheridan
takes up a subject concerning which I am better
qualified to form an opinion. The article was
suggested by the work of my friend, Mr. Fraser
Rae, "already well known," Mr. Gladstone says,
"to political readers as the author of a useful
volume in which he associated the name of
Sheridan with those of Fox and of Wilkes," and
who brought out a recent biography of Sheridan
for the purpose of proving that full justice had
never been done in this country to the memory
of the author of the "Begum Speech" and the
"School for Scandal."

Mr. Gladstone thoroughly agrees with the views
of Mr. Fraser Rae. "The path of a biographer,"
he says, "may be a flowery path, but it is beset
with snares, especially as to the distribution of
his materials and the maintenance of a due proportion in presenting the several aspects of his
subject. These, in the case of Sheridan, were
especially numerous and diversified. He was a
dramatist, a wit, and something of a poet. He
won his wife by duelling and by a trip which
might be called an elopement. In society he

quickly grew to be a favorite, almost, indeed, an
idol. He came into Parliament by means which,
if open to exception in point of purity, were due
to no man's favor, but thoroughly independent.
While a representative of the people he sustained
in a marked manner the character of a courtier,
though the scene of his practice lay at Carlton
House and not at Windsor." Carlton House, I
should say, was the residence of the Prince Regent, afterwards George the Fourth. "Here have
been enumerated parts enough to fill the life of
an ordinary, nay, of something more than an
ordinary man. But interwoven with these and
towering high above them were his claims as an
orator, a patriot, and a statesman. It is in these
respects, and especially in the two last, which are
the most important of them, that, as Mr. Rae
considers, justice has not been fully done . to
Sheridan. His main purpose, therefore, is one of
historical rectification. No aim is of more dura-
ble consequence, and I cannot but think that in
a great measure it has been attained."

I do not want to quote too much of this most interesting article. It would be interesting and worth
studying if it had been written by a perfectly obscure author. There would not seem to be much
on the surface of Sheridan's character which could
attract a man so profoundly earnest as Mr. Glad-

stone. But Mr. Gladstone goes far beneath the
surface and boldly brushes aside the commonplace
and conventional notions of Sheridan as a mere
writer of plays and unpaid jester to the Prince
Regent, and shows him in his true rank as an
orator of the highest Parliamentary class, as a
statesman and as a patriot.

I cannot forbear from quoting a few closing
lines which Mr. Gladstone devotes to the memory
of Mrs. Sheridan, the wonderful singer Miss Lin-
ley, who has often been called the Saint Cecilia
of her day. "It is impossible," says Mr. Gladstone, "to close this rapid and slight sketch without one word at least on Mrs. Sheridan. One of
the strong titles of Sheridan to the favor of posterity is to be found in the warm attachment of
his family and his descendants to his memory.
The strongest of them all lies in the fact that he
could attract and could retain through her too
short life the devoted affections of this admirable
woman, whose beauty and accomplishments, remarkable as they were, were the least of her
titles to praise. Mrs. Sheridan was certainly not
strait-laced; not only did she lose at cards fifteen
and twenty-one guineas on two successive nights,
but she played cards, after the fashion of her
day, on Sunday evenings. I am very far from
placing such exploits among her claims on our

love. But I frankly own to finding it impossible
to read the accounts of her without profoundly
coveting, across the gulf of all these years, to
have seen and known her. Let her be judged
by the incomparable verses (presented to us in
these volumes) in which she opens the flood-gate
of her bleeding heart at a moment when she
feared she had been robbed, for the moment, of
Sheridan's affections by the charms of another.
Those verses of loving pardon proceed from a
soul advanced to some of the highest Gospel at-
tainments. She passed into her rest when still
under forty, peacefully absorbed for days before
her departure in the contemplation of the coming
world."

It seems to me that there is something in the
tender and melancholy compassion and toleration
of these kindly words not unworthy of the pen
of Thackeray. Mr. Gladstone wrote, among other
things, an article on minor poets, of whom he
must have known a good many in his time; but,
as we have already seen, he had known Wordsworth in his early days, and he knew Tennyson
and Browning to the end of either man's life.
Nobody could have admired more than I did Mr.
Gladstone's versatility and activity as an orator
and a statesman, but I confess that I am almost
equally impressed by the healthy vitality of the

man who, at the age of eighty-six, having retired altogether from Parliamentary life, can yet enter with so profound and practical an interest into almost every question which concerns men and women, and can absolutely refuse to exile himself from any manner of controversy, theological, literary, or political, on which there was a word to be said in season. In truth, we never lost Mr. Gladstone, even when he had no longer a place in the House of Commons or on the political platform.

On Monday, June 1, 1896, the public of England were penetrated by an unexpected sensation. It came in the form of a statement made by Mr. Gladstone and communicated to the world by the Archbishop of York, on the subject of the unity of Christendom and the validity of Anglican orders. It ought to be said in explanation of Mr. Gladstone's letter that the question of unity or union among the Christian churches had been lately pressed upon public attention by Pope Leo the Thirteenth. The Pope had addressed a letter to the English people, appealing for something like a reunion with the Church of Rome. The letter was full of interest, was grave and dignified and sympathetic. A movement, having for its purpose the same general result, had been going on for some time among clergymen and laymen who be-

longed to one section of the Anglican Church. Lord
Halifax, who was the chairman of a great Anglican organization, the English Church Union, had
taken a prominent part in the movement.   He
went to Rome, had interviews with the Pope and
with the Pope's councillors, and he endeavored
to ascertain how far Rome on the one hand and
the English Church on the other were willing to
advance toward a basis of union.   One of the
questions which came up for discussion was that
of the validity of Anglican orders ; that is,
whether Rome would or could recognize the
right of an Anglican clergyman to seek, as such,
admission to the clerical order in the Roman
Church, if any change of opinion should lead him
that way.

Mr. Gladstone's letter concerns itself almost altogether about that one part of the whole subject, but
his utterances are full of interest, even as regards
the grave possibilities of the greater subject. "The
question of the validity of Anglican orders," he
says, "might seem to be of limited interest if it
were only to be treated by the amount of any
immediate, practical, and external consequences
likely to follow upon any discussion or decision
that might now be taken in respect to it. For
the clergy of the Anglican communions, number-
ing between thirty thousand and forty thousand,

and for their flocks, the whole subject is one of settled solidity. In the Oriental Churches there prevails a sentiment of increased and increasing friendliness toward the Anglican Church, but no question of actual intercommunion is likely at present to arise, while, happily, no system of proselytism exists to set a blister on our mutual relations. In the Latin Church, which from its magnitude and the close tissue of its organization, overshadows all Western Christendom, these orders, so far as they have been noticed, have been commonly disputed, or denied, or treated as if they were null. A positive condemnation of them, if viewed dryly in its letter, would do no more than harden the existing usage of reordination in the case, which at most periods has been a rare one, of Anglican clergy who might seek admission to the clerical order in the Roman Church."

It ought to be explained that the particular object of Mr. Gladstone's interest was the report, widely spread over the world, that the question of the validity of Anglican orders was then actually the subject of a formal investigation by the authorities at the Vatican. On this point Mr. Gladstone goes on to say that "very different indeed would be the moral aspect and effect of a formal authorized investigation of the question at Rome, to whichever side the result might incline. It is to the last degree improbable that a ruler of known wisdom would at this time put in motion the machinery of the Curia for the purpose of widening the breach which severs the Roman Catholic Church from a communion which, though small in comparison, yet is extended through the large and fast increasing range of the English-speaking races, and which represents in the religious sphere one of the most powerful nations of European Christendom.

WILLIAM HENRY GLADSTONE
(From a photograph by Maull & Fox)

According to my reading of history, that breach is indeed already a wide one; but the existing schism has not been put into stereotype by any anathema or any expressed renunciation of communion on either side. As an acknowledgment of Anglican orders would not create intercommunion, so a condemna-

tion of them would not absolutely excommunicate;
but it would be a step, and even morally a stride,
toward excommunication; and it would stand as a
practical affirmation of the principle that it is wise
to make the religious differences between the
churches of Christendom more conspicuous to
the world, and also to bring them into a state of
the highest fixity, so as to enhance the difficulty
of approaching them at any future time in the
spirit of reconciliation.   From such a point of
view an inquiry, resulting in a proscription of
Anglican orders, would be no less important than
deplorable."

Mr. Gladstone goes on to say that the information which he had received from Lord Halifax
dispelled from his mind every apprehension of
that kind, and convinced him that if the investigations of the Curia did not lead to a favorable
result, wisdom and charity would in any case
arrest them at such a point as to prevent their
becoming an occasion and a means of embitter-
ing religious controversy.

Mr. Gladstone then sets out very frankly his
own point of view.   "And now I must take
upon me to speak in the only capacity in which
it can be warrantable for me to intervene in a
discussion properly belonging to persons of com-
petent authority.   That is the capacity of an

absolutely private person, born and baptized in the Anglican Church, accepting his lot there as is the duty of all who do not find that she has forfeited her original and inherent privilege and

WILLIAM HENRY'S SON, PRESENT HEIR
(From a photograph by Webster of Chester)

place. I may add that my case is that of one who has been led by the circumstances, both of his private and of his public career, to a life-long and rather close observation of her character, her fortunes, and the part she has to play in the grand history of Redemption.

Thus it is that her public interests are also his personal interests, and that they require or justify what is no more than his individual thought upon them. He is not one of those who look for an early restitution of such a Christian unity as that which marked the earlier history of the Church. Yet he even cherishes the belief that work may be done in that direction, which, if not majestic or imposing, may nevertheless be legitimate and solid; and this by the least as well as by the greatest. It is the Pope who, as the first Bishop of Christendom, has the noblest sphere of action; but the humblest of the Christian flock has his place of daily duty, and according as he fills it, helps to make or mar every good or holy work."

Mr. Gladstone declares that he "has viewed with profound and thankful satisfaction, during the last half-century and more, the progressive advance of a great work of restoration in Christian doctrine. It has not been wholly confined within his own country to the Anglican communion, but it is best that he should speak of that which has been most under his eye. Within these limits it has not been confined to doctrine, but has extended to Christian life and all its workings. The aggregate result has been that it has brought the Church of England from a state externally of halcyon calm, but inwardly of deep stagnation, to one in which, while buffeted more or less by external storms, subjected to some peculiar and searching forms of trial and even now by no means exempt from internal dissensions, she sees her clergy transformed (for this is the word which may advisedly be used), her vital energies enlarged and still growing in every direction, and a store of bright hopes accumulated that she may be able to contribute her share, and even possibly no mean share, toward a consummation of the work of the Gospel in the world. Now the contemplation of these changes by no means unfortunately ministers to our pride. They involve large admissions of collective fault. This is not the place, and I am not the proper organ, for exposition in detail. But I may mention the widespread depression of evangelical doctrine; the insufficient exhibition of the person and the work of the Redeemer; the coldness and deadness, as well as the infrequency, of public worship; the relegation of the Holy Eucharist to impoverished ideas and to the place of one (though doubtless a solemn one) among its occasional incidents; the gradual effacement of Church observance from personal and daily life. In all these respects there has been a profound alteration, which is still progressive, and which, apart from occasional extravagance or indiscretion, has indicated a real advance in the discipline of souls and in the work of God on behalf of man. . . .

" Certain publications of learned French priests," Mr. Gladstone went on to say, " unsuspected in their orthodoxy, which went to affirm the validity of Anglican ordinations, naturally excited much interest in this country and elsewhere. But there

was nothing in them to ruffle the Roman atmosphere, or invest the subject in the circles of the
Vatican, with the character of administrative
urgency.   When, therefore, it came to be understood that Pope Leo the Thirteenth had given his
commands that the validity of Anglican ordinations
should form the subject of an historical and theological investigation, it was impossible not to be
impressed with the profound interest of the considerations brought into view by such a step, if interpreted in accordance with just reason, as an effort
toward the abatement of controversial differences.
There was, indeed, in my view, a subject of thought
anterior to any scrutiny of the question upon its
intrinsic merits which deeply impressed itself upon
my mind.   Religious controversies do not, like
bodily wounds, heal by the genial course of nature.
If they do not proceed to gangrene and to mortifi-
cation, at least they tend to harden into fixed facts,
to incorporate themselves with law, character, and
tradition, nay, even with language; so that at last
they take rank among the data and presuppositions
of common life, and are thought as inexpugnable as
the rocks of an iron-bound coast. . . .

"What courage must it require in a Pope, what
an elevation above all the levels of stormy parti-
sanship, what genuineness of love for the whole
Christian flock, whether separated or annexed, to

enable him to approach the huge mass of hostile and still burning recollections in the spirit and for the purpose of peace! And yet, that is what Pope Leo the Thirteenth has done, first in entertaining the question of this inquiry, and, secondly, in determining and providing, by the infusion both of capacity and impartiality into the investigating tribunal, that no instrument should be overlooked, no guarantee omitted for the possible attainment of the truth. He who bears in mind the cup of cold water administered to 'one of these little ones' will surely record this effort, stamped in its very inception as alike arduous and blessed. But what of the advantage to be derived from any proceeding which shall end or shall reduce within narrower bounds the debate upon Anglican orders? I will put it upon paper, with the utmost deference to authority and better judgment, my own personal and individual, and, as I freely admit, very insignificant reply to the question.

" The one controversy which, according to my deep conviction, overshadows and, in the last resort, absorbs all others, is the controversy between Faith and Unbelief. . . . This historical transmission of the truth by a visible Church with an ordained constitution is a matter of profound importance, according to the belief and practice of fully three-fourths of Christendom. In these three-fourths I include the Anglican churches, which are probably required in order to make them up. It is surely better for the Roman and also the Oriental Church to find the churches of the Anglican succession standing side by side with them in the assertion of what they deem an important Christian principle than to be obliged to regard them as mere pretenders in this belief and *pro tanto* reduce the 'cloud of witnesses' willing and desirous to testify on behalf of the principle. . . . I may add that my political life has brought me much into contact with those independent religious communities which supply an important religious factor in the religious life of Great Britain, and which, speaking generally, while they decline to own the authority, either of the Roman or the National Church, yet still allow to what they know as the Established religion no inconsiderable hold upon their sympathies. In conclusion, it is not for me to say what will be the upshot of the proceedings now in progress at Rome. But be their issue what it may, there is, in my view, no room for doubt as to the attitude which has been taken by the actual head of the Roman Catholic Church in regard to them. It seems to me an attitude in the largest sense paternal, and while it will probably stand among the latest recollections of my lifetime, it will ever be cherished with cordial sentiments of reverence, of gratitude, and of high appreciation." The letter was dated Hawarden, 1896.

I have quoted much of Mr. Gladstone's letter because it is a document full of living and also of enduring interest. The earnest feeling which

HERBERT GLADSTONE
(From a photograph by Russell & Sons)

he threw into the question is proved by the evidence of the physical labor it must have given a man of his years to write with his own hand a letter which occupied two columns of the London daily papers. Of course it did not escape controversy and censure. One of the London daily papers, counted amongst those most devoted to Mr. Gladstone, dryly said that "the Christian reunion which begins at Rome will inevitably lose as much at one end as it gains at the other." The allusion is to the attitude of some leading Nonconformists toward Mr. Gladstone's letter.

Dr. Guinness Rogers, one of the most distinguished and influential Nonconformist leaders and teachers in Great Britain, indignantly denied that Nonconformists had any sympathy with a state-established religion. Dr. Rogers declared that upon his sympathy the Established Church had not the very faintest hold. He honored real Christian men in the State Church, but for a religious establishment he had no sympathy and no respect. He declared himself puzzled to know how a great and subtle intellect like Mr. Gladstone's could occupy itself for a single moment as to whether the Pope did or did not recognize the validity of Anglican orders. What meant, he asked, this silly craving for recognition from Rome? What right have these Anglican clergy, who belonged not to a private church, to betray the liberty purchased by this country by this weak and childish sighing after recognition by the Pope? Many other distinguished Nonconformist ministers talked in the same strain, and at one meeting of Nonconformists the mention of Mr. Gladstone's name was received with some hisses, which were promptly rebuked by the voice of the chairman and by the cheers of the great majority of the audience. I am not going into the controversy, but it is only right to record the fact that a serious controversy did arise.

CHAPTER XXXIII

Mr. Gladstone was beset by letters, calling on
him to give some explanation of the position which
he had taken up with regard to the Pope and the
Anglican orders. I may quote a few sentences
from one letter, which will speak for many, a letter from a well-known Baptist minister, the Rev.
Walter Wynn. After paying some well-deserved
compliments to the profound interest and the ability of Mr. Gladstone's letter, the writer goes on to
say: "As a Nonconformist minister, however, I am
perplexed by this latest demonstration of your genius. If your reasoning is right, the whole basis
upon which Nonconformist Church policy is built
up is unscriptural and insecure. Any one of less
importance and ability than yourself could not have
produced upon my mind the shock such a thought
gives me. I venture in all sincerity to ask would
you, if your heart's desire were fulfilled, see the
whole of Christendom under the sway and rulership of the Pope? If not, why discuss his opinion
as to the validity of Anglican orders, or his sanc-

tion in particular of any form of ministry? May I ask also whether your reference to our Churches as 'separate religious communities' implies a dogmatic dislike of them?"

Mr. Gladstone in his reply said: "The tone of your kind letter commands my sympathy. But I do not yet comprehend the mental process by which my paper has been alarming to any one. My proposition is simply this — the more we, the separate bodies of Christians, are able to acknowledge as sound the truth or usages held by any of us, the more is our common Christianity strengthened. I will endeavor to illustrate.

"The Church of Rome recognizes as valid (when regularly performed) baptism conferred in your communion and ours. By this acknowledgment I think that Christianity is strengthened in face of non-Christians. For baptism read orders (for the purpose of the argument), and the same proposition applies, though unhappily in this case only to us, not to you. No harm that I can see is done to any one else. The settlement of this matter is a thing of the likelihood of which I cannot even form an opinion. But I honor the Pope in the matter, as it is my duty to honor every man who acts as best he can with the spirit of courage, truth, and love. My answer to your question is in the negative."

I think there can be no doubt in the mind of any fair-minded person that in writing this letter on the Anglican orders Mr. Gladstone acted, as he had done in so many other cases, the best he could with the spirit of courage, truth, and love. Considering his peculiar position, his letter might be set down by some as a rash utterance, but then it has to be remembered that many of the noblest words he ever uttered might be regarded as rash utterances. Probably it did not occur to him to think that he, a believer in the Anglican Church, could desire to see the whole of Christendom under the sway and rulership of the Pope. What Gladstone always did desire was, that the Christian Churches should all draw as near to one another as possible, and should make a common stand against irreligion, against infidelity, against atheism, and against indifference. Mr. Gladstone did not see any enemy to his faith in any Christian Church or sect or denomination. He saw the enemies of good in boorish ignorance and in cultured indifference and agnosticism. With him Christianity was a living force, and more than that, a force essential to the true life of everything. In this spirit, and in none other, he gave forth his utterances on the Anglican orders and the possibility of a nearer approach between the Church of Rome and the Church of England.

The Pope shortly after issued an Encyclical
which was undoubtedly in great part meant as a
reply to Mr. Gladstone's letter. Nothing decisive
and final was said as to the subject of the Anglican orders, but, of course, the Pope made it clear
that on the part of Rome there could be no
compromise of religion or principle. Indeed, the
letter was little more than a continuation of a
former Encyclical addressed directly by the Pope
to the English people. In that Encyclical the
Pope made an appeal full of friendliness and even
affection to the English people, inviting them to
return to the religion of the Roman Catholic
Church. But he did not offer any concession or
compromise on any matter of importance. The
more recent Encyclical merely emphasized the
same views. This was exactly what any thoughtful person might have expected. The vital principle of the Roman Catholic Church is, of course,
the maintenance of its own doctrines. It is certain that Mr. Gladstone's letter and the Encyclical
in reply to it could only tend to produce a kindlier
feeling between Anglicans and Roman Catholics.
But I am much mistaken if the letter and the
Encyclical did not bring about a feeling of sore-
ness and of deep regret among many of the
Nonconformists of Great Britain. Their historical
position, too, it is easy to understand. But I am

sure that some of them, at least, did not quite comprehend or do full justice to the generous impulse of Mr. Gladstone.

Following out, as I have been trying to do, the story of Mr. Gladstone's career, I may own that I am less concerned about the public possibilities of his letter than with the extraordinary evidence it gives of that indomitable interest in the great affairs of humanity which was ever and always the predominant instinct of his nature. Age could

REV. STEPHEN GLADSTONE
(From a photograph by Elliott & Fry, London)

not wither that great emotion in him. He saw a chance, a possibility, of uniting two of the great forces of Christianity in a common war against irreligion and indifference, and he came to the front of the field and called on all who felt with him to follow him. That is simply the meaning of his letter. It was but another testimony, if any such were needed, to his absolute sincerity.

On Friday, June 26, 1896, there was a peculiarly interesting ceremonial at Aberystwith, in Wales, in honor of the installation of the Prince of Wales as Chancellor of the new Welsh University. The Prince of Wales, in his new capacity, received an address from the University Court and was presented with a key of the university, the seal and a copy of the Charter and the statutes. Among the recipients of honorary degrees were the Princess of Wales and Mr. Gladstone. A description of the scene when the Prince of Wales presented his wife with the degree said that "Her Royal Highness, rising to confront the Prince face to face, the Chancellor clasping his wife's hand, was an interesting episode, and it seemed to amuse immensely the Princess of Wales, who had a difficulty in keeping her countenance while the Prince, speaking in Latin, as is the ceremonial of such occasions, said, 'Altissima Principissa, admitto te ad gradum doctoris in musica et ad omnia privilegia hujus dignitatis.' When Mr. Gladstone's turn came," said the same report, "the cheering was so fast and furious that the Chancellor had to wave his velvet gold-laced mortar-board with authority before he could gain a fair hearing."

There was a luncheon given afterward at which the Prince of Wales made a most sympathetic and graceful reference to the honor conferred on Mr. Gladstone. "You will all join with me," the Prince said, " I am sure, in thanking the veteran statesman and eminent scholar, Mr. Gladstone, who, notwithstanding his advanced age, has undertaken a journey, necessarily fatiguing, in order to pay a compliment to the University of Wales and to myself as its Chancellor. I may truly say that one of the proudest moments of my life was when I found myself in the flattering position of being able to confer an academic distinction upon Mr. Gladstone, who furnishes a rare instance of a man who has achieved one of the highest positions as a statesman and at the same time has attained such distinction in the domain of literature and scholarship. His translation of the Odes of Horace would alone constitute a lasting monument to him even had he not accomplished so much besides which has rendered him illustrious. Nor do we extend a less warm welcome to Mr. Gladstone's ever faithful companion and helper during the many years of his busy life."

Mr. Gladstone, of course, has his home in Wales, and therefore his position as recipient of honors from the University of Wales through the voice of the Prince of Wales was a peculiarly appro-

priate, and must have been a very grateful, ceremonial. Mr. Gladstone had already been loaded
with honors of all kinds, but I am sure that no
honor was ever more welcome to him than this

MR. AND MRS. GLADSTONE, WITH ALL THE CHILDREN AND GRANDCHILDREN
(From a photograph by Mr. Watmough Webster, of Chester)

tribute from the Welsh University, given through
the medium of the heir of the Crown who bears
the title of the principality. The reception offered
to Mr. Gladstone by the crowd as he returned to
his special train was something which might have

given a new throb of feeling to even the proudest
of men.   To Mr. Gladstone who had always borne
his honors meekly, it must have been a peculiarly
touching and thrilling welcome.   The long political struggle was over and done.   The heat of
opposition this way and that had gone out forever,
and Mr. Gladstone had none left but friends on
both sides of the political field.   Probably that
ceremonial, that installation of the Prince of Wales
as Chancellor of the Welsh University, was the
last occasion on which Mr. Gladstone would consent to make an appearance on a public platform.
It was a graceful close to such a great career; an
honor paid to a scholar by the people in whose
midst he lived; a tribute to a statesman's genius
and to a noble life.

Later on Mr. Gladstone came back into London
and into London society for a short time, not to
a platform but to a great ceremonial occasion.   It
was on July 22, 1896, when he and Mrs. Gladstone
came to be present at the marriage of one of the
daughters of the Prince and Princess of Wales
to Prince Charles of Denmark.   Mr. Gladstone,
it is not too much to say, shared public attention
with the Sovereign and the young bridegroom
and bride.   Everybody was delighted to see how
well he was looking and how vivid and active
was his personal interest in every incident that

belonged to the occasion. Many noted with deep regret that the sight of one of his eyes was sadly dimmed, — those eyes that long were so piercing and so thrilling in their gaze and even in their glance, — but, so far as the ordinary conditions of health were concerned, the great old statesman seemed to have moulted no feather. The day after the royal wedding he went back to Hawarden — a long journey — and declared himself to be not in the least wearied by his travel to London, or by his attendance at the protracted and formal ceremonial.

CHAPTER XXXIV

IT is well understood that Mr. Gladstone on his retirement from public life received from the Sovereign the offer of an earldom with, of course, a seat in the House of Lords. Mr. Gladstone gratefully and gracefully declined the title and the position. No one could have been surprised at his decision. He had already made a name which no earldom or dukedom or any other rank could have enhanced. "Posterity," says Lord Macaulay, "has obstinately refused to degrade Francis Bacon into Viscount St. Albans." In the same sense, the contemporaries and the posterity of William Ewart Gladstone would have declined to accept for him the title of Earl of Hawarden or Earl of any other place. He is fixed in the affection and the admiration of his countrymen as William Ewart Gladstone.

One title he has indeed received by the universal accord of the public of England and the public of all the world. I do not know, and I suppose nobody knows, who invented this title for him, but it was conferred upon him and it will always remain with him and with his memory. He was called the Grand Old Man and the Grand Old Man he always will remain. Never was there a character which more aptly deserved that title, sacred to age and to grandeur of genius, of purpose, and of career.

I do not know whether English Parliamentary history records greater doings of any man. In different paths of political work other men may have been as great as he. So far as one can judge by the writings of contemporaries there may have been orators and debaters in Parliament who were equal to him. Probably Fox was his equal in Parliamentary debate. There is a magnificent phrase of Henry Grattan's, himself hardly surpassed as a Parliamentary orator, in which he describes the eloquence of Fox as "rolling in resistless as the waves of the Atlantic." I have often thought of that description when listening to some of Mr. Gladstone's greatest speeches. I have said to myself:—This makes me understand the force and the meaning of Grattan's superb phrase. This is indeed eloquence rolling in resistless as the waves of the Atlantic. The elder Pitt was probably as great an orator as Mr. Gladstone. The younger Pitt was probably his equal in the statelier forms of declamation. But not Fox nor Chatham nor William Pitt had anything like Mr. Gladstone's capacity for constructive legislation, and the resources of information possessed by Fox or Chatham or Pitt were poor indeed when compared with that storehouse of knowledge which supplied Mr. Gladstone's intellectual capacity.

Mr. Gladstone was possessed through his life with an eager passion to do the right thing at all times. Sometimes, no doubt, he took a wrong view of things ; but never was swayed by any but the most rightful motives. No human interest was indifferent to him, and the smallest wrong as well as the greatest aroused his most impassioned sympathy and made him resolve that the wrong should be righted. I have mixed with most of Mr. Gladstone's contemporaries, his political opponents as well as his political followers, and I have never heard a hint of any serious defect in his nature and his character, or of any unworthy motive influencing his public or private career. Defects of temperament, of manner, and of tact have, no doubt, been ascribed to him over and over again. He was not, people tell me, always successful in conciliating or playing up to the weaknesses of inferior men. He was not good, I am told, at remembering faces and names. In this peculiarity he was unlike what we all used to believe of the great Napoleon, who never, it once was the common belief, forgot a face or a name. Later historians, how-

ever, have corrected public opinion a good deal
on this subject, and we now know that the great
Napoleon was very carefully "coached" both as
regards faces and names, and made many fine theatrical effects on the strength of some quietly administered hint.

Such defects, however, in Mr. Gladstone's nature
or temperament count indeed for little or nothing
in the survey of his career. He was loved by his
friends, he cannot but be honored, even by his
political enemies — for personal enemies he never
could have had. The name conferred on him, by
nobody knows whom, will be borne by him to all
time, and so long as the history of Queen Victoria's
reign remains in the memory of civilization, he will
still be "the Grand Old Man."

The year now drawing to a close was made
memorable to England and, indeed, to all the civilized world by the celebration of what was called
the Diamond Jubilee of Queen Victoria's reign —
the sixtieth year of her sovereignty. Every civilized
state took some share in the tribute of regard thus
paid to Queen Victoria. Even the Nationalists of
Ireland, who felt bound to take no part in the dem-
onstrations, abstained for purely political reasons
and had no thought of disrespect for the ruler,
whom I have already described as the first and only
Constitutional Sovereign of Great Britain. The

Queen was seventy-eight during the year of the
Diamond Jubilee, and was, therefore, some ten
years younger than Mr. Gladstone or Pope Leo the
Thirteenth. Mr. Gladstone's health did not allow
him to take any conspicuous part in the Jubilee
celebration; but we may be sure that no heart
beat more fervently than his for the Queen, and
for her happiness, and that of her family, and for
the glory of the reign which he himself had done
so much to make illustrious and successful.

INDEX

2 F   433

ALFRED LORD TENNYSON.

A MEMOIR

BY

HIS SON.

Two Vols. 8vo. Cloth. In Box. Price, $10.00, net.

These volumes of over 500 pages each contain many letters written or received by Lord Tennyson, to which no other biographer could have had access, and in addition a large number of Poems hitherto unpublished.

Several chapters are contributed by such of his friends as Dr. Jowett, the Duke of Argyll, the late Earl of Selborne, Mr. Lecky, Professor Francis T. Palgrave, Professor Tyndall, Mr. Aubrey de Vere, and others, who thus express their Personal Recollections.

There are many Illustrations, engraved after pictures by Richard Doyle, Samuel Lawrence, G. F. Watts, R.A., etc., in all about twenty full-page Portraits and other Illustrations.

COMMENTS.

"The biography is easily the biography not only of the year, but of the decade, and the story of the development of Tennyson's intellect and of his growth — whatever may be the varying opinions of his exact rank among the greatest poets — into one of the few masters of English verse, will be found full of thrilling interest not only by the critic and student of literature, but by the average reader." — *The New York Times.*

"Two salient points strike the reader of this memoir. One is that it is uniformly fascinating, so rich in anecdote and marginalia as to hold the attention with the power of a novel. In the next place, it has been put together with consummate tact, if not with academic art. . . . It is authoritative if ever a memoir was. But, we repeat, it has suffered no harm from having been composed out of family love and devotion. It is faultless in its dignity." — *The New York Tribune.*

THE MACMILLAN COMPANY,

66 FIFTH AVENUE, NEW YORK.

THE LETTERS OF MATTHEW ARNOLD.

1848-1888.

Collected and Arranged by GEORGE W. E. RUSSELL.

Two Vols. 12mo. Cloth. $3.00.

(Uniform with Matthew Arnold's Works.)

" These two volumes constitute, from the point of view of literature, the most important publication of the season — or, for that matter, of several seasons. A man of letters of such distinction belongs, however, to the world which he has stirred, stung, or charmed, and some personal account was needed. That account is furnished by these letters, written largely to those who stood nearest him, and covering the whole period of his active life. The letters are so entirely in accord with the published works that they form a connecting link to bind them together, and they also supply the key to them. As biography, these letters are of a great and lasting interest; as literature, they will take their place beside ' Culture and Anarchy ' and ' Essays in Criticism.' " — *The Outlook.*

" There is not a dull line in his correspondence. Their substance is one of the rarest in epistolary literature, and their style is unique, for in the smallest matters, as in the greatest, Matthew Arnold gave the best of himself to his task; even as a letter writer his motto was ' Noblesse oblige.' " — *New York Tribune.*

" They constitute a valuable contribution, and give one a peculiar insight into the spirit of the scholar and the man." — *New York Herald.*

" ' The Letters of Matthew Arnold' show us a more fascinating character than we knew to be his. As a man he exceeds himself as a scholar, and, with our few opportunities for seeing the human side, we naturally have thought mostly of the scholarly. That kept us at arm's length. The letters bring him close and make him dear." — *Chicago Times-Herald.*

LETTERS OF EDWARD FITZGERALD

TO

FANNY KEMBLE.   1871–1883.

Edited by WILLIAM ALDIS WRIGHT.

16mo. Cloth. $1.50.

" The volume is full of intensely interesting matter, and allusions to authors and their work. It is one of the notable books of the season." — *Boston Daily Advertiser.*

" The letters are charming; not too long, almost purely personal, yet not too much so for printing purposes; funny, pathetic, and characteristic." — *Chicago Times-Herald.*

" These letters are rich in literary gossip, touches of shrewd criticism, and fine strokes of unstudied observation. It is a book to be read and kept for its kernels of wholesome human nature as well as for its little bachelor bizarreries which are not so wholesome, but, like salted almonds, quite appetizing." — *New York Independent.*

" The book will be a delight to all who love character revealed in correspondence. There is not a dull letter in the collection, and that cannot be said of many such collections." — *Minneapolis Journal.*

" These letters give us at least a partial insight into the purest, the noblest, the grandest personality this old world of ours has held for a long time, and they should be prized accordingly." — *Chicago Evening Post.*

THE MACMILLAN COMPANY,

66 FIFTH AVENUE, NEW YORK.